SOUTH CAROLINA
WOMEN WRITERS

PROCEEDINGS
OF THE
REYNOLDS CONFERENCE
UNIVERSITY OF SOUTH CAROLINA
October 24–25, 1975

SOUTH CAROLINA
WOMEN WRITERS

edited by
JAMES B. MERIWETHER

Published for the Southern Studies Program
University of South Carolina

THE REPRINT COMPANY, PUBLISHERS
SPARTANBURG, SOUTH CAROLINA
1979

Copyright © Southern Studies Program 1979

Published: 1979
The Reprint Company, Publishers
Spartanburg, South Carolina

ISBN 0–87152–292–6
Library of Congress Catalog Card Number: 78–31300
Manufactured in the United States of America on long-life paper.

Library of Congress Cataloging in Publication Data

Reynolds Conferences, 2d, University of South
    Carolina, 1975.
    South Carolina women writers.

    1. American literature—South Carolina—History
and criticism—Congresses. 2. American literature
—Women authors—History and criticism—Congresses.
I. Meriwether, James B. II. South Carolina. Uni-
versity. Southern Studies Program. III. Title.
PS266.S6R4   1975   810'.9'9287   78–31300
ISBN 0–87152–292–6

CONTENTS

FOREWORD

"South Carolina Women Writers" was the topic of a conference held on October 24–25, 1975, sponsored by the Southern Studies Program of the University of South Carolina. It was the second of a series of annual conferences dealing with various aspects of South Carolina intellectual and cultural history made possible by the generosity of Mrs. John S. Reynolds, through a gift to the University of South Carolina Educational Foundation.

It was Mrs. Reynolds' intention to provide, by these annual conferences and their published proceedings, a memorial to her husband, John S. Reynolds, and her daughter, Joan Reynolds Faunt. The first conference, "South Carolina Journals and Journalists," was held in May 1974, and its proceedings were published the following year. Both conferences followed the same format, with graduate students in the Southern Studies Program and in several departments of the University joining established scholars in the presentation and discussion of papers.

The topic for this conference was chosen after discussions with a number of scholars familiar with the history and especially with the literary history of this state. South Carolina is fortunate in having had many women writers whose work, in several different fields, is significant and in some cases distinguished. Most of these writers, however, have been relatively neglected. In the three quarters of a century that have elapsed since A. S. Salley, Jr., compiled his "A Bibliography of the Women Writers of South Carolina,"[1] almost nothing has been published about most of the writers he listed—although in most cases the resources for their study have been readily available.

The intent of this conference, then, was to demonstrate the significance of a number of women writers of this state who merit more attention—or a different kind of attention—than they have previously received. Those chosen for treatment are representative. Though some—Mary Boykin Chesnut and Julia Peterkin, for example —achieved real distinction, many are minor writers and were selected

---

[1] *Southern History Association Publications*, VI (1902), 143–57.

from a far larger group of possible subjects. Ample opportunities exist for further research on these and other South Carolina women writers, as the papers and discussion sessions of the conference make clear.

The entire proceedings of the conference were taped, and the tapes transcribed. The authors of papers were given the opportunity to make minor revisions and corrections and add footnotes, and the comments made during the discussions were edited, by the participants and by the editor, in order to condense and occasionally to clarify them. However, one session of this conference—three papers with subsequent discussion—is omitted from the proceedings published here. Thanks are due to Professors Anna Katona and Nan Morrison of the College of Charleston, for presenting at this session papers on Elizabeth Allston Pringle and on Caroline Gilman's *Rose Bud*, respectively; and special thanks are due to Miss Anna Wells Rutledge, of Charleston, for her lecture upon and display of early Charleston cookbooks. Though not appropriate for inclusion in the published proceedings, these papers were, with the discussions they stimulated, a valuable part of the conference itself. This session too was taped and transcribed; the edited typescript is preserved in the files of the Southern Studies Program at the University of South Carolina and may be consulted there.

During their preparations for the conference, students in the Southern Studies Program and the staff of the South Caroliniana Library compiled notes upon many of the South Caroliniana Library collections containing letters and papers of women writers. These notes are also available in the files of the Southern Studies Program.

The cooperation of a number of faculty and staff members and friends of the University of South Carolina made possible this conference and the publication of its proceedings. First of all, most grateful thanks are due Mrs. Reynolds for her constant encouragement and support. Funds from the Bostick Charitable Trust, also made available to the Southern Studies Program through the Educational Foundation, were used for graduate and undergraduate student research assistantships and to help defray the costs of publishing the conference proceedings. For their help in all matters involving finances, Mr. C. Wallace Martin, Vice-President for Development, and Mr. W. Thomas Jervey, Trust Officer, are to be thanked. Grateful acknowledgment is made to Professor Noel Polk, Visiting Bibliographer of the Southern Studies Program, and Mr. David Moltke-Hansen and Mrs. Beverly Scafidel, Research Assistants, for their work upon the exhibition, "South Carolina Women Writers," mounted in the Kendall Room of the South Caroliniana Library, October 1975-March 1976. For assistance with the preparations for the conference and for the exhibition, thanks are due Mr. E. L. Inabinett, Director of the Library, and his staff, especially Mr. Allen H. Stokes, Jr. And finally, for their help in preparing the proceedings for publication, the editor wishes to thank Mrs. Ellen Arnold, who first transcribed the tapes, and Mrs. Jean Patterson and Ms. Alleene Walker, who typed the final camera-ready copy for offset printing.

J. B. M.

"Jeanie Drake":
A South Carolina Writer Overlooked

by

Dianne Luce Anderson

    "Jeanie Drake" was active for a period of almost
thirty years, from 1890 until 1918. During that time she
is known to have produced two novels, a novelette, two
poems, and thirty short stories in various periodicals.[1]
She was apparently well educated: her novels show the
results of considerable research and of intelligent
absorption in the life she could observe around her, and
she knew Latin, Spanish, French and German well enough to
use them all in her work. She was well travelled, inti-
mately familiar with South Carolina from the low country
to the mountains, with New York City and State, and with
the provinces of Western Europe. Alsace; Martres, France;
St. George, Winyaw; New Orleans; the American West and the
Arctic circle all serve as settings for her stories. She
knew people as well as places: Northern socialites,
Southern planters, Blue Ridge Mountain folk, provincial
Frenchmen, emancipated black men and urban immigrant
families are treated with greater or lesser degree of
intimacy and almost always convincingly in her fiction.
In fact, local reviewers of her books, set in Charleston
and in New York, recognized in her characters many actual
people indigenous to those cities.[2] What is ironic is
that in spite of what seems to have been her full life,
her long writing career, and the number of places and
people she knew, no one now, and perhaps few people
during her lifetime, knew Jeanie Drake--at least not
under that name.

1

Nor can I give you the last word on Miss Jeanie Drake, but only, I'm afraid, a few initial stammerings. My research is still in progress, and I have reached that intriguing but frustrating stage at which I am convinced that "Jeanie Drake" is indeed a pseudonym, but I have not quite cracked it yet. This conviction is based on a little positive information and quite a lot of negative evidence. First, the Charleston *News and Courier*'s review of Miss Drake's first novel, *In Old St. Stephen's*, states that she is "of this city," but gives no further information about her in what is for that newspaper a very long and detailed book review.[3] Significantly, none of the sources of data on residents of Charleston and the surrounding parishes around the turn of the century includes anything on a "Jeanie Drake." As a matter of fact, "Drake" seems to have been a very uncommon name in that area: the Charleston City Directories for the 1890's list only a couple of Drake families in the city, and the 1880 census records for the surrounding parishes contain not a single reference to any Drake family. Finally, the reviewer for *The Literary World*, with the air of one who knows much more than he's telling, calls our author "a new writer who signs herself Jeanie Drake," and subsequently he places the name in quotation marks.[4]

Having abandoned the assumption held by the very few bibliographers who have listed her work[5] (that is, that "Jeanie Drake" was indeed Jeanie Drake) we are left with a new set of questions and a few clues. By way of telling you what can be tentatively inferred about Miss Jeanie Drake's identity, then, it is these questions and clues, rather than any definitive answers, that I would like to share with you today.

Miss Drake's earliest discovered publication is the short story "And Peace on Earth" which appeared in January of 1890.[6] Assuming that she was at least in her twenties at this time, she would have to have been born no later than 1870--probably in the 1860's. For a date of death we can postulate some time after early 1918, the time of her last known publication.[7] However, this might be misleading. Being possibly as young as fifty in 1918, Miss Drake could easily have retired from writing and lived up to thirty or forty years longer. Her publishing record for the years from 1905 to 1918 lend some support to this possibility: after several years of quite regular contributions to *Catholic World*, averaging three or four stories

per year, she drops to one or two contributions per year
from 1911 through 1914. In the latter year she published
one original story[8] and one, entitled "On Pigeon River,"
that had been written and published fifteen years earlier
in *The Black Cat*,[9] a magazine of original short stories
published in Boston. Miss Drake had been awarded a first
prize of 250 dollars for this in the *Black Cat*'s story
competition, and it was republished without authorial
revision in *Catholic World* in 1914.[10] There followed a
silence of three and a half years, and finally Jeanie
Drake's last story, "Major Münchausen of the Gap,"
appeared in April of 1918. There is a pattern here which
certainly suggests gradual retirement, but neither is this
an inevitable and necessary conclusion from the evidence.
Miss Drake may have died as early as 1914, in which case
"On Pigeon River" and "Major Münchausen" were revived from
earlier publication or from the *Catholic World* files and
published posthumously by the editor. It may be significant in light of this hypothesis that through a mistake
on the part of printer or editor, *Catholic World* attributes
the latter story to "Jennie Drake." Incidentally, a check
of the volumes of *Catholic World* from 1914 through 1926
reveals no notice of the death of Jeanie Drake, though it
was a normal practice for this journal to print tributes
to its deceased contributors soon after their deaths. Nor
does this journal, still in existence, have now any files
on Jeanie Drake.[11]

We can console ourselves with at least one relatively
certain "fact." Jeanie Drake was, in the early years of
her writing career, living in South Carolina. Besides the
claim to that effect of the *News and Courier* review
already cited, and the internal evidence of her novel *In
Old St. Stephen's*, which displays an intimate knowledge
of the history, traditions and local characteristics of
Charleston and the low country, there is an early story,
"Under the Bôdhi-Tree," published in 1891, a year before
the novel, to which is ascribed the location of composition, "Charleston, S.C."[12] In 1896 when *The Metropolitans*
appeared, the *News and Courier* was still claiming for
Charleston a share of pride in her achievement,[13] though
the New York City setting of this novel, and its acceptance
by New York critics as being authentic in its portrayal of
the social aspects of that city,[14] would suggest that
Jeanie Drake might then have been spending more time there
than in Charleston. If so, this would probably not have
been her first exposure to the metropolis. Her first and

third published stories, "And Peace on Earth" and "Under
the Bôdhi-Tree," had their settings in or near New York,
while her second and fourth, "Tartuffe in Ebony"[15] and
"Ancient and Honorable,"[16] were set in South Carolina.
Although in her later works specific locales are less
frequently pinpointed, the stories set in New York and
in South Carolina are about evenly balanced throughout
Jeanie Drake's career. So it may be that she drifted at
will between the two places rather than removing permanently from one to the other.

In 1906 and 1907 *Catholic World* serialized Miss
Drake's novelette, "Narcissus."[17] The first half of this
piece is set in the ancient little provincial town of
Martres in France and has for its backdrop the traditions
of the local saint, Vidian, and the villagers' ceremonial
recreation of the medieval battles there between the
Christians and the Saracens. This marks Jeanie Drake's
first extensive use of a European background for her
fiction, a practice she continued increasingly later in
her career ("The Brother of Mercy," 1905,[18] had been set,
only incidentally, in England). All this would suggest
that whoever was Jeanie Drake, she perhaps led something
of a wanderer's life. It may well be that she spent the
years of World War I in Europe, and possibly she died
there.

An obvious clue to the identity of this writer is the
fact that all but three of her known periodical publications appeared in *Catholic World*.[19] But it may be wise
not to take for granted Miss Drake's Catholicism. It seems
that whatever her religion, she was quite deliberately
writing for a specific audience when she wrote her *Catholic
World* stories. Only a few of these are overtly religious
stories; those which are are usually set in the Christmas
season and deal with a character's ability, or lack of it,
to apply the meaning of the ritual celebration to his own
life. It is probably significant that the first story
Jeanie Drake published in *Catholic World* is one of these,[20]
but in all of her work there is very little to mark her
stories as specifically "Catholic" except for the almost
off-hand provision of details which identify their characters as Roman Catholic. And it is striking to notice
that in the two novels and the three stories not published
in *Catholic World*, only one incident, the conversion in
In Old St. Stephen's of the daughter of the family by
Bishop John England of Charleston, gives any hint of the

author's possible Catholicism. If she was indeed Catholic,
this dichotomy may result from her recognition of religious
prejudices still manifest in the general American populace
at the turn of the century; if she was not Catholic and
had simply found a ready market for her fiction in *Catholic
World*, this might go far toward explaining her use of a
pseudonym.

The most tantalizing clue to the identity of Jeanie
Drake is that in the copy of *In Old St. Stephen's* from the
W. G. Hinson collection in the Charleston Library Society
is pasted a clipping of an obituary from the Charleston
News and Courier, March 28, 1894. It reports the death of
Charles Sinkler, of Belvidere Plantation in St. John's
Berkeley, and names his five surviving children, three of
them daughters.[21] A little research into the Sinkler
ancestry reveals that Charles Sinkler's great grandmother
was a woman named Ann Drake.[22] It is quite probable that
Hinson, a South Carolinian who lived from 1838 until 1919,
knew who Jeanie Drake was and perhaps even knew her per-
sonally. And it would most likely have been he who pasted
the obituary into her novel. There is, of course, no
mention of the name "Jeanie Drake" in this clipping, but
the circumstantial evidence all points to the possibility
that Jeanie Drake was somehow connected with the Sinkler
family.

However, a representative of the family who knew the
three Sinkler daughters very well, has told me that to her
knowledge none of them ever published any fiction, that
although two of them moved to Philadelphia they had never
lived in New York, and that no one in her family had ever
been a Catholic.[23]

This leaves us with more questions unanswered, but
with many avenues for further exploration. The most important question, however, at a conference on South Carolina
writers, is "What about her fiction: what does she achieve:
how good is she?" And that one can be answered, partially,
for we do have Jeanie Drake's work.

It won't surprise anyone to hear that Jeanie Drake is
not a hitherto undiscovered literary genius. She is a
pretty good writer of popular fiction--if an arbitrary distinction can be drawn between that and what, for lack of an
adequate term, I'll call "artistic fiction." Miss Drake
is an intelligent woman with an occasionally acute insight

into the intricacies of human relationships, and possessing
well developed habits of observation, which are reflected
in her flair for effectively using local detail and dialect
in her fiction. But her work is weakened by certain sentimental attitudes which appear again and again and tend to
falsify what is often otherwise a quite fine sense for
situations with good dramatic potential. She seems com-
pelled, especially in her magazine fiction exploring human
relationships, to close each piece by placing in a character's mouth a mildly witty or ironic summary statement
which, while never quite a moral, is always as anticlimactic as one. And where there is a romantic involvement, whether really integral to the plot or not, the
endings tend to consist of sentimentally sweet reunions
or reconciliations. For example, the story "To Men of
Good-Will" is a relatively well-controlled depiction of a
young couple, provincial Alsatians, who are engaged to be
married. Each has a profound but simple confidence in his
place in the world and in his betrothed. The young man
has learned, with his fiancée, to believe of his fellow
men that "'There is nothing unpardonable, . . . or how
could any of us dare to die when the time comes? Peace
is always and forever best.'"[24] When he responds to his
duty to defend his homeland, he learns gradually to accept
the necessity of fighting; but on Christmas Eve when defeat
is inevitable he walks serenely into the no-man's-land
between the armies and sings a French hymn into the night,
to which a German voice soon responds with a hymn in its
own language, and shouts of Christmas greetings swell from
each intrenchment. Though this scene itself holds some
potential for the sentimental, Miss Drake does not let it
get away from her. But instead of moving quickly to close
the story, she has the soldier "fatally" wounded but
miraculously nursed back to life by his fiancée, who
materializes suddenly wearing a field nurse's insignia.

In many of the stories, and even in *The Metropolitans*,
romantic love is portrayed as a sort of earthly reward for
a character's virtue. It is only in her first novel, *In
Old St. Stephen's*, which is the best-plotted of her works,
that the reverse is true. Anthony Ashley has a destiny to
fulfill--that of living up to the ideals of the gentleman
inherited through his father from his ancestor Landgrave
Ashley. He succeeds, though it means silently relinquish-
ing to his brother Miles a girl he loves and still relin-
quishing her after Miles has been killed in a duel by a
man she had thoughtlessly encouraged. In this situation

virtue and honor are incompatible with a consummation in
marriage of romantic and passionate love. Having suffered
deeply at the loss of the objects of both his brotherly
and his passionate love, Anthony is shown to have reaped
nevertheless some modest rewards for his victory over com-
promise in a pretty, gentle wife whom he learns to love,
in the love of his children and in the emulation of his
grandson. But even this is given a complicating poignancy
by the fact that Anthony Ashley is the last of his kind:
the social order in which ideals like his have had their
roots is gone by the time of his death, and he fulfills
his destiny in an alien land, whether the South of Reconstruction or the North, to which he moves.

Though in her later fiction Miss Drake learns to flesh
out her characters a little more fully than in *In Old
St. Stephen's*, she never again achieves anything quite as
sustained or as disciplined as her first novel. *The
Metropolitans* is little more ambitious than her magazine
fiction--only longer. It is the typical story of lovers'
misunderstandings and wavering fortunes which all come
right in the end. Again Miss Drake uses a specific location, New York City, as background for her fiction, but
with less feeling for its essential flavor and with less
success.[25] She may have realized this herself, for though
the second novel follows within four years of the first,
she writes no more of them, but concentrates on the magazine fiction instead.[26]

These stories are sometimes little moral tales
pointing to some ideal of behavior, but they are often
carefully drawn sketches of interesting characters in
amusing, exotic or difficult situations. A number of
character types recur: strong, useful and independently-
minded women; weak and selfish "society" people--especially
in the New York fiction; clever journalists; neo-
Abolitionists who are taken in by black role-playing;
simple and self-sacrificing mountain folk. Certain basic
plots and conflicts tend to resurface throughout the work,
though Miss Drake varies her characters and settings to
create an impression of freshness. Few of the stories
work really well as coherent wholes, but almost every one
has some good touches of imagination to recommend it.

Jeanie Drake, though not the best writer South
Carolina has ever produced, still deserves more than the
oblivion to which she has been consigned, and which she

may well have courted, herself. Beyond the immediate question of her identity, and the examination of any literary
papers which may be unearthed once the problem of her
pseudonym is solved, her work seems worthy of one or two
extended critical studies, say of master's thesis length.
It would be worthwhile to determine her relationship to
other South Carolina and New York fiction writers of her
time. And a study of her use of Charleston and low-country
history and tradition in *In Old St. Stephen's* might prove
interesting. Or a consideration of the career itself—a
career of popular literary production which from the outset
was addressed, apparently by choice, to quite circumscribed
audiences. The writing of Jeanie Drake is a virtually
untouched topic for investigation. Though as yet we know
very little of its author, the body of fiction is there to
be read and studied, posing some intriguing questions of
its own.

Notes

[1]See the appended checklist of her writings.

[2]See, for example, the review of *In Old St. Stephen's* in the Charleston *News and Courier* (23 October 1892), 4:2; and that of *The Metropolitans* in *Bookman*, 4 (December 1896), 372-73.

[3]Sunday, 23 October 1892, 4:2.

[4]23 (22 October 1892), 368.

[5]Miss Drake is mentioned in the *Library of Southern Literature*, XV: "Biographical Dictionary of Authors" (Atlanta: Martin and Hoyt, 1910), p. 126; and in A. S. Salley, Jr., "A Bibliography of the Women Writers of South Carolina," *Publications of the Southern History Association*, VI (1902), p. 150. Her two novels are listed in Lyle H. Wright, *American Fiction, 1876-1900* (San Marino, Cal.: The Huntington Library, 1966), p. 165.

[6]*Catholic World*, Vol. 50, 472-83.

[7]"Major Münchausen of the Gap," *Catholic World*, 107 (April 1918), 96-104.

[8]"Lucerne, Modern and Mediaeval," *Catholic World*, 99 (June 1914), 367-74.

[9]No. 44 (May 1899), 1-12.

[10]100 (October 1914), 35-44.

[11]Letter of 9 October 1975 from Robert Heyer, managing editor of *New Catholic World*.

[12]*Catholic World*, 52 (January 1891), 586.

[13]Anonymous review of *The Metropolitans*, Sunday, 15 November 1896, 5:1.

[14]The reviews, both anonymous, appearing in *Bookman* 4 (December 1896), 372-73, and *The Critic* n.s. 27 (19 June 1897), 425, remark on Miss Drake's use in *The Metropolitans*

of recent occurrences in the social affairs of the city.

[15]*Lippincott's Magazine*, 46 (July–December 1890), 512–20.

[16]*Catholic World*, 69 (May 1899), 248–54.

[17]83–84 (May 1906–January 1907), 202–19, 315–31, 483–96, 598–611, 733–45; 21–35, 161–75, 314–25, 440–52.

[18]*Catholic World*, 82 (November 1905), 158–65.

[19]The exceptions all occur in the first half of her writing career: "Tartuffe in Ebony," *Lippincott's Magazine*, 46 (July–December 1890), 512–20; "On Pigeon River," *The Black Cat*, no. 44 (May 1899), 1–12; "The Price of Jonathan," *Pearson's Magazine*, 15 (February 1906), 161–65.

[20]"And Peace on Earth," *Catholic World*, 50 (January 1890), 472–83.

[21]Charles Sinkler's daughters were Elizabeth Allen (Mrs. Charles) Coxe, author of *Memories of a South Carolina Plantation During the War* (privately printed, 1912), Mary (Mrs. Charles) Stevens, and Caroline Sidney Sinkler.

[22]Joseph S. Ames, "Cantey Family," *South Carolina Historical and Genealogical Magazine*, 11 (October 1910), 203–258; Anne Sinkler Fishburne, *Belvidere: A Plantation Memory* (Columbia: University of South Carolina Press, 1949), p. 109.

[23]Telephone interview with Mrs. Laura Manning, 22 October 1975. Moreover, neither the memoirs of Elizabeth Sinkler Coxe nor of her niece, Anne Sinkler Fishburne (see notes 21 and 22), reveal a connection between the Sinklers and "Jeanie Drake."

[24]*Catholic World*, 88 (December 1908), 357.

[25]The social satire in the novel is superficial and artificial, symptoms of her never having genuinely come to terms with the society; her characters seem to be abstractions, types, rather than caricatures of real, living people.

[26]Her decision to abandon the novel form may very well
have been influenced by the critical reviews *The Metro-*
politans elicited. As opposed to *In Old St. Stephen's*,
which was received very favorably locally, *The Metropoli-*
tans was reviewed for the most part condescendingly and
even insultingly by the New York journals. See, for
example, the reviews in *Bookman*, 4 (December 1896), 372-73,
and in *The Nation*, 64 (28 January 1897), 71. Even *Catholic*
World gave its regular contributor a very mixed review
[65 (August 1897), 701-702]. If *The Metropolitans* was
Jeanie Drake's bid for a wider or more lucrative readership, she could have found little encouragement in its
reception by that audience.

A Checklist of the Writings of Jeanie Drake

I. Books:
   1. *In Old St. Stephen's.* New York: D. Appleton, 1892.
   2. *The Metropolitans.* New York: Century Co., 1896.

II. Contributions to periodicals:
   1. "And Peace on Earth," *Catholic World*, 50 (January 1890), 472-83.
   2. "Tartuffe in Ebony," *Lippincott's Magazine*, 46 (July-December 1890), 512-520.
   3. "'Dios te Guarde,'" *Catholic World*, 51 (July 1890), 438.
   4. "Under the Bôdhi-Tree," *Catholic World*, 52 (January 1891), 570-86.
   5. "Ancient and Honorable," *Catholic World*, 69 (May 1899), 248-54.
   6. "On Pigeon River," *The Black Cat*, no. 44 (May 1899), 1-12.
   7. "The Dream of her Life," *Catholic World*, 80 (February 1905), 592-98.
   8. "Miss Ferrill's Diploma," *Catholic World*, 81 (May 1905), 157-61.
   9. "June," *Catholic World*, 81 (July 1905), 483-4.
   10. "Tobias Greene, Tonsorialist," *Catholic World*, 81 (August 1905), 623-35.
   11. "The Brother of Mercy," *Catholic World*, 82 (November 1905), 158-65.
   12. "Hired Wedding Garments," *Catholic World*, 82 (February 1906), 670-82.
   13. "The Price of Jonathan," *Pearson's Magazine*, 15 (February 1906), 161-65.
   14. "A Determined Celibate," *Catholic World*, 83 (April 1906), 32-42.
   15. "Narcissus," *Catholic World*, 83-84 (May 1906-January 1907), 202-19, 315-31, 483-96, 598-611, 733-45; 21-35, 161-75, 314-25, 440-52.
   16. "Cinderella's Sister," *Catholic World*, 85 (June 1907), 366-76.
   17. "An Uncivil Engineer," *Catholic World*, 86 (November 1907), 189-97.
   18. "A Mountain Griselda," *Catholic World*, 86 (March 1908), 769-78.

19. "Pink Lemonade, a Bear, and a Prodigal," *Catholic World*, 87 (June 1908), 376-83.

20. "With a White Stone," *Catholic World*, 88 (October 1908), 13-24.

21. "To Men of Good-Will," *Catholic World*, 88 (December 1908), 356-62.

22. "By the Waters of Babylon," *Catholic World*, 88 (March 1909), 735-44.

23. "For Sport," *Catholic World*, 90 (October 1909), 50-63.

24. "His Neighbor," *Catholic World*, 90 (December 1909), 329-40.

25. "As It Happened," *Catholic World*, 90 (March 1910), 776-87.

26. "The Drum Major's Daughter," *Catholic World*, 91 (April, May 1910), 28-38, 160-71.

27. "The Wayside Stations," *Catholic World*, 92 (December 1910), 340-52.

28. "The Cross of the Legion," *Catholic World*, 94 (December 1911), 345-58.

29. "The Postboy," *Catholic World*, 96 (November 1912), 170-79.

30. "The City of Goodwill," *Catholic World*, 96 (January 1913), 487-99.

31. "The Rainbow Crystal," *Catholic World*, 97 (June 1913), 360-73.

32. "Lucerne, Modern and Mediaeval," *Catholic World*, 99 (June 1914), 367-74.

33. "On Pigeon River," *Catholic World*, 100 (October 1914), 35-44.

34. "Major Münchausen of the Gap," *Catholic World*, 107 (April 1918), 96-104.

The Unpublished Diaries of
Mary Moragné Davis

by

Delle Mullen Craven

It is well known that diaries from the early years of
American history comprise a large segment of the literature
of this time. Such diverse personalities as William Byrd,
Samuel Sewall, John Woolman, and Sarah Knight are revealed
through their diaries with a candor possible only to writing intended solely for the private eye. On becoming ac-
quainted with some of these diaries early in my teaching
career, I began to look again at the diaries of my great-
grandmother, Mary Moragné Davis, which I had read while in
high school. I found them of undoubted value in depicting
the times and personalities of a relatively unexplored
locale and era of Southern history---the South Carolina
upcountry in the 1830's and 1840's. Oral family history
from my grandfather, Robert McCheyne Davis, and his sister
Kate had already interested me in the personalities of
their parents and their childhood home near Willington in
what is now McCormick County. In graduate school I met
with encouragement by professors at the universities of
North Carolina and Tennessee and by the University of
South Carolina Press. In 1951 the diaries for the years
1836-1842 were published under the title of *The Neglected
Thread: A Journal from the Calhoun Community, 1836-1842.*

Mary Elizabeth Moragné was born in December, 1816, on
her father's plantation, "Oakwood," near New Bordeaux,
South Carolina. Her father, Isaac, was the youngest son of
Pierre Moragné, who had come to this country as a Huguenot
from Bordeaux, France, in 1765 and helped to found the
short-lived town of New Bordeaux. Her mother, Margaret

15

Blanton Caine, daughter of William and Mary Vaughn Caine,
was of English ancestry. Mary was the eldest of eleven
children. Although all of her brothers received a professional education in law or medicine, her own formal
schooling was limited to the neighborhood schools and female academies of her locality. Her literary bent, however,
early showed itself in her lengthy diaries, which she began
presumably in her late teens, and in her preoccupation with
reading and studying.

Up to 1838 Mary Moragné's activities followed the
usual pattern for Southern girls: parties, dancing, visiting, flirting---and in her case reading and writing. Early
in 1838 she made a six-weeks' visit to Augusta, Georgia,
forty miles away, the metropolis of the area, which one of
its literary editors, William Tappan Thompson, called "the
Philadelphia of the South." Later in that same year
Thompson awarded Mary Moragné first prize for the best
"tale"---of novelette length---submitted to the *Augusta
Mirror*. This historical romance was *The British Partizan*,
based on the life of her great-great-uncle, a British
sympathizer during the American Revolution.

The following year, however, saw a decided change in
Mary Moragné's life. Two deaths in her family brought
about a profound religious conversion. Then, by 1842, because of church disapproval and her marriage to a
Presbyterian minister, she stopped writing stories. Her
husband, the Reverend William Hervey Davis, pastor of
Willington Presbyterian Church, was born in North Carolina
and reared in East Tennessee. As pastor at Willington he
succeeded the venerable Moses Waddell, famed Willington
schoolmaster and president of the University of Georgia.

The Davises remained at Willington for thirty-three
years after their marriage. Nine children were born to
them. During these years Mr. Davis was also schoolmaster
and Mary Moragné joined him intermittently in 1863 and con-
tinuously in 1867. By 1875 both church and community had
been so depleted by deaths and removals that the Davises
removed to Georgia and finally to Talladega, Alabama.

Mary Moragné continued to write to the end of her long
life, contributing many articles and poems to religious
periodicals and newspapers. Her collected poems, *Lays from
the Sunny Lands*, were published in 1888. She died early in
1903 in Talladega in her eighty-seventh year and was buried

in Oak Hill Cemetery there.

As a literary figure, Mary Moragné's reputation rests,
not on her poetry and fiction, but on her diary. Brought
into sharp focus by her trenchant pen is the world of such
diverse elements as the camp-meeting and the Augusta
theatre, Senator McDuffie and the Moragné's overseer, a
Presbyterian conscience and the easy-going society of the
rural South.

The journals exist, in more or less fragmentary form,
from 1834-1842, 1863, 1867, and 1899-1903, only a short
while before her death.[1] The romantic froth of her earliest years, which masks reality, is a far cry from the terse,
methodical entries of an aged woman concerned mainly with
medicines, the weather, and the comings and goings of
family members and her daughters' dressmaking customers and
music pupils. Yet even from 1834, when she was seventeen,
there is a carefully detailed description of the ruins of
the Revolutionary fort at Ninety-Six, showing how her
imagination was stimulated by local history. Her early
bent for philosophical musing is interwoven with comments
on the character of her acquaintances. Of a woman who lost
all her possessions in a fire, she writes:

> . . . It is amusing amid all her lachrymose ex-
> pressions of grief to see her entertain her company
> with the same ceremonious pride on a few old
> wooden chairs & picked up spoons, as when she
> moved in mahogany & silver--but pride is fire
> proof![2]

Her reflections after 1839 were directed by religious influences, and the diary becomes more introspective, running
the gamut from the exultation of her first Communion to
remorse over a fit of bad temper.

Her intellectual and literary interests continued,
however, and were put to the practical use of teaching
school in her father's home, the beginning of a lifelong
occupation as her pupils changed from her brothers and
sisters to her own children, and finally to a formal
community school. Sometime during the latter years of her
life she wrote and evidently intended for publication two
textbooks, one on Biblical characters called "Bible
Sketches, or Half hours with the Ancients" and the other
on astronomy, entitled "Facts & Fancies in the Material

Universe, or God's Glory in the Heavens." The latter contains surprisingly accurate scientific information. But
its market value as a textbook was probably diminished by
the very quality which captivates the literary historian:
her inclusion of occasional personal anecdotes and her own
views on cosmology. For instance, she writes thus of the
fright caused by a spectacular meteor shower in 1833, when
she would have been sixteen years old:

> I was aroused from sleep at four o'clock A.M. by
> the doleful voice of the old patriarch of the
> blacks, at the door: "Master! Come out here,
> Master! There's something dreadful to pay!"
> That Master had never seen a work on Astronomy,
> but he was a Natural Philosopher; and taking a
> short survey of the Heavens, he replied: "some
> change in the elements, Jim;" & went quietly
> back to bed. Through an open window, I gazed on
> the grand panorama; but with that ignorant & panic
> fear, which almost paralyzed my nerves, to the
> splendor of the amazing scene.[3]

Whatever the subject of her writing, it was pursued with
thoroughness, vivacity, and a flair for dramatic incident.

The unpublished journal fragments which are my chief
concern at this time are from 1863 and 1867. The first
covers only three months, May, June, and December. The
second is much more extensive, running from April through
December. These show family and community life during
this period in a place which did not experience the dis-
location and destruction of the fighting. The effects of
war are seen throughout these pages, but its action is
always offstage.

In 1863 Mary Moragné was forty-six years old, her
husband fifty-five. Their oldest child, Margie, was
twenty, and the youngest, Ellie, was not quite four. In
the Moragné family, of the six daughters and five sons
living during the years covered in *The Neglected Thread*,
four daughters and only one son were alive in 1863. War
had already taken its toll with the death of John in the
Mexican War, and of William, a Confederate colonel of the
Nineteenth South Carolina Regiment, in 1862.

Mr. Davis had in the preceding year resigned the
pastorate of the Willington church evidently because of a

schism, the details of which are obscure. At this time
he was supplying several churches in the surrounding area.
He was also conducting a school with his wife as substitute teacher when his preaching engagements required him
to be away. She seemed to welcome the opportunity to
teach after so many years of child-bearing and household
management. An entry on May 1, 1863, shows what this
household management involved:

> During all this time that the "school *mistress* has
> been abroad" my children's wardrobe has been in
> "statu quo"--I must now reel & carry my thread
> to the weaver to supply their summer clothes. I
> must set the house in order--make a barrel of
> vinegar-work in the garden, etc.[4]

1863 was a year of crisis in the conduct of the war:
the death of Stonewall Jackson occurred in May, and the
outcome of the battles at Gettysburg and Vicksburg was to
seal the fate of the Southern cause by the end of the year.
Communication of news to Willington was fairly prompt.
The telegraph extended to Abbeville, and Willington received mail from there daily. When Jackson died on May 10,
Mary Moragné was writing of it in her journal on the 11th.
Also there were frequent reports of conditions in other
parts of the South. Her brother Nat and his family were
driven from their home in Palatka, Florida, on the St.
John's River by an attack from a Yankee gunboat, evidently
aimed at a Confederate camp close by. The family, however,
escaped without injury or destruction of the home.

Once when the Davises returned home after a walk,
they found the household in a flurry of alarm because of a
rumor that the Yankees were only five miles away. Young
John, nine years old, declared he knew the Yankees would
go for him since he would soon be a man! But even when
the news was reported, people doubted it because there was
no Union military activity in South Carolina at this time
except for sporadic attacks in the Low Country. Some women
from Elbert County, Georgia, were blamed for starting the
rumor. The sentiments of all were probably voiced by
little Ellie as she asked her nurse, "Don't you wish this
war was over, Marthy?"

Sometime in 1863 between June and December the
Davises' oldest son Willie, age seventeen, enlisted in the
Confederate army and was assigned to guard an arsenal at

Augusta. The main event of the last month of the diary
for this year deals with his efforts to get home for
Christmas. His adventure was caused not by the hardships
of the military but by teen-age impulsiveness and determination, along with bad weather conditions. Although his
father had sent him money to come home on by relatives
going to Augusta (his mother's married sister lived there),
the young soldier left before hearing from home, hopping a
freight train for Abbeville. Due to unusual delays caused
by a record flood, the train took twenty-four hours to
reach Abbeville at six o'clock in the evening. Unable to
procure a horse, Willie set out on foot, carrying his va-
lise and blanket roll, to walk the sixteen miles home.
But when he reached Calhoun's Mill, the bridge was out;
still determined, he endeavored to ford the river by rock-
hopping as he had often done in the past. The depth of
the water, however, forced him to swim to a rock big
enough to offer some security, and here, wrapped in his
blanket, he slept until dawn, when he was discovered and
rescued by some Negroes. Surprisingly, he suffered little
from this ordeal and was able to join in the festivities
of what was probably, for these young people, the last
merry Christmas in quite some time.

Throughout this journal Mary Moragné comments on the
reports from battles and the qualities of the leaders on
both sides. While she seemed hopeful of military success
in June, she was very discouraged at the end of December
as she writes of the woes of the time:

> Under these circumstances, when I have so much im-
> perilled, how dark is the gloom that overshadows
> the country! When I think of the defection of our
> men at Lookout Mountain when 20,000 threw down
> their arms & ran, when I hear that one half of
> our armies are coward & play out of every engage-
> ment, when I see so many deserting or bribing fur-
> loughs & loitering about home while the Yankees
> are overrunning us. . . I lose all faith in *man*;
> & when I see extortion & speculation preying like
> greedy vultures upon the vitals & life-blood of
> this Confederacy--when I see public opinion dis-
> regarded, charity, benevolence, good faith & all
> the amenities of society bowing before the demon
> of selfishness. . . I seem to be trembling on
> the brink of a precipice. . . .[5]

Few service-connected deaths are recorded in 1863,
though we learn from her collection of obituaries that
several of the young men in her family connection did not
survive 1864. But deaths and funerals from the native
population are a major item of entry. The victims ranged
in age from a tiny infant to a hundred-year-old Negro and
included young ladies of her daughters' age, a young
mother with her husband at war, taken with a sudden
seizure, and Mr. Davis' older brother Robert, whose son
had been killed in battle the preceding year. In reading
the constant chronicle of these deaths, much as in any
nineteenth-century diary, one is struck by the helpless-
ness of people in the face of disease, the way they accepted sorrow as an inevitable part of life, and the way
they tried to prepare the dying person for his or her
demise. Mary Moragné always noted with thankfulness if
the dying person had made a profession of Christian faith,
and consoled herself with his having gone to a better life.

Mary Moragné's religious convictions, as in the last
years of *The Neglected Thread*, are of paramount importance
in these journals. Faith was her bulwark against despair
during years of anxiety and sorrow. More than once she
lifted herself from the despondency to which she was often
prone because of her sense of duty to her family and the
necessity of attending to her household and her school.
As an earnest Calvinist, ever conscious of man's sinful
state, she regarded the afflictions of the present as evidence of the chastening hand of God. To endure without
questioning the will of the Almighty and maintain faith
in the goodness of his ultimate Providence was the course
that kept her going. Christianity was her frame of
reference for her other studies. Her joy in nature, which
she described in connection with her study of botany in
1867, was related to the wonder of God's creation; her
interest in astronomy prompted her to sympathize with the
pagans, who, without benefit of revelation, worshipped the
stars.

The church services dealt with in greatest detail
were those of the Methodist revival at Zoar in 1867. This
church, which was within earshot of the Davis home,
prompted much the same reaction from Mary Moragné as had
the camp meeting she attended in 1839. She deplored the
noisy emotionalism of a preacher whose "zeal has somewhat
outstripped his knowledge," but admitted his popularity:
"The farmer has left his plough, the shoemaker his bench,

42675

the housewife her broom & distaff, and all. . . have run to
the scene of expectation."[6] The revival attracted young
people from Presbyterian families, and some parents feared
that they were being proselyted. But Mary Moragné respected the revivalists' sincerity and hoped that if they set
her children to thinking, it would be "the first step on
the ladder of grace."

This revival was followed by Presbyterian meetings at
Willington and Hopewell, similar in intent but more sedate
in tone. The Davises were overjoyed when their daughter
Margie joined the church at this time.

Turning to the social life of the time, in 1863 we see
that entertaining soldiers provided the chief spur for
parties. On the way home from church one day the Davis
girls met some young cavalrymen and, arriving home, sent
them some strawberries and cream. The young men later
called at the Davis home, but one of them from Georgia
committed the *faux pas* of asking for piano music on the
Sabbath and thereby provoked Mary Moragné's acid comment
in her diary on the decadent state of Sabbath-keeping in
Georgia! She had equally sharp comments on parties at
which dancing took place, having long before abjured the
pleasure of dancing which she herself had described in her
pre-conversion days of 1837.[7]

Christmas of 1863 with Willie and the other boys at
home seems to have been a gay time. Mary Moragné gave a
dinner party for her children's friends with a large
turkey and eggnog. They enjoyed singing to the piano and
guitar and pulling candy. The mother watched the young
people with an observant eye and noted with interest and
some satisfaction who was courting or flirting with whom.
Willie had sufficiently recovered from his exposure on the
river to ride four miles to see Miss Cary Noble home, and
similar hospitality was extended at other houses. It all
reminds me of a song from one of the great-aunts, "And the
Captain with his whiskers took a sly glance at me."

By 1867, however, extending hospitality had become
much more difficult. Help was unpredictable or non-
existent, and provisions were scarce. Yet old friends came
to visit and sometimes to make a lengthy stay. One couple
at least, the Stokes, were paying guests, but others like
Mrs. DeGraffenreid, who had lost everything in the war,
came as a refugee. At one time Mary Moragné writes that

there were sixteen at the table, while shortages were growing acute:

> The prospect is truly dark:--we have no bacon,--
> no Lard, nor butter, only as is scantily purchased
> at 25ct pr [1b] . . . we have no milk at present;
> yet to such as *we* he [God] says, "use hospitality
> without grudgeing"; & sweetly cheers us on in this
> duty, by saying; "Whoso giveth to the poor
> *lendeth to the Lord*"![8]

Household affairs, which were seldom mentioned in 1863,
were a major concern four years later. Servants had left
or were undependable, sometimes leaving at a time of crisis
to go to a meeting. Once when company came, Mary Moragné--
evidently teaching at or near her home--had to dismiss her
school and go to the kitchen. She writes of having to take
over the syrup-making, at which she was assisted by the
children:

> Our little girls Susie, Minnie, and my own Katie
> and Ellie--are my good little fairies--drive the
> horses, skim the boiler, strain the juice, run on
> errands. . . and that too with so much sweetness
> & alacrity, that they remind me of the "Merry Puck
> who held himself ready to put a girdle about the
> earth in forty minutes."[9]

Growing their own wheat provided them with bread as long as
the crop lasted, but by Christmas the supply was exhausted.
That Christmas the festivities were confined to the blacks
while the Davises brought in their own wood and water.
Mary Moragné earlier wrote: "If only I had a stove, a well,
and a washing machine, I should be tolerably independent. . . ." But somehow they managed to survive.

Mary Moragné's chief source of pleasure in 1867 was
her teaching, especially the study of botany. She devoted
several pages of her first entries for April of this year
to a description of the various plants to be found in her
locality. Her systematic mind took readily to botanical
classification as evidenced by two herbaria, which are
still in a well-preserved condition. She enjoyed rambles
in the woods and fields with her children in search of new
specimens, and the seven-mile drive to church at Hopewell
did not seem tedious because she was identifying plants
along the way. Mary Moragné would have abhorred Thoreau's

politics, but she would surely have agreed with his statement, "There can be no very black melancholy to one who lives in the midst of Nature." Incidentally, her daughter Kate became a florist and supported herself and two sisters with a successful business up to the last years of her life.

The diarist contrasts their pleasant pastoral situation in the lush countryside of April with the turmoil and suffering in other sections of the state. Yet as the year went on, the effects of the political and economic upheaval were painfully evident here also. Labor for the fields as well as for the house gave trouble. Willie, as the oldest son, was living apart from his family in a lonely cabin as he rented land and tried to farm, but he was hampered by a crochety and overbearing landlord as well as strikes by his hands—a discouraging beginning for a rather moody, introspective young man.

> The cry of "Bread," [his mother writes] the first
> ever known in this country, is now owing to the
> want of labor during the past year & it must
> continue while there are so many non-producers
> preying upon the vitals of the land. . . .[10]

There was anxiety about the frequent meetings of the blacks, at one time led by a trouble-maker who had been run off some time before, but there was no account of rioting or violence. The picture given by the diarist of the blacks is one of pathetic confusion. Promises of their own land never materialized, and the magical vote seemed even to its new possessors an uncertain blessing. One Negro was indignant to discover that he could not vote for the white men he knew because they were disenfranchised!

The diarist notes, "Cousin D. M. Rogers, the best farmer, & once the richest man in this community is seen ploughing and hoeing now to save his crop."[11] The point is that he *did* plow and hoe and presumably he *did* save his crop. Adversity was testing the mettle of this people, even as it had tried their Huguenot ancestors a century before. It is true, as Mary Moragné bitterly writes, that poverty bred selfishness, and unguided and misguided emancipation bred flagrant irresponsibility. But, even in these times, the good things in life had not been completely eclipsed. One also sees lively children in a hay-filled wagon going on a nutting expedition; the enthusiasm of a

middle-aged woman, who is both teacher and student, im-
mersed in her new study; a family sharing its meagre resources with an impoverished friend. And, as 1867 ends,
Elize, a Negro woman, pays a visit to the Davises, bringing a basket of cakes for the children.

Mary Moragné Davis thought of herself as old at fifty.
She was to live another thirty-six years, through the
wrench of leaving her home surroundings of nearly sixty
years, through the vicissitudes of several temporary homes
and many bereavements. Always making do with limited
financial resources, she sustained herself and her family
with her remarkably durable intellectual and spiritual
resources. Words continued to flow from her pen up to her
very last years in the form of letters, poems, obituaries,
articles, and, of course, her diary. She remained the head
of her family until her death: a proud, versatile, strong-
minded woman who had outlived, not only her own generation,
but the very social and economic structure of her time.

Notes

[1]The journals from the years 1836 through 1842 are located in the South Caroliniana Library, Columbia, South Carolina. All other journals and manuscripts mentioned in this paper are in the possession of Mrs. Delle Mullen Craven, Knoxville, Tennessee.

[2]Mary E. Moragné, journal of 1834.

[3]Mary E. Moragné Davis, "Facts & Fancies in the Material Universe," manuscript textbook, pp. 186-187.

[4]Mary E. Moragné Davis, journal of 1863.

[5]*Ibid.*

[6]Mary E. Moragné Davis, journal of 1867.

[7]Mary E. Moragné, *The Neglected Thread: A Journal from the Calhoun Community, 1836-1842*, ed. Delle Mullen Craven (Columbia: University of South Carolina Press, 1951), p. 25.

[8]Mary E. Moragné Davis, journal of 1867.

[9]*Ibid.*

[10]*Ibid.*

[11]*Ibid.*

Mary Moragné's *The British Partizan*

by

Karen A. Endres

Mary Moragné lived from early in the 19th century (1816) into the 20th century (1903). In her early to middle twenties (1838-42) she published both prose and poetry, primarily in the *Augusta Mirror*. William Tappan Thompson, editor and publisher of the *Mirror*, liked her writing, praised it highly, encouraged her to write further sketches, stories, and poems, and, it appears, published whatever she sent him. Thompson counted on her as a regular contributor, and in at least two issues of the *Mirror* (April 24 and May 8, 1841) he included three and four pieces by her, giving her in one issue five out of a total of eight pages, in the other six out of eight pages. Material of Mary Moragné's that was published in the *Mirror* at this time includes: two short novels, *The British Partizan* (December 15, 1838 through January 26, 1839) and *The Rencontre* (April 24, May 8, 1841); at least three selections from her journal, titled "Extracts From My Journal" (December 12, 1840; "The Preacher" December 26, 1840; "The Dutch Wedding" April 24, 1841); one long and quite good poem, published in three issues, entitled "Joseph" (May 8, July 3, September 11, 1841); and a variety of shorter poems, of varying merit.

After her early success in writing and publishing, however, Mary Moragné decided for religious reasons not to write any further fiction, and turned her energies in 1842 to marriage and raising a family of nine children. In 1888, when she was 72 years old, she published a book

of poetry, *Lays from the Sunny Lands*,[1] which includes poems
from both the early and the later periods of her life.
During the later period, she also wrote two textbooks, each
over 200 handwritten pages; one is on Biblical history, the
other on science. Mrs. Craven has indicated a belief that
a primary purpose of writing them was an attempt on Mary
Moragné's part to earn money from their publication. They
were never published, however.

Despite acclaim by her contemporaries, Mary Moragné's
contribution to our knowledge of South Carolina history was
unknown in this century until 1951, when her great granddaughter, Mrs. Delle Mullen Craven, transcribed the manuscript journals covering the period 1836-1842 and published
about two-thirds of this material as *The Neglected Thread*.[2]
The journal covering this period seems to be the most
important of all of Mary Moragné's writing. In her preface
Mrs. Craven points out the value of the journal as a record
of a part of Southern life often overlooked although quite
common. She says

> this was not the South of pillared mansions but
> of plain, substantial frame houses, the homes
> of small plantation-owners, of country preachers
> and teachers. It was an up-country region close
> to the frontier; yet the . . . people. . . were
> neither crude nor ignorant.[3]

Additionally, the early journal records the daily and
yearly tasks of a young woman of Mary Moragné's economic
class in the 19th century, her educational and social
activities, and her developing religious and philosophical
ideas. It also shows a young 19th century writer's self-
education by means of wide reading, and her strong ambition.

Second in importance only to the journals are Mary
Moragné's two short novels. While the journals reveal a
quiet region of plain houses and small farms of the 1830's
and 1840's, the novels portray the same region fifty years
earlier (1780-81), when the area was more primitive and
more rural and yet was more violent--when the Revolutionary
War was in progress. In both novels, Mary Moragné uses a
brief historical outline of events as a basic framework
within which to write of human emotions. In *The Rencontre*,
which is a shorter story than *The British Partizan*, she
seems more limited by the historical event, especially in

the telescoped ending; but even here, she masterfully
controls and uses the tension between past, present, and
future time.

My purpose here is to discuss *The British Partizan*:
its reception, its texts, its publishing history, and,
finally, some of its themes and images.

In the second issue of the *Augusta Mirror* (May 19,
1838) William T. Thompson offered several prizes for original material submitted to him. One was for a historical
tale "founded upon incidents connected with the early
history of Georgia or South Carolina."[4] Mary Moragné
entered this contest at her brother William's suggestion.[5]
According to her journal, she received the *Mirror* adver-
tisement from her brother on July 22, 1838, and she wrote
The British Partizan in the next two months, sending it
off to Thompson on September 21.[6] She won the complete
works of Sir Walter Scott, plus a year's subscription to
the *Mirror*; Augustus B. Longstreet was one of the judges.[7]
Her story, *The British Partizan, A Tale of the Times
of Old*, was published in the *Mirror* in four issues,
December 15, 1838 through January 26, 1839.[8]

Less than a month after its inclusion in the *Mirror*,
Thompson published the novel in book form.[9] He explains in
his preface that readers of the *Mirror* have requested "its
publication in a more convenient form."[10] He further indicates that Mary Moragné reluctantly gave consent for its
re-publication, and that she did not revise it.[11] Her lack
of revision was no doubt caused by Thompson's haste in publishing the book rather than unwillingness on her part, for
she made extensive improvements in her journal sketches
before their publication in 1840. It seems that she also
wrote a dedication for *The British Partizan* which did not
reach Thompson in time to be included in the book. His
preface is dated February 10, and her journal indicates
that she wrote a letter to him on February 15, 1839,

> concluding, I hope, the *business*, of the
> *dedication*, the *book* he informs me will be
> out next Wednesday. . . .[12]

Apparently 5,000 copies of the book were printed, which
Thompson hoped to sell for one dollar each.[13] He relates
in his preface to the 1864 edition of the novel that "the

greater part" of the 1839 edition was destroyed in a flood in Augusta.[14] The flood, however, was more than a year later, in May, 1840,[15] and it is likely that many copies were sold during that year. Thompson certainly advertised the novel well, praising it frequently in the editorials of the *Mirror* and reprinting notices of it by other newspapers and periodicals. Mary Moragné was not aware of the loss of the copies of the book, for in a letter to R. Means Davis in 1898, she blames Thompson for publishing so small an edition:

> His extreme caution, or it may be, his poverty, caused him to publish a small Edition, for which he was much censured at the time. Many calls were made for the Book, which could not be supplied.[16]

The novel was re-published once more. In 1864, Burke, Boykin & Company of Macon, Georgia, published it, in paper covers, from the *Mirror* text, with a new preface by Thompson. The subtitle was changed to "A Tale of The Olden Time," and Mary Moragné's name was replaced with "By a Lady of South Carolina." In the same letter to R. Means Davis, a Professor of History at South Carolina College in 1898, Mary Moragné points out what she calls "many printers errors" in the 1864 edition.[17] A partial collation of the texts of the two editions reveals the usual expected variants in punctuation and spelling, though they are more frequent than expected. But many word changes are revealed as well. In fact, three major word changes occur on the same page. The 1839 edition has "revulsion" (29.15) and the 1864 edition has "convulsion" (26.14-15) in the phrase "with what a sickening revulsion its whole weight is thrown back upon the heart." The word "comprised" (29.18) is changed to "compressed" (26.19) in the sentence "In that first moment of exquisite anguish, a life time is comprised." The word "restore" (29.20) appears as "return" (26.21) in "to restore its withered pulses to their freshness again." These changes are not authorial, and they are probably not Thompson's, as, according to Mary Moragné, he had sold the rights to the material to Burke, Boykin & Company in 1841;[18] thus he probably had no part in this edition beyond writing a preface. The heavy editorial hand perhaps shows that word usage had changed by 1864 and that a diligent copy editor was making the words match current usage. Outdated word usage does not, however, explain the change from "the

purple muscodine" (30.19) to "the purple wild grape"
(27.21-22), as "muscadine" is still a good word, even
today. Since these variants are not corrections of
obvious errors but deliberate editorial revisions without
the author's approval, and in the absence of the original
Mirror text, the 1839 edition is the definitive text.

Mary Moragné's contemporaries viewed her novels
favorably. A short review of *The British Partizan* which
appeared in *The Knickerbocker* in May of 1839 and which was
reprinted in June in the *Mirror*, says in part:[19]

> We commend the little book, therefore, to our
> readers, for many positive as well as negative
> merits, and as better worth perusal than one
> half of the republications of trans-atlantic
> fictions, the labors of small minds, and
> written by the score for the London market.

Sarah Lawrence Griffin, editor of the *Family Companion*, in Macon, Georgia, when asking Mary Moragné to
send material for the *Family Companion* in 1842, wrote her,
saying:

> I do not flatter, when I say, that you can
> command a name which shall rank as high as
> any writer in the country, if you choose to
> do it. . . .[20]

And, of course, Thompson had only praise and encouragement for Mary Moragné's writing. A letter in 1842
informing her of the merger of the *Mirror* with the *Family
Companion* conveys appreciation for her work:

> I *do* admire your style of composition above
> all those who have contributed to the Mirror. . . .[21]

Six weeks later, soliciting material for the merged magazine, he wrote:

> I am the more anxious to see your name on the
> cover of our magazine because I regard you as
> the chief literary patron of the Mirror.[22]

In the *Mirror* in May, 1841, he refers to *The Rencontre*,
concluded in that issue, as belonging to "that class of
literary productions we prize above all other orders of

fiction." He goes on to say:

> ... we hold it worth volumes of the mawkish
> romance and sickly sentimentality which has
> of late become a merchantable commodity with
> a great portion of the literary world.[23]

Thompson uses *The Rencontre* as an example of the high
quality of Southern literature, and he urges the Southern
public to support both the literature and his magazine.

In 1854 William Gilmore Simms, novelist and editor,
listed "Miss Moragné" as one of the South Carolina writers
he recommended for inclusion in Duyckinck's anthology of
American literature.[24] But she was not included.

Another opinion of Mary Moragné's writing is given in
1913 in a letter of John M. McBryde, who lived in the area
the novel is set in. The letter is quoted in George A.
Wauchope's *Literary South Carolina*:

> While a little crude and lavish in description,
> there is a good deal of merit in the work of so
> young a writer. Especially is this true of the
> characterization of Ferguson. Our Southern
> writers almost without exception have described
> him as a rough, brutal partizan. She portrays
> him as chivalrous, ambitious, generous, and
> gallant.[25]

Of other 20th century comments on the novel, we have
only Mrs. Craven's, in her introduction to *The Neglected
Thread*. Her emphasis, like McBryde's, is on the novel's
historical content. She finds it "noticeably the work of
an amateur," however. She feels that it is too loose in
in structure, that it should be more tightly woven so that
no character or incident is extraneous to the plot.[26]

Thompson's approach to *The British Partizan* seems a
good place to begin a discussion of its themes and purposes. He suggests that we let the author lead us "with
the wand of an enchantress, through this beautiful romance
of the 'olden time.'"[27] The tone of the novel is nostal-
gic; the action is in a distant past which we are not able
to see into too clearly because of the time span in
between. And because of the distance in time, people may

appear simpler than they really were; for example, Ralph Cornet seems almost too good, and Hugh Bates may seem an unalleviated villain. People seem to meet by chance and characters may seem one-sided. But I think part of Mary Moragné's purpose is to show that we cannot see history exactly as it was, and in our re-creation of it in imagination, it may take on aspects of a dream; that is, it may lose its complexity and its realistic qualities. Historical events may appear symbolic rather than realistic. Past history certainly has a large part in the novel; the reader is aware always of the fact that many towns like the Vienna, South Carolina, of the novel no longer exist except in ruins.

The opening scene of the novel establishes this historical aspect and the dreamlike atmosphere, and it also points out the Savannah River as an important image. At the core of the world in the novel is a magical river, "where the shadows of painted barges and smoking engines pass over it like the illusions of the enchanter's mirror." (13) The idea that there is disparity between appearance and reality is initiated here, both in relation to the reader and in relation to the characters. The author seems to put the reader under a spell in which the action and scenes of a past time will rise up as if out of the mist or out of a dream. The calm untroubled waters of the river, from which the story seems to rise, are deceptive to the characters in the novel as well. Because their town is so outwardly peaceful, the people in the fictional Vienna feel that the Revolutionary War, which they hear about from a distance, does not concern them. However, Mary Moragné indicates that the arrival of British officers does not bring the war to them but that it merely stimulates friction which already exists among the inhabitants of the town.

The opening scene further shows how the river functions as a symbol. As in the quotation from Sir Walter Scott which begins the novel, the river survives the scenes of war. "Steel-clad warriors" no longer ride along Scott's river Teviot; no evidence of war or even of civilization remains. It looks as if it has always been pastoral. Civilization, and its accompaniment, war, might have been an illusion, as the American Indian civilization on the land of Mary Moragné's Vienna might well have been an illusion. The river, the representative of nature, renews itself and survives while war and civilization fade away.

The author sets up the contrast between this point on the
river where the water is deceptively calm and a connected
point, in Habersham county, Georgia, where the precipices
and rocks are closer to reality. The Savannah connects
the two areas, and this is the path Ralph Cornet travels
when he is wounded and outcast. It is at Tallulah Falls,
in Habersham county, that he undergoes a profound experience where he loses his illusions and is healed both
mentally and physically. It is in Ralph's re-aligning
himself with the renewing power of nature and in leaving
the battlefield that he, too, survives.

The river is also used to separate civilization and
the wilderness. The town is on the South Carolina side of
the river; the Georgia side is wilder, and uncivilized.
The difference between the two sides is clearly shown:

> The Georgia bank is high, and mostly rugged;
> but on the other side is a vast extent of
> rich and fertile lowland. . . . [14]

Another description is given when Annette Bruyésant's
father is attacked by Tories:

> Perhaps, no where could have been found a
> greater number of desperadoes than the
> extreme western part of this district,
> aided by the Georgia side of the Savannah,
> afforded; men, who eagerly accepted the
> favor of the British as an excuse for
> indulging their lawless propensities. [37]

A group of these desperadoes is camped in a flood plain
right on the river, between it and the banks leading to
civilization, when two frightened but curious young women
approach the camp, after these men have ransacked their
home. The area is wild; the men are completely at home
on the river.

> Its naturally gloomy aspect was now rendered
> fearfully wild, by the effect of the various
> lights scattered through it; around which,
> sat or stood, about thirty or forty ferocious
> looking beings, in every variety of grotesque
> attitudes. [69]

Since the two sides of the river are established so clearly as opposites, the frequent crossings and recrossings of the Savannah take on added meaning. After Ralph has joined the British, he comes across from the Georgia side to see Annette, his fiancee, to whom he is a traitor to his country. Ralph's father is safe for a while in the middle of the river, on an island, but he is killed there and his attackers flee into Georgia afterwards. When Ralph is wounded and unconscious at one point, on the Georgia side, his horse carries him across the river, where he is found and cared for by his old friend, Juba. Ralph, who is allied with the wilderness from his youth, crosses into Georgia for his real healing at Tallulah Falls. And, as he cannot live in the tame, civilized town, at the end of the story, he and Annette cross into Georgia for the last time, turning their backs on civilization.

In addition to sustained tone and river symbolism, Mary Moragné uses other sophisticated fictional devices that illustrate her competent handling of the novel form.

Ralph's horse in a way represents his manhood. After he gives his horse to his British officer and friend, Ferguson, he goes through his worst periods of suffering and trouble; when he is reunited with the horse, the horse leads him to Tallulah Falls, where he is healed. When Annette and her friends discover the horse on an island in the river, it is as though Ralph himself were present. And as Ralph comes boldly to claim Annette as his bride at the end of the novel, it is the horse which attracts the attention and admiration of the townspeople:

> He was riding a horse of prodigious size and
> beauty, which seemed to yield to every motion
> of the rider, as his graceful, swan-like neck,
> obeyed the impulse of the rein. [147]

It seems here that Ralph, who had forsaken his fiancee for glories of war portrayed by the British officer Ferguson, now is able to see that love and sex should have been his primary goal. It was not right for him to throw away his manhood on a cause he did not deeply feel.

Mary Moragné's most successful achievement in this novel seems to me to be Ralph's Tallulah Falls experience. He joins the British side in the war for no sound reason. He is deceived by the appearance of Ferguson, who wears

fine clothes and a shining sword. Ralph knows the ways of
the forest, but not those of civilized society, and he is
deluded by the apparent simplicity of war. Having lived
his early life instinctively, he is subdued by a superior
intellect and a superior dream-maker:

> His youthful reason, which had never been taught
> to raise its eagle eyes to the sun of truth, was
> blinded by the splendid illusions conjured up by
> this master spirit. . . [24]

Ferguson's mental capacity overcomes Ralph's native
instincts; he tricks Ralph into a wrong decision. Ralph
makes a wrong choice in a very serious matter, and he
suffers greatly for it. He then goes through a process of
re-education similar to that of Shakespeare's King Lear
after *his* wrong decision, which has also been made on the
basis of the way things appear. Ralph, like Lear, begins
a search for what is real; he progressively loses layers
of socialization and of his individual personality until
all that is left is his humanity. At this point, Ralph is
guided by his horse across the river from civilization
back into the wilderness. He goes, seeking

> the stern and terrible, that he might hide
> from himself in the subduing presence of that
> nature which had ever been his god. [121]

When he has no layers of personality left, but only his
deepest psychic self, he arrives at the falls. In the
reality of the falls, he undergoes a spiritual experience.

> [He] drank in the roaring of the waters, until
> his strained eyes ached almost to bursting, and
> his brain whirled round with ecstasy. Scarcely
> could he refrain from throwing himself headlong,
> in sympathy with the torrent, down--down into
> its eddying pool; so fascinating--so impelling
> to his soul were those elements of the beautiful
> and terrible. [122]

There are no illusions here. He has gone beyond misery,
pride, fear, or any other human emotion; he is at one with
the cosmic force of nature. He faces death, but death
too is natural. It is in his thus experiencing, in a non-
theoretical way, his basic tie with nature, the "stern
and terrible" reality, that he is healed.

It is for Mary Moragné's power to engage us in scenes such as this one that we regret, with Thompson, "that one so gifted has not given to the literature of her country and the world, the fruit of her maturer years."[28]

Notes

[1]Mrs. Mary E. Moragné Davis, *Lays from the Sunny Lands* (Buffalo: Moulton, Wenborne and Company, 1888).

[2]Mary E. Moragné, *The Neglected Thread: A Journal from the Calhoun Community*, ed. Delle Mullen Craven (Columbia: University of South Carolina Press, 1951). Mrs. Craven's introductory material consists of "Preface" and "Backgrounds."

[3]Craven, Preface, p. vii.

[4]Bertram Holland Flanders, *Early Georgia Magazines: Literary Periodicals to 1865* (Athens: The University of Georgia Press, 1944), p. 34.

[5]Moragné, *The Neglected Thread*, p. 101.

[6]p. 101, 104.

[7]Flanders, p. 34, 35.

[8]p. 35, 254n.

[9]M. E. Moragné, *The British Partizan, A Tale of the Times of Old* (Augusta, Ga.: William T. Thompson, 1839). Thompson's preface is dated February 10, 1839. Quotations from this novel are placed in the text.

[10]Thompson, preface to 1839 edition, p. ii.

[11]p. ii, iv.

[12]Moragné, *The Neglected Thread*, p. 113.

[13]p. 122. Mary Moragné received this information from a cousin who had just visited Thompson in Augusta.

[14][Mary Moragné], *The British Partizan: A Tale of the Olden Time*, By a Lady of South Carolina (Macon, Ga.: Burke, Boykin & Company, 1864), p. [3]. Thompson's preface, "To the Reader," is dated Savannah, June, 1864.

[15]*Augusta Mirror*, May 30, 1840, p. 175.

[16]Mary E. Moragné Davis to R. Means Davis (Talladega, Alabama, January 1, 1898), p. [1]. Letter is in South Caroliniana Library.

[17]p. 2.

[18]p. 2.

[19]*The Knickerbocker*, XIII (May, 1839), p. 464. Quoted in part in Craven, Backgrounds, p. xxxvii. In the *Mirror* reprinting (June 29, 1839, p. 31), "fiction" appears instead of "fictions."

[20]Sarah Lawrence Griffin to Mary Moragné Davis (Macon, Ga., October 8, 1842), p. [1-2]. Letter is in South Caroliniana Library.

[21]William T. Thompson to Mary Moragné (Macon, Ga., February 4, 1842), p. [2]. Letter is in South Caroliniana Library.

[22]William T. Thompson to Mary Moragné (Macon, Ga., March 21, 1842), p. [1]. Letter is in South Caroliniana Library.

[23]*Augusta Mirror*, May 8, 1841, p. 79.

[24]*The Letters of William Gilmore Simms*, Vol. III, eds. Mary C. Simms Oliphant and T. C. Duncan Eaves (Columbia: University of South Carolina Press, 1954), p. 297.

[25]George A. Wauchope, *Literary South Carolina*. Bulletin of the University of South Carolina, No. 133 (December, 1923), p. 33.

[26]Craven, Backgrounds, p. xxxvi.

[27]Thompson, preface to 1864 edition, p. 4.

[28]p. 4.

Session I: Discussion

UNIDENTIFIED SPEAKER: Karen, what sort of library did Mary Moragné have at her disposal?

MISS ENDRES: Many books she knew well are listed in Mrs. Craven's introduction to *The Neglected Thread*; some of the books were histories of the war. She uses an incident from Dr. Charles Caldwell's *Memoirs of the Life and Campaigns of the Hon. Nathaniel Greene* for the plot of *The Rencontre*. *The British Partizan* uses knowledge that was in her family, that came down from her ancestors. I don't think that she set out deliberately to do much research; she knew already most of the historical facts she needed.

MR. MERIWETHER: Should we assume that she had a pretty good family library to draw on?

MRS. CRAVEN: Yes, yes, I think so, and she certainly read and thoroughly absorbed whatever was at hand. She had, for instance, her grandfather's diaries, which were quoted at some length by her brother William in one of his addresses. And that I believe would be the primary source, her grandfather's diaries.

MR. ARNOLD: Mrs. Craven, I think Miss Endres mentioned that Mrs. Davis sometimes took sections from her journal and revised them for publication. In the journals themselves do you ever find her becoming consciously literary? Does she ever fill scenes using direct quotes, extended dialogue?

MRS. CRAVEN: Yes, I think she does, though I think she does it as a way of natural self-expression. And her later use of some of those early sketches which were published in *The Mirror* is news to me. I've never seen them before myself.

MISS ENDRES: These sketches are not signed, and I am able to attribute them to Mary Moragné only because Mrs. Craven has some of the manuscripts. I compared the manuscript of "A Christmas Jaunt" with a selection from it published in *The Mirror*---in some parts *The Mirror* sketch follows the journal word for word, but in other parts it is revised. She added generalizations about the

41

incidents and added an introduction and an ending to
make it tell a better story.

MR. ARNOLD: What other kind of additions would she make?
Would she add dialogue, for instance?

MISS ENDRES: She would have already had some dialogue in
her original sketch. She added quotations, and a kind
of interpretive judgment at the beginning.

MR. MERIWETHER: To continue Mr. Arnold's question, then
you are saying that the diary was used from time to time
as a source book or a sketchbook, that she's working up
material in her diary that she's probably already planning to do something else with?

MRS. CRAVEN: I wouldn't say that she had been planning to
do something else when she wrote it. Rather, she wrote
it and then simply used it later on. The material that
you're talking about was quite early, prior to 1836; but
it was not published until 1840.

MISS ENDRES: Going back to this idea of using the journal
as a source book: I think frequently in letters she
copied out from her journal things to send to family
members, or friends.

MISS GREGORY: Does Mrs. Davis ever indicate why she's
writing a diary, or why she's keeping a journal? Does
she have any practical motive, or do you think it's just
in the tradition of Puritan examination of conscience?

MRS. CRAVEN: I think she just wrote because she liked to
write, just as a means of self-expression.

MISS GREGORY: That long passage that you quoted---during
the war, when she's viewing all of the cowardice, all the
corruption and grief---sounds very much to me like a
Puritan meditation, a kind of a meditation on the evils
of the world, and the evils of the spirit.

MR. POLK: I'm curious about Mrs. Davis's textbooks, your
opinion of their quality, their usefulness at the time
that they were written---their potential usefulness, at
any rate.

MRS. CRAVEN: Well, I started to include something about
the textbook on science, but I realized I didn't have
time. That's something that I have just recently read,
because I thought, well, what point is there in reading
a book written about astronomy in the 1880's? But I
have read it with especial interest because my husband
is a professor of astronomy, and he's been fascinated by
the accuracy of her information back then. And I think
that the qualities that made it unsuitable for a textbook are most interesting now because she includes
personal anecdotes. For instance, she has a good account of a spectacular meteor shower in 1833, which she
saw, and she describes the consternation that it caused
among the blacks on her plantation and neighboring plan-
tations.

SEVERAL VOICES SIMULTANEOUSLY: "The year the stars fell."

MR. DASHER: Karen, you emphasized the role of nature in
The British Partizan. Do you also see any indication of
her turn towards religion and away from fiction, away
from natural kinds of spirituality?

MISS ENDRES: No, I don't.

MRS. CRAVEN: I might say that nature was always one of her
greatest interests. The study of nature in 1867 was one
of her prime delights, especially flowers, botany.

MR. RICHARDS: She was knowledgeable about astronomy---was
she aware at this time of the revolution going on in the
biological and natural sciences?

MRS. CRAVEN: Yes. She has some interesting comments on
science and theology that we didn't have time to go into
here.

MR. MOLTKE-HANSEN: Mrs. Anderson, you mentioned the element of nostalgia in some of the writings of Jeanie
Drake---in *In Old St. Stephen's*, for instance. How much
of this nostalgia is historical? What element of history
does she include?

MRS. ANDERSON: Well, it seems to me that she's trying to
do something like what Simms was doing in the Revolutionary novels, without doing the kind of life-long research that he had done. It was almost imposed on the

surface of her novel, rather than coming up from the
center of it, the way it is in Simms' things. And she
will include local details about Charleston: buildings,
people, places. She has a string of personages running
through this novel---John Calhoun, Lafayette, Bishop
England---who simply appear and then fade back into the
background. Basically it's a fictional treatment.
It's interesting that she makes her main character a
descendant of Landgrave Ashley, but I haven't found any
evidence that he is based on any man actually living at
that time; I think basically she's just drawing on what
she knows, as Miss Moragné was, and perhaps did a little
bit of research in the newspapers of the time to set
things in their proper chronological periods.

MR. MOLTKE-HANSEN: What did the Charleston reviewer have
to say about this aspect of her work?

MRS. ANDERSON: He talked mostly about contemporary figures
in the book or figures within his lifetime that he could
identify. There's a schoolmaster whom she names Yorick
Sterne Gordon, and he says that the name is a thin dis-
guise of some actual character around Charleston.
Apparently he was a notorious drunkard and was dismissed.

MR. INABINETT: Dianne, what evidence do you have that
Jeanie Drake was not an imported South Carolinian, that
she married into a South Carolina family, and was, say,
a New Yorker by background?

MRS. ANDERSON: That's a possibility. This first novel is
told in retrospect, and it's told by the New York
grandson of Ashley, a family that had moved out of
South Carolina during Reconstruction, and was still
familiar with it because they travelled back and forth.

MR. INABINETT: In continuing your research, I might point
out that the index to *The State* newspaper which covers
the years 1891 to about 1913 just might possibly have a
clue for you, or maybe an actual identification. That's
an oft overlooked source, and I might also suggest that
you look into the Yates Snowden papers, if you haven't
already. He collected a great deal of material on South
Carolina writers of that same period, and we also have
an extensive collection of the papers of Mayor Courtenay
of Charleston, and it's highly likely that Jeanie Drake

in her real name may have written to, or even sent
copies of her work to Mayor Courtenay.

MRS. ANDERSON: Thank you.

MR. INABINETT: Mrs. Craven, I would like to ask you a
question. Do the diaries of Miss Moragné's grandfather
still exist?

MRS. CRAVEN: No. I've always wished they did. The only
excerpts I know are contained in William Moragné's address on the ninetieth anniversary of the landing of
the French Huguenots. There is a children's story, or
story for younger readers, called "Azalie of Old
Bordeaux," which I looked at recently. It's published,
I think, by a company at Greenwood, South Carolina, and
it is based on this very colony and takes some excerpts
from Pierre Moragné's diary.

MR. INABINETT: But Mary herself had access to the diary?

MRS. CRAVEN: Evidently.

MR. INABINETT: And the figures in *The British Partizan*
are real? Is Ralph Cornet really---

MRS. CRAVEN: ---William Caine, Mary Moragné's grandfather's uncle. His brother James, who was killed, who was
wounded and died in a battle, on the American side, was
a direct ancestor of Mary Moragné. William and James
are the two brothers. And her Huguenot grandfather was
supposed to have been the model for the Huguenot there,
Bruyésant.

MR. INABINETT: And what Karen sees as a great deal of
symbolism in the novel---Karen, do you think it's really
that, or did Mr. Caine cross the Savannah River as many
times as she said?

MISS ENDRES: I doubt that that's the kind of detail that
would have been handed down in the family. The trip to
Tallulah Falls I feel quite sure is created completely.
I doubt that the ancestor went to Tallulah Falls.
There are some accounts of Mary Moragné's own trips
there, which are similar in description to the one in
the novel, and I feel that it made such a profound impression on her that she wanted to use it in some way,

and did.

MR. RICHARDS: Mrs. Craven, I know now that the name of
the author of *The British Partizan* is Mary Elizabeth
Moragné Davis. But when I first saw the name in connection with *The British Partizan*, it was Kate Moragné.
Is that a mistake?

MISS ENDRES: That's in Wauchope's book. He has Kate,
wrongly.

MRS. CRAVEN: She had a sister named Katherine Bersheba,
but she was never called Kate. She had, of course, a
daughter named Kate, Katherine.

Caroline Carson

by

Beverly Scafidel

Caroline Carson is an unpublished writer. Who she
was, what she wrote and why, are interesting from a
literary standpoint, because she attempted to create a new
literary form. Her life and writings are interesting also
from a psychological standpoint, for they reveal a picture
of a misfit; the daughter of a South Carolina Unionist
(James Louis Petigru), and sister to a gifted and somewhat
aggressive novelist (Susan Petigru King), she was politi-
cally and temperamentally out of place in her family and in
her society. Her works reflect a person in search of
stability through the understanding of human nature and
human relationships.

She was born in Charleston, in 1820,[1] the second child
of James Louis Petigru, the brilliant lawyer. Throughout
her life she appears to have functioned as a sometime
secretary and housekeeper for her father,[2] and upon his
death she became one of the executors of his will.[3] The
available facts of her life are few. In 1841 she married
William Augustus Carson, a rice planter of Dean Hall plantation[5] (on the Cooper River). They had two sons, William[6]
and James.[7] Her husband died in 1854, leaving a large
estate to her and her children.[8] Afraid of insurrection,
she moved to New York in 1861, and lived there during the
war;[9] her eldest son, a Southern sympathizer, returned to
America from Germany, much to her dismay,[10] and her
youngest son remained in South Carolina against her
wishes.[11] Finding herself isolated from her family and

47

without cash, she was obliged to go to work to support herself at this time,[12] and she did so again, after the war,
in order to pay for her father's tombstone.[13] She died in
1892, and is buried at the Protestant Cemetary in Rome.[14]

Today she is best known as the person primarily
responsible for the most important study that has been made
of her father's life. She preserved many letters and
speeches, and had already furnished notes and recollections
for an earlier attempt at a biography; when a box of her
father's private papers was discovered in a Charleston law
office, she inspired her son James to prepare the *Life,
Letters and Speeches of James Louis Petigru*,[15] published in
1920. She was a talented artist and poet herself, but few
of her papers remain---many of them were in her father's
house in Charleston when it burned in 1861.[16]

There are, however, two manuscript albums[17] which
reveal something of her accomplishments and her thoughts.
Albums like hers were often kept by young ladies, usually
as autograph books. They are unlike diaries, for the owner
requested her friends to write something, usually verse, in
the book, and to sign their names. Carson's practice was
to have blank pages with her whether she was at home or
visiting friends, to get the verses and autographs she
wanted, and later to transcribe them into her book. She
accompanies one entry with a note explaining that these
lines of verse were given to her by a friend at a ball.[18]

The books themselves were bound volumes with hard
covers. Some of the pages were colored, and some had
ornate drawings or raised scrollwork in the shape of a
frame for a picture. These "picture-pages" were protected
by a sheet of tissue. The exteriors of the books ranged
from very plain to ornate, with mother-of-pearl decorations.
Carson had one of each.

The striking thing about her albums is that she
planned the general format and arranged the contents with
some deliberation, so that they form a kind of literary
diary. It is clear that she did not begin either book by
filling the first page and moving through the following
pages in sequence: intermittent pages throughout each
album are blank, and some pages are only partially filled.
Instead, since almost every entry is in her own hand, it
seems to me that she transcribed each passage she chose
onto a page designated for it.

She received the plain book in 1837,[19] when she was seventeen years old, but evidently didn't conceive of organizing its contents until later. The earliest work it contains is a didactic poem that she wrote during her school-days, on the pains of getting out of bed on a cold morning; it is dated 1834,[20] and the latest entry in the book is dated 1857.[21] Sometime during those years she formed her idea about the kind of book she was creating, and she wrote this inscription on the first page:

> I got this book several years ago, when I was very, very happy, and some persons I liked very much drew some little specimens in it, that I might always remember that time. Therefore I value the old book in spite of its coarse paper and shabby binding; and I advance it to the dignity of containing such original fragments, and quaint or pleasing passages as may chance to strike my fancy from time to time in reading. All those scraps which may in the end serve to show me what it is that *really* pleases or interests me. I have some curiosity to know what I do like---what I am like---For as I have hitherto never known my own mind, so it is not wonderful that I never know how to profit by happiness when I had her in my grasp; and so when the heavenly visitant has flown away I stand all wonder and amazement to find she had been so near. It may be that out of the confusion of this scrap book I may discover order---And by finding what things touch my fancy and sympathy, I may learn what is the real bent of my inclinations. And so, though I fail to attain happiness, I may at least have the sad satisfaction of knowing by what mistake I have thrown it away.[22]

This promising beginning is followed by quotations from 18th and 19th century poems, novels, and essays; by axioms, by biblical passages; by original poems, and by one sermon. The first quotations are idealistic---they deal with perfect love, an ideal marriage, human dignity, reason, and the perception of the truthfulness of Christianity (this is a difficult passage which she notes that she does not understand). Gradually the quotations become more realistic: instead of perfect love, she describes the lady who has been deceived; instead of the comradship of husband and wife, she quotes a passage about the silence that creeps into a marriage and separates the two. Instead of Christian truth she quotes passages about submission, meekness, and death.

Her own poems are usually somewhat lighter in nature than the quotations she selects. She includes poems written to accompany gifts, to commemorate birthdays, to invite friends to dinner. In her most thoughtful and best efforts, though, the theme of lost love is prevalent. During the summer of 1848, which was a period of convalescence from a long illness,[23] she translated some sonnets from Dante which repeat the theme of love and death, and which, of all her efforts, seem to have been the most important to her: they reappear, with a few of her other favorite poems and quotations, in the second album. One of the best of these translations is a description of love, ending with these lines:

> Imaginary pleasure! which Nature sends,
> Power of the Heart with which no force contends,
> Wealth which surpassing all things---too soon ends.[24]

At the bottom of the page appears a note saying, "so much out of humour today!"[25]

The few biographical facts suggest two possible sources of her unhappiness at this time---she was weak from a long illness, and her husband was a chronically unsuccessful planter. In a letter to his sister (Caroline's aunt) James Louis Petigru says that Carson is a failure who seems "incapable of change as of Reformation," and that Caroline's children are her only comfort.[26]

The conclusion of her first album is a prose passage quoted from de Tocqueville. It indicates a change in the person who once wrote about getting up on a cold morning:

> My contemporaries tread paths so different from mine, often so contrary, that our feelings & opinions are scarcely ever the same. I do not complain of them, we live on good terms, but there is a gap between us. They care nothing for what is most dear to me. I despise or am indifferent to their new idols, while my views of life are no longer comprehended by them. We do not oppose but, we do not understand one another. I have relations, & neighbors, and friends, but my mind

has not a family or a country.[27]

The sense of isolation this passage suggests might be
attributed to her father's unpopular sympathies with the
Union, and his opposition to secession. However, we cannot
be sure. The three major studies of her father's life give
information about Carson's life only incidentally, and at
that the information comes from only one source, her father.
Petigru is certainly a reliable and qualified source, but
in his published letters he mentions little about Caroline
except to describe her poor health. He says nothing of her
social activity, her reputation as a wit, or her accomplishments. Her son, in the *Life, Letters and Speeches of James
Louis Petigru*, naturally describes her in the most flattering terms, but gives no real information.[28] Her cousin
(by marriage) Joseph Blyth Allston includes, in his biography of Petigru, letters that imply some of her difficulties,[29] but these letters do not supply full information. One must infer, then, what caused this growing
tendency toward realism in her selection of materials for
her album.

She was sick throughout her life. Her health problems
are not specifically described, but in 1860 Petigru says of
her: "I wish she could be made to believe in the healthy
character of Badwell [the Petigru family home], but I am
afraid her faith in that direction is gone, and even if
Badwell should be exempt from all other complaints, it
would still suffer in her mind from the infliction of
ennui."[30] This boredom might have been caused partly by
her frequent illnesses, and partly by the Byronic pose
popular at that time. Its result can be seen in the gloom
of the late quotations, and in the theme of lost love which
pervades her poems.

Another possibility for her gradual loss of idealism
is that family relations may have been strained. Her
father does not seem to have had much faith in her
husband's business sense, or in his ability to take care of
her. And her sons distressed her by their active support
of the Confederacy. James, in fact, refused to join her in
the North, afraid that she would not allow him to return to
South Carolina.

Illness, fashionable world-weariness, money and family
problems are all sound reasons for her developing sense of
melancholy. Also, her father's opposition to nullification

and secession were supported by few South Carolinians.
Whereas Petigru was respected, he, and by extension his
family, were members of a very small political minority.
One can only speculate about the effect of his position on
his children, but certainly the final quotation in her
first album reveals a feeling of loneliness which, given a
knowledge of her background, is understandable: "my mind
has not a family or a country." This feeling is as
apparent in her second album as in the first.

The second album is the more impressive in both
appearance and content. It is a smaller volume, bound in
glossy black leather with decorations on front and back.
Although it is smaller, it contains more material, and of a
greater variety than the first. She includes, for example,
several of her drawings, some of which are tinted. Many of
her quotations are in Italian, as well as the French and
English of the first album. Some of her poems from the
first volume reappear in a revised form. One of the most
impressive changes is that the touching prose introduction
to the first volume has become a poem with a less romantic,
more detached tone. The last of the four quotations reads:

> So this book, a trap is set
> My own mind wherein to catch
> Ten to one that I fail yet---
> Who'd be taken on the watch?[31]

Although the poem of the second volume bears an
earlier date than the prose passage of the first, it seems
to reflect a later choice. Judging from the dates of her
poems, from the nature of the revisions she made,[32] and
from the appearance of the two books, I believe that she
kept the two albums concurrently, using the plain one as a
kind of rough draft, and the ornate one as a finished product. W. H. Hurlbut, an old family friend, places both
these collections in a useful perspective when he refers to
the second one as her "new work on Life."[33]

Though the books bear roughly the same dates and some
of the same works, there is a marked difference in the
general tone of the two. In the second one she does not
include the biblical passages or the frequent references to
Christian humility, meekness, and submission. Instead, she
uses many more and much shorter quotations, and they are
axiomatic or proverbial in nature. That is to say, the
second volume leans more heavily on the wisdom of man than

on faith in God.

Another aspect of the second volume is the interest it reflects in the nature of woman, absent in the first album. Most of these quotations are cynical observations about women and their relationships with men. Women are shown as vain, coquettish, and yet angelic;[34] woman's mind is irrational, and yet she can make a fool wise;[35] she destroys her lover's tranquility, and yet she allows him to become a tyrant.[36] Perhaps the most interesting conflict of ideas appears in two passages, one early and one late in the book: the first, from Byron, states that man and woman can be either friends or lovers, but not both. The second, that a wife is her husband's best friend.[37] Most of her quotations about women are made by men and are sometimes contradictory. Perhaps for this reason she includes a poem she wrote on a Southern woman,[38] and ends the album with a quotation from a woman.[39]

Looking back to the intentions she stated at the beginning of each album, one might ask if Caroline Carson accomplished what she set out to do. These were to be books through which she would learn to know her own mind in order to gain happiness. From her deliberate selection and organization of material, it is clear that she did analyze the passages she chose to include in the albums. The changes of subject matter between the first and second books suggest that there were changes in her personality, and that she was aware of them. Her tendency to select realistic, pithy quotations over abstract, idealistic ones reflects a person in the process of maturing. Her interest in the nature of women and in the way men see women indicates an awareness not only of her own place in society, but also of the social role of woman. We cannot know if she finally achieved happiness, because little is said of her after the time at which she worked to pay for her father's tombstone. The latest date in the second album is 1856.[40] She was soon to move North in fear of war, to suffer isolation if not estrangement from her family, and to experience severe financial difficulty. The climax of this period was the death of her father. These were not happy times for her, and until more is known about her life we must hope that at least she profited by the self-knowledge she gained.

Her literary accomplishment is small. She encouraged her sister Susan Petigru King to publish her short stories

and novels,[41] but as far as I know Caroline Carson made no
attempt at publication herself. However, it is possible
that she continued both writing and anthologizing in the
second half of her life.[42] The poems she wrote in her
youth are competent, and some are well above average. Her
effort to make a commonplace book into a history of her own
ideas and development is an ambitious and imaginative
undertaking. The talents she possessed were not fully
realized; they are indicated by her achievements, which are
interesting by themselves and significant in their promise.

Notes

[1]James Petigru Carson, *Life, Letters and Speeches of James Louis Petigru* (Washington, D. C.: W. H. Lowdermilk & Co., 1920), p. 488.

[2]Carson, pp. 67-68, 207.

[3]University of South Carolina copy of *Charleston County Will Book N 1862-1868*, Will of James L. Petigru, pp. 54-57.

[4]Carson, p. 207.

[5]Harriette Kershaw Leiding, *Historic Houses of South Carolina* (Philadelphia: J. B. Lippincott Company, 1921; repr. 1975), p. 35.

[6]Joseph Blyth Allston, "Life and Times of James L. Petigru," (Charleston) *News and Courier* (Feb. 11, 1900), letter of J. L. Petigru to his sister Jane North, dated Jan. 6, 1843.

[7]Leiding, p. 35.

[8]The same.

[9]Allston, letter of Petigru to Jane North, dated Jan. 20, 1861.

[10]In a letter from Jane North to her sister Mrs. R. F. W. (Adele) Allston, dated April 13, 1864 (located in the R. F. W. Allston Papers, South Carolina Historical Society, Charleston, S. C.), Mrs. Carson is said to have written to the house where William was employed in Germany, asking that her son not be allowed to leave the country. This house was probably a counting house in which Petigru says (in a letter to Jane North, June 28, 1862; see Allston, *News and Courier*, May 18, 1900) that Mrs. Carson hoped to get William a place.

[11]Allston, *News and Courier* (May 6, 1900), letter of J. L. Petigru to Jane North, dated Jan. 29, 1862.

[12]Allston, *News and Courier* (May 20, 1900), letter of
J. L. Petigru to Jane North, dated Dec. 4, 1862. Petigru
reports Caroline as saying she can support herself by her
work: he does not identify the type of work she did. It
is possible that she received financial aid from friends to
supplement her income, for Jane North tells Mrs. R. F. W.
Allston in her letter of April 13, 1864 (see #10) that
people in New York and Boston made up sums to build a monument to James Louis Petigru, who died March 9, 1863.
Caroline was to have the interest from this money until the
end of the war.

[13]Carson, p. 477.

[14]Carson, p. 488.

[15]Carson, p. xii. The earlier attempt at a biography
of Petigru was made by Edward Everett. Among the James
Petigru Carson Papers (South Carolina Historical Society,
Charleston, S. C.) is a letter of July 25, 1863, from
Edward Everett (signed E. E.) to Caroline Carson, stating
that for lack of material he has not yet finished his
memoir of James Louis Petigru.

[16]Allston, *News and Courier* (May 6, 1900), letters of
Petigru to Jane North, dated Dec. 13 and Dec. 16, 1861.

[17]Located in the Manuscripts Room, South Caroliniana
Library, University of South Carolina, Columbia, S. C.

[18]This appears in the ornate album, which I shall refer
to as Album #2. These words appear on the verso of leaf
[44].

[19]Album #1, leaf [3], recto. The first two pages are
blank. On the third appear the words, "Caroline Petigru
West Point 1837."

[20]Album #1, leaf [36], recto.

[21]Album #1, leaf [40], verso.

[22]Album #1, leaf [5], recto and verso. This entry is
dated 1852, but the date and the entry are written in two
different hands.

[23]In July, 1845 (see Carson, p. 243) Petigru took his daughter, her child, and the child's nurse to White Sulphur Springs, Va., to seek a cure for Caroline's illness. By August, 1847 (see Allston, *News and Courier* [Feb. 25, 1900], letter of Petigru to Jane North), Petigru describes her as an invalid. The poems referred to below are dated August, 1848, from Sullivan's Island, where Petigru had a summer home.

[24]Album #1, leaf [60], recto. This poem is entitled "Love." In Album #2, Carson further identifies it as Dante's Sonetto LII. The translation in both albums is dated September 2, and in both albums this work is placed near other translations from Dante dated 1848.

[25]Album #1, leaf [60], recto. The note does not accompany this poem in Album #2.

[26]Letter of J. L. Petigru to Mrs. R. F. W. Allston, Dec. 16, 1851, in the R. F. W. Allston Papers, South Carolina Historical Society, Charleston, S. C.

[27]Album #1, leaf [78], recto.

[28]See, for example, Carson, 207.

[29]See, for example, Allston *News and Courier* (April 15, 1900), letters from J. L. Petigru, dated June 15, 1860; Jan. 20, 1861; Feb. 19, 1861; (May 20, 1900) letter from J. L. Petigru, dated Dec. 4, 1862.

[30]Allston, *News and Courier* (April 15, 1900), letter of J. L. Petigru to Jane North, dated June 15, 1860. He continues: "She is the prey of discontent and nervous irritation to an alarming degree. . . ."

[31]Album #2, leaf [1], recto.

[32]While her revisions are not extensive, in several instances she did make a few changes in her poems. The one she worked with the most bears no title; the first line reads, "Ah! who could have fancied my beautiful flowers!" Between the two versions there are four substantive and ten accidental changes. The version in the smaller album is the improved one; among other changes, she makes a verb conform in its tense with the rest of the poem (l. 5 will [did), she inserts (and sometimes removes) punctuation in

an effort to clarify the meaning of the sentences (And now tho, all scentless [though all) and she chooses the more precise of two words (So love should/though we silently hopelessly cherish [So love though we silently, hopelessly cherish).

[33]Album #2, leaf [4], verso.

[34]Album #2, leaf [3], verso; leaf [38], recto; leaf [45], verso; leaf [25], recto.

[35]Album #2, leaf [38], recto; leaf [4], recto.

[36]Album #2, leaf [72], recto; leaf [25], recto.

[37]Album #2, leaf [6], recto; leaf [36], recto.

[38]Album #2, leaf [45], recto.

[39]Album #2, leaf [96], recto.

[40]Album #2, leaf [4], verso.

[41]The dedication of King's *Busy Moments of an Idle Woman* (Appleton, 1854) reads:

> To MY SISTER, who the first commended these trifles I dedicate them; and I call upon her to bear with me the fate which (if noticed at all) may befall them; for though to our owlish eyes these fledglings seem "very pretty birds indeed," yet to the eagle glances of critics, and to indifferent readers, they will probably appear stupid good-for-noughts, only fit to be disposed of at one fell swoop.

[42]Her obituary in the *New York Times* (Sept. 15, 1892) reads:

> Like her father, she was devoted to the cause of the union, but with the old order of things passed away her home, with the friends and the associations that were part of her life and she went forth into a changed world. She resided for some years in New York, but circumstances brought about a removal to Rome. There she cultivated painting, always her favorite pursuit, and lived to the end in an atmosphere that soothed in some degree the bitterness

of separation from her native land and the
familiar faces of friends.

A World Introduced:
The Writings of Helena Wells
of Charles Town,
South Carolina's First Novelist

by

David Moltke-Hansen

At the South Carolina Inter-State and West Indian
Exposition of 1901-1902, there was a "Women's Department"
with a small library of writings by and about South
Carolina women. Alexander Salley's bibliography of this
collection included only one eighteenth-century writer
and three posthumously published eighteenth-century
diarists and letter writers. Relative to the total
number and range of the entries, this was a fair showing;[1]
for women did not begin to publish much in South Carolina,
after all, until the second quarter of the nineteenth
century.[2]

Nevertheless, there is more to the eighteenth century
than Salley's bibliography indicated. There were also
periodical contributions,[3] newspapers published and edited
by women,[4] the tracts of a woman Quaker "preacher,"[5] and
a gardening handbook.[6] Then too, there were, at the end
of the century, didactic novels and essays by a loyalist
refugee from Charleston, the subject of this paper.

These materials have yet to be fully studied. The
relevant reference works are incomplete, and the relevant
histories cursory.[7] No satisfactory explanation has been
given, for instance, of the fact that, in the eighteenth
century, women published newspapers in South Carolina, but
in the nineteenth, they did not.[8] Neither have the careers
and contributions of the eighteenth-century women publishers been examined in detail. Though it is reasonable

61

to assume that, because they were women, these publishers
had common experiences in business which set them apart
from their male counterparts, this assumption has still to
be explored fully. Similarly, the peculiar experiences
of women evangelists in the colony remain largely unex-
amined.[9] Even the career and writings of the well-known
exhortatory pamphleteer and Quaker "preacher," Sophia
Hume, still have to be considered in detail. Yet these
and other gaps in our knowledge and understanding have to
be filled in before an overall historical and critical
assessment of the eighteenth-century women publishers and
authors of South Carolina can be made. And such an assessment is necessary before the cultural and social roles of
these women, taken individually and collectively, can be
interpreted.

When such an interpretation is eventually made, the
works of Helena Wells of Charles Town will be found
revealing. South Carolina's first novelist,[10] her books
are artistically of little interest or importance, but
they do provide insights into the concerns and interests
of a middle-class woman from late eighteenth-century
Charles Town. Some of the ways in which Helena Wells's
world is illuminated by her writings will be briefly considered here. First, though, her career and the publishing history and critical reception of her works should
be reviewed.

I

Helena Wells was born in the decade after 1757 in
Charles Town, South Carolina.[11] The youngest of five
children, she grew up in a culturally active family.
Robert Wells, her father, was a newspaper publisher and
the principal bookseller in the colony.[12] A competent
Latinist, who had been schooled in Dumfries, Scotland,
he was active in the Charles Town Library Society, and
according to Alexander Hewatt, was responsible for introducing "many of the most distinguished authors" to the
colony.[13] Indeed, he became the first large-scale book
publisher in the South-East.[14] Because of her father's
contact with numerous "literary characters," Helena once
noted, she was made sensitive to literature and the language arts by exposure to them at an early age,[15] and
though she did not follow her brothers to school in
Scotland, she became an avid reader.[16]

Like a sister, Helena must have worked in her father's shop.[17] Like other members of her family, too, she must have been involved in the life of the Scottish community in the city; for her father, who came from south-west Scotland, was ardent in his filial patriotism, and the family worshipped at the First Scots Presbyterian Church a few blocks from their home.[18]

The family was a large one. Brothers of both Robert Wells and his wife Mary were established in Charles Town as merchants and planters.[19] Like Robert and Mary, they came there from Scotland, as did many of Robert Wells's business associates, and even an apprentice of his.[20] Not surprisingly, Robert Wells apprenticed his own sons to Scots. The elder went to Edinburgh to work at Donaldson's Printing House. The younger returned to Charles Town after his premedical training at the University of Edinburgh to work for Alexander Garden, the eminent naturalist and physician from Birse parish near Aberdeen, Scotland.[21]

Like Garden and many other Scottish-born colonials, the Wellses were loyalists in the American Revolution.[22] Robert Wells, in particular, was outspoken in his views, and so, according to his younger son, soon after the battles of Lexington and Concord he "found it prudent to leave [America] and to return to Great Britain."[23] His three daughters followed their parents to London in 1777 and 1778.[24]

In 1779 Helena was helping her sister Louisa supervise the remodeling of the home their father had leased in London.[25] At the time this lease was taken, Robert was prospering. He was doing so well by 1780, in fact, that the government reduced the family's war pension from £150 to £60 per year. Despite this reduction, Robert had, by the end of the Revolution, realized about £20,000. Soon after the War, however, he suffered a serious reversal in his fortunes. "Thro' the Speculations of some Correspondents in Georgia and the injustice of others in the West Indies," Louisa recalled, "he was under the necessity of delivering up his effects to his Creditors...," who "allowed £170 for the support of the Family." To this sum "[the] Government added £30 per annum"[26] plus £1200 compensation, in all, for property losses. The South Carolina General Assembly also awarded the family a small income from some confiscated property in Charles Town.[27] Nevertheless, at Robert's death in 1794 "his Widow and two daughters," according to Louisa, were "totally unprovided for...."[28]

The two daughters had already started to provide for themselves, however. In 1789 Helena and Griselda opened a boarding house "for those young gentlewomen of fortune who are without female relations to introduce them into life...."[29]

It was a year or two later, apparently, that Helena began to write. What inspired her, according to the *Gentleman's Magazine*, was the appearance of *Letters Written in France in the Summer of 1790*, by Helen Maria Williams, whom Wolfe Tone called "Miss Jane Bull completely," but whom the Reverend Richard Polwhele described as "an intemperate advocate of Gallic licentiousness" because of her support of the French Revolution.[30] Helena Wells, the conservative daughter of a conservative father, agreed with the Reverend, and wanted "to counteract the pernicious tendency of modern philosophy" exemplified by Miss Williams' *Letters*.[31] To rebut the *Letters*, she wrote a moral tale in which, she said, she was "desirous of delineating characters from *real life*, and of alloting to them stations, though difficult and arduous, yet making the sustaining of them with propriety, to be within the bounds of probability."[32] The title of this work was *The Step-Mother: A Domestic Tale, from Real Life*. Though the writing of one volume was completed about 1791, the two volume novel was not published until 1798, after Helena had given up teaching because of bad health.[33] The work received restrained praise from the *Critical Review* and the *Monthly Review*.[34] The *Gentleman's Magazine*, which Helena's brother William Charles Wells occasionally contributed to,[35] was more encouraging in its reception, as were other periodicals.[36] Also encouraging was the fact that the work sold well. Less than a year after the appearance of the first edition, a second edition was called for.[37]

On the last page of this second edition, two further works by Helena Wells were advertised. The first, *Letters on Subjects of Importance to the Happiness of Young Females*, was already "in the press." The second, "a novel, in three volumes," was being prepared "for publication by subscription." A poem from it, however, was separately published in a periodical before the work was completed.[38]

The *Letters on Subjects of Importance to the Happiness of Young Females* appeared in 1799. It, too, had been a long time in composition, for the first letters date back to 1794. A collection of Helena Wells's correspondence with her pupils, the *Letters* were meant to draw "the attention of the younger part of [the female] sex from frivolous pursuits to objects hitherto disregarded by many of them...," namely, "the interests of religion, as connected with the happiness of the human race."[39]

The three volume novel, *Constantia Neville; or, the West Indian* had a similar purpose.[40] Like *The Step-Mother*, it was well received,[41] and it sold well, the preface to the first edition being dated "April 15, 1800" and the preface to the second edition, "August 30, 1800."

After this quick succession of works and her marriage in 1801, Helena Wells only published, so far as is known, twice more before her death in 1824.[42] In 1807, a second edition of the *Letters* appeared, and in 1809, her *Thoughts and Remarks on establishing an Institution for the Support and Education of Unportioned Respectable Females* was published.[43] A plea for the government to support "protestant nunneries" to shelter, educate, and employ impoverished gentlewomen, the volume did not attract much attention.[44]

II

By the time of her death in 1824, Helena Wells's works were largely forgotten. A few literary historians have since written briefly of her novels but only to dismiss them because they found the characters and plots of *The Step-Mother* and *Constantia Neville* clumsy and dull, and their language sententious.[45] I agree. While there are episodes, like the masqued ball in chapter ten of *Constantia Neville*, which have vitality and charm, these do little to liven the deadly didacticism of the fiction. This didacticism pervades and shapes everything--the plots, the dialogues, the characterizations. As a result, even the heroines of the two novels never become full-bodied characters but are two dimensional stereotypes. The embodiments of virtue, these paragons neither change nor develop but remain fixedly, unrelentingly virtuous. Though their temptors are tempted by them, they resist every

impropriety of thought and action. Advocates of the
virtue they practice, furthermore, they fill their con-
versations with observations on and appeals to virtuous
conduct. These appeals often fall on deaf ears. Nevertheless, virtue triumphs in the end. After various vicissitudes, the heroines finally achieve the happiness they
so richly deserve. They do so, unfortunately, without
ever having excited the reader's interest in their fates.
It is not surprising, therefore, that *The Step-Mother* and
Constantia Neville are now all but forgotten. Both art-
less and artificial, they should not be simply dismissed,
however; for whatever their literary limitations, they are
serious works dealing with serious questions in biographi-
cally and historically significant ways.

The principal questions addressed are these: How
should children be raised? What should be the roles of
women in society? How should women be educated to assume
their roles? What are the problems inherent in women's
social condition? How should these problems be dealt
with? The answers to these questions are illustrated by
the lives of the heroines of both *The Step-Mother* and
Constantia Neville. In these novels, we follow the up-
bringing of the heroines, their entries into society,
their confrontation and surmounting of personal, family,
business, and social problems, and their conduct as children, students, friends, teachers, and wives. The lessons
learned are essentially the same in both books. Based on
the instruction being given then in female academies and
on contemporary educational theory, they reflect Helena
Wells's concerns as a governess/teacher.[46] Let me list a
number of the points made.

From infancy, the child should be close to its
parents, who should treat her with understanding love
rather than with unbending discipline. At the same time,
however, it is the parents' duty to shape the child's
inclinations to worthwhile pursuits and responsible
behavior. What the specific pursuits and responsibilities
are to be depends on the social and cultural background
of the parents. Of course, the Church sets norms common
to all.

Social fripperies, painted faces, seductive twitch-
ings are to be scorned; though external graces, *per se*,
are not bad. In fact, young ladies who have the opportunity should learn to dance, play a musical instrument,

and sing to the best of their abilities. They should
remember, however, that these accomplishments, like
beauty of form and dress, are only made worthwhile by the
inward graces of mind and spirit. These inward graces are
initially shaped through early moral and emotional training, but continued cultivation of them is necessary. For
the leisured classes, liberal learning is the core to such
training, being a much more likely route to continued
mental and moral growth than the careful accumulation of
gossip, fashions, and the latest romances.

Liberal learning by itself does not insure proper
growth, however. For a liberal education to do any good,
it must be pursued in the proper frame of mind. But even
that is not enough. Such learning does not fit a lady for
work; though often circumstances force gentlewomen to seek
work. Gentlewomen should, therefore, be schooled for
employment as well as for marriage.

When confronted with the problem of making a living,
ladies should be on their mettle, but they should not
ignore society's norms in their determination to achieve
a competence. Women should let the wisdom of conventions
control their passions and should repudiate the philosophy
of writers like Mary Wollstonecraft,[47] because the wilful-
ness they advocate only disturbs the moral and social
orders. This is not to say, though, that women should
either submit to society's wrongs against women and woman-
kind or betray their sense-of-self and sense-of-morality.
Rather, women should maintain their integrity within not
without social norms.

These observations, though hardly original, were
vital, growing as they did out of Helena Wells's life.
Neither *The Step-Mother* nor *Constantia Neville* is auto-
biographical. Both, however, deal with the problems
Helena Wells faced after the decline of her father's
fortunes. Furthermore, because it was her aim to copy
"existing manners," both novels are built on observation
of her own sphere.[48] In addition to suggesting some of
what she thought, therefore, the novels also tell us a
good deal about the world she lived in--what its horizons
were, who peopled it, what went on in it, and what
Helena's place in it was.

Helena Wells lived in the world of middle-class
gentility between the unfashionable respectability of
the petit bourgeois and small freeholder, on the one
hand, and the elegance of the grand bourgeois and the
aristocrat, on the other. She did not, however, hold a
commanding position in her world. Well-bred and well-
read, she was not wealthy enough to be fashionable in her
gentility. While she was knowledgeable about fashionable
society, therefore, she was at the same time a bit removed
from it. In being thus removed, she had a vantage point
from which to survey her world. It is this vantage point
which she gave to her heroines.[49]

Helena Wells and her heroines have more in common
than point of view, however. All three women were left
more or less penniless by the deaths of their fathers; all
served as governesses; and all lived in London, among other
places, and were involved with people having mercantile
interests and international business and social connections. The nature of these connections is suggested by
the subscription list in the first edition of *Constantia
Neville*. This list is divided into three parts: subscribers in the British Isles, subscribers on the Continent--
particularly, in North Germany--and subscribers in South
Carolina. All in all, it is an impressive list, including
senior officers in the British army and navy, American
diplomats, members of both Houses of Parliament, Prussian
royalty, and numerous barristers, doctors, professors, and
merchants, as well as libraries. To be noted are the
large number of Scottish names. Included in the South
Carolina section, of course, are the Rowands, Helena's
mother's brother's family.[50] Other South Carolina subscribers were old family acquaintances.[51] Among the Scots
are William Charles Wells's close friend, David Hume,
Professor of Civil Law at the University of Edinburgh.[52]
Presumably many others on the British and Continental
lists were also known by the Wellses; though their connections with the family have, in most cases, still to be
established.[53] My guess is that some of the members of
the British community in Hamburg, Germany, included had
been business associates of Robert Wells at one time;
though their connections with the Wellses have still to
be established as well. Other subscribers may have been
from families whose daughters Helena Wells had taught.

It was such familial, social, and business ties which
defined Helena Wells's world and the world of her heroines.

Such imperial and international ties were, of course, important to South Carolina before the Revolution, and though weakened by the War, they continued to be important after it.[54] Helena Wells may have left Charles Town as an adolescent, never to return, but there was justice, nevertheless, in her being called "Helena Wells of Charles Town, South Carolina" on the title page of the second edition of *The Step-Mother*. Though she had left Charles Town, she continued to live in the same world. Because this is the world she writes about, her novels tell us a good deal about its culture and social life.

The novels are particularly informative on attitudes. Worth remarking, for instance, is the attitude towards slaves and slavery. Slavery is condemned but so is abolitionism. The argument is that slavery is bad, because it exposes the owners to the lascivious and slovenly behavior of the slaves; while abolitionism is wrong, because it is based on the utopian notion of the equality of blacks and whites.[55]

This attitude towards blacks, which angered some of Helena Wells's critics,[56] is illuminated by Isaiah Thomas. A former employee of Robert Wells, he wrote that Wells's slaves in his Charles Town printing shop were often drunk and were as often chastized by their owner,[57] who was, according to his son William Charles, "a man of great sobriety."[58]

Helena Wells's understanding of slavery is only one aspect of her mind and background to be brought out in the novels. Another is her perception, as a young colonial just arrived in England, of social relations. At one point in *Constantia Neville*, for example, the author observes: "...[W]here poverty is scarcely known, and a white person reduced to a state of servitude is a phenomenon, the squalid wretchedness which daily presents itself to the eyes of Americans or West Indians on their arrival in Europe, must have a powerful effect."[59]

Though clumsily phrased, this is a suggestive observation. There are many others—on Liverpool merchants, fashionable behavior, literature, and a variety of other things. The novels, though, go beyond giving impressions of places, people, and activities, and recording attitudes towards institutions, social classes and customs. They also analyze (if somewhat simplistically) social, economic,

and psychological pressures on women like Helena Wells.
The pressures *The Step-Mother* deals with are principally
those rising out of social inequalities, concupiscence,
marriage, war, widowhood, and motherhood. *Constantia
Neville*, on the other hand, deals more with how a woman's
life is impinged upon by business and the law. In fact,
the novel is remarkably informative on stock jobbing,
credit manipulation, international marketing, bankruptcy
proceedings, debt collection practices, and the like.

*   *   *

Much fuller information on these subjects can, of
course, be gotten from other sources, and there are much
more sophisticated presentations of the problems confronting Anglo-American gentlewomen in the late eighteenth
century than *The Step-Mother* and *Constantia Neville*.
However, these novels and Helena Wells's non-fiction still
merit study. Together, in fact, her works form one of the
most important bodies of writings by any eighteenth-century
South Carolina woman. Not only do they bulk larger than
the extant writings of any other woman from her colony,
if the newspapers published by Elizabeth and Anne Timothy
and Mary Crouch are excluded, but they are the only large
body of writings by a woman of the Charles Town merchant
class.[60] Furthermore, they are the most extensive treatment of women by any eighteenth-century South Carolinian.

This treatment is valuable not merely because it is
extensive, but more importantly, because it is both realistic and, at the same time, prescriptive: Helena Wells's
works tell us what women of her class did and what they
were supposed to do. In addition, they tell us how women
were educated to their roles, how their education shaped
their actions, and how their experiences modified their
understanding of their roles. In doing so, Helena Wells's
writings tell us something which the writings of better-
known eighteenth-century South Carolina women like Eliza
Lucas Pinckney do not.

Eliza Lucas Pinckney was an extraordinary woman, and
her writings record the actions, thoughts, and perceptions
of an extraordinary woman.[61] Helena Wells, if only because
of her accomplishments, was also extraordinary, but her
writings intentially record the actions, thoughts, and
perceptions of the ordinary women of her class. Paradoxi-
cally, her writings succeed in doing so because literarily

they are bad. Her characters conform to rather than rise
above stereotypes. As a result, they are thoroughly representative. They show not only how women typically saw
themselves but how they projected themselves. In doing so,
they make for uninspired reading but have a lot to offer
the historian.

Other elements in Helena Wells's writings deserve
commentary.[62] However, enough has been said to indicate
how her works serve to introduce a world and to illuminate
the roles played by Anglo-American gentlewomen in the late
eighteenth century. In time, I hope this potential of
these works will be capitalized on.

Notes

Unless otherwise noted, all references to Helena Wells's
works are to the first editions.

[1]A. S. Salley, "Bibliography of South Carolina Women
Writers," *Publications of the Southern History Association*,
8 (1902), 143-157. Thirty-nine authors are represented by
seventy-four titles, eighty entries. For information on
the Exposition and its "Women's Department" see *The Exposition Magazine*, which was published in 1901-1902.

I would like to thank Professors Stephen Meats, James
Meriwether, and George Rogers as well as Ms. Elisabeth
Muhlenfeld for their criticisms of earlier drafts of this
paper. I would also like to thank Mr. E. L. Inabinett,
Director of the South Caroliniana Library, University of
South Carolina, Columbia, South Carolina, both for the
South Caroliniana's purchase, at my suggestion, of micro-
films of Helena Wells's works and for his calling my
attention to Virginia Young (see below, note 8).

[2]See William Stanley Hoole, *A Check-List and Finding-
List of Charleston Periodicals, 1732-1864* (Durham, North
Carolina: Duke University Press, 1936); Jeanne Denyse
Mosimann, "A Check List of Charleston, South Carolina
Imprints from 1731-1799" (M.S. thesis, Catholic University,
1959); Lucy Eastham, "A Preliminary Check List of Imprints:
Charleston, South Carolina, 1800-1810" (M.S. thesis,
Catholic University, 1961); Miriam D. Meacham, "Check List
of South Carolina Imprints for the Years 1811-1818" (M.S.
thesis, Catholic University, 1962); Sister M. Odelia Koenig,
"A Check List of Charleston, South Carolina, Imprints for
the Years 1819-1825" (M.S. thesis, Catholic University,
1959); Barbara Butts Dunn, "Check List of Charleston, South
Carolina, Imprints for the Years 1826-1830" (M.S. thesis,
Catholic University, 1967); George Armstrong Wauchope,
Literary South Carolina (Columbia, South Carolina: Univer-
sity of South Carolina, 1923); George Armstrong Wauchope,
The Writers of South Carolina (Columbia, South Carolina:
The State Company, 1910). See also the essays on Mary
Moragne and Susan Petigru King in this volume.

[3]Julia Spruill, *Women's Life and Work in the Southern
Colonies* (Chapel Hill, North Carolina: University of North
Carolina Press, 1938), 153; Hennig Cohen, *The South
Carolina Gazette, 1732-1775* (Columbia, South Carolina:

University of South Carolina Press, 1953), 200, 224-225.

[4]*Ibid.*, 238-241, 247; Ellen M. Oldham, "Early Women Printers of America," *Boston Public Library Quarterly*, 10 (Jan., April, July 1958), 6-26, 78-92, 141-153, especially 6-8, 16-21, 146-150.

[5]*British Museum General Catalogue of Printed Books* (London: The Trustees of the British Museum, 1962), CIX, cols. 114-115; Amelia Mott Gummere, ed., *The Journal and Essays of John Woolman* (New York: Macmillan & Co., 1922), 589-590, 596; Henry J. Cadbury, *John Woolman in England* (London: Friends Historical Society, 1971), 57-58; Stephen Beauregard Weeks, *Southern Quakers and Slavery* (Baltimore: Johns Hopkins University Press, 1896), 140-141.

[6]See Edwin Arnold's discussion of Martha Logan in this volume.

[7]A useful bibliography of the historical literature is Eugenie Leonard *et al.*, compilers, *The American Woman in Colonial and Revolutionary Times: 1565-1800* (Philadelphia: University of Pennsylvania Press, 1962). The study of woman's history has mushroomed since 1962, but little has been done on South Carolina women, as a quick review of the annual bibliographies of writings on Southern history in the *Journal of Southern History* shows. See also Lewis Pinckney Jones, *Books and Articles on South Carolina History* (Columbia, South Carolina: University of South Carolina Press, 1970).

[8]Anne Timothy, who died in 1792, appears to have been the last woman to publish or edit a newspaper in South Carolina until the 1890's, when Mary Hemphill became co-editor of the Abbeville *Medium* and Virginia Young became associate editor of the Fairfax *Enterprise*. See Clarence S. Brigham, *History and Bibliography of American Newspapers, 1690-1820* (Worcester, Massachusetts: American Antiquarian Society, 1947), II, 1023-1053; Mary Wescott and Allene Ramage, compilers, *A Checklist of United States Newspapers (and Weeklies before 1900) in the Library of Duke University* (Durham, North Carolina: Duke University, 1936), 813-884; the Fairfax *Enterprise*, 16 November 1898, in the South Caroliniana Library, University of South Carolina, Columbia, South Carolina. On the work of Young and of Mary Hemphill's husband in the Woman's Suffrage Movement see Antoinette Elizabeth Taylor, "South Carolina

and the Enfranchisement of Women: The Early Years," *South Carolina Historical Magazine*, 77 (1976), 115-126. See also Foy Stevenson, "Virginia Durant Young--Pioneer for Woman's Rights," *Sandlapper: the Magazine of South Carolina*, February 1974, 36-38, 41-42. About 1890, according to Stevenson (p. 37), Young "bought the Varnville *Enterprise* and started publishing the Fairfax *Enterprise*, a weekly, in her own home." Young was a prolific journalist, frequent public speaker, and a novelist, as well as a publisher and editor.

[9]For an overview of Quaker women ministers see Janis Calvo, "Quaker Women Ministers in Nineteenth-Century America," *Quaker History*, 63 (Autumn 1974), 75-93. On the role of women in religious affairs in the eighteenth-century South, generally, see Spruill, *Women's Life and Work*, 245-254.

[10]See Robert Turnbull, *Bibliography of South Carolina, 1563-1950*, 5 vols. (Charlottesville, Virginia: University of Virginia Press, 1956-1960), I, for a bibliography of South Carolina-related materials published before 1815. The first fiction by a South Carolinian included (p. 438) is Edmund Botsford's *Sambo and Tony* (1808). Helena Wells does not treat South Carolina in her fiction. The first novelist to do so seems to have been the Englishwoman Jane West. See her *The History of Ned Evans*, 4 vols. (London: G. G. & J. Robinson, 1796).

[11]William Charles Wells, *Two Essays ... with a Memoir of his Life* (London: Archibald Constable and Co., 1818), [vi]. See Frances M. Ponick, "Helena Wells and Her Family" (M.A. thesis, University of South Carolina, 1975), 10. I wish, here, to express my appreciation to Mrs. Ponick for making her thesis available to me before it was bound for the University Library.

[12]Isaiah Thomas, *The History of Printing in America*, 2 vols. (Worcester, Massachusetts: Isaiah Thomas, Jr., 1810), II, 152-153, 369-370. See Calhoun Winton, "The Colonial South Carolina Book Trade," *Proof*, 2 (1972), 80.

[13]William Charles Wells, *Two Essays*, viii; Committee Minutes and Journals of the Proceedings of the Charles Town Library Society in the Charleston Library Society, Charleston, South Carolina; Alexander Hewatt, *An Historical Account of the Rise and Progress of the Colonies of South*

Carolina and Georgia, 2 vols. (London: Alexander Donaldson, 1779), II, 296.

[14]Richard Parker Morgan, *A Preliminary Bibliography of South Carolina Imprints, 1731-1800* (Clemson, South Carolina: Clemson University, n.d.), 23-26, lists Robert Wells's 1774-1775 publications. It was in those years that Wells published large numbers of books. See Walter Edgar, "The Libraries of Colonial South Carolina" (Ph.D. dissertation, University of South Carolina, 1969), 66. *Cf.* Winton, "The Colonial South Carolina Book Trade," 73. Robert Wells's book publishing is the subject of my paper "Filaments of Imperial Culture: Robert Wells and the Eighteenth-Century Reprint Trade" to be published in the proceedings of the third annual Reynolds Conference.

[15]Helena Wells, *Letters on Subjects of Importance to the Happiness of Young Females* (London: L. Peacock, the Juvenile Library no. 259, 1799), 100.

[16]William Charles Wells, *Two Essays*, viii-ix; Helena Wells, *Letters*, 94.

[17]Obituary of Alexander Aikman, *Gentleman's Magazine*, 10, n.s. (Nov. 1838), 556, cited in Ponick, "Helena Wells and Her Family," 9.

[18]William Charles Wells, *Two Essays*, viii-ix; Alexander S. Salley, Jr., ed., *Register of St. Philip's Parish, Charles Town, South Carolina, 1720-1758* (Charleston, South Carolina: printed for the author, 1904), 101, 145.

[19]Louisa Susannah Wells, *The Journal of a Voyage from Charleston, S.C., to London, Undertaken During the American Revolution* (New York: New York Historical Society, 1906), 1, 76; Judgement Rolls, South Carolina Court of Common Pleas, box 47A, no. 213A, microfilm in South Carolina Department of Archives and History, Columbia, South Carolina; Duncan Clinch Heyward, *Seed from Madagascar* (Chapel Hill, North Carolina: University of North Carolina Press, 1937), 8.

[20]Judgement Rolls, South Carolina Court of Common Pleas, box 41A, no. 213A, microfilm in South Carolina Department of Archives and History, Columbia, South Carolina; Isaiah Thomas, *The History of Printing in America*, II, 160; obituary of Alexander Aikman, 556.

[21]Isaiah Thomas, *The History of Printing in America*,
II, 168; William Charles Wells, *Two Essays*, ix-x.

[22]Ian Graham, *Colonists from Scotland* (Ithaca, New
York: Cornell University Press, 1956), 153; Edmund
Berkeley and Dorothy Berkeley, *Dr. Alexander Garden of
Charles Town* (Chapel Hill, North Carolina: University of
North Carolina Press, 1969), 262 *et seq.*; Isaiah Thomas,
The History of Printing in America, II, 159, 394.

[23]William Charles Wells, *Two Essays*, xi.

[24]"Izard-Laurens Correspondence," *South Carolina
Historical and Genealogical Magazine*, 22 (April 1921), 39;
Louisa Susannah Wells, *Journal*, 1, 30, 49.

[25]*Ibid.*, 11.

[26]*Ibid.*, 79-80. See William Charles Wells, *Two Essays*,
xxx.

[27]A.O. 12/51, 365 *et seq.*, microfilm in the Library of
Congress, Washington, D. C.; Louisa Susannah Wells,
Journal, 79-80; Account Book of the Commissioners of For-
feited Estates, 1782-1783, in the South Carolina Historical
Society, Charleston, South Carolina; "The Petition of
Robert Rowand of Charleston, on behalf of his Sister Mary
Wells, the wife of Robert Wells, formerly of Charleston,
but now of London," 28 Nov. 1792, and "The Humble Petition
of Charles Pinckney," 4 Dec. 1798, both among the South
Carolina General Assembly Petitions, South Carolina
Department of Archives and History, Columbia, South
Carolina.

[28]Louisa Susannah Wells, *Journal*, 79-80.

[29]Mary Beth Norton, *The British-Americans: The Loyalist
Exiles in England, 1774-1789* (Boston: Little, Brown and
Co., 1972), 235-236; Mary Beth Norton, "Eighteenth-Century
American Women in Peace and War: The Case of the Loyalists,"
The William and Mary Quarterly, 3rd series, 33 (July 1976),
401; Louisa Susannah Wells, *Journal*, 71. There is some
confusion about the name of the sister with whom Helena
opened the boarding school. She is referred to not only
as Griselda, Grissel, and Grissie, but as Pricilla. See
Ponick, "Helena Wells and Her Family," 22-23; "Izard-
Laurens Correspondence," 39; William Charles Wells, *Two*

Essays, viii.

[30]Review of Helena Wells, *The Step-Mother: A Domestic Tale, from Real Life*, 2 vols. (London: T. N. Longman, 1798), in the *Gentleman's Magazine*, 68 (June 1798), 516, quoted in Ponick, "Helena Wells and Her Family," 39. The *Letters* were published in London in 1790. The characterizations of Helen Maria Williams by Tone and Polwhele are quoted in M. Ray Adams, "Helen Maria Williams and the French Revolution," *Wordsworth and Coleridge: Studies in honor of George McLean Harper*, ed. by Earl Leslie Griggs (Princeton, New Jersey: Princeton University Press, 1939), 117 and 115, respectively.

[31]Helena Wells, *The Step-Mother: A Domestic Tale, from Real Life*, 2nd ed., 2 vols. (London: T. N. Longman and O. Rees; and Edinburgh: W. Creech, 1799), I, v-vi.

[32]*Ibid.*, I, vi.

[33]Note 30 above; Helena Wells, *Letters*, 126.

[34]Review of *The Step-Mother* in the *Critical Review*, 24 (Oct. 1798), 237, and in the *Monthly Review*, 26 (Aug. 1798), 459, cited in Ponick, "Helena Wells and Her Family," 40.

[35]William Charles Wells, *Two Essays*, xlii, lxv-lxvi; John Nichols, *The Rise and Progress of the Gentleman's Magazine* (London: John Nichols and Son, 1821), lxxviii.

[36]Ponick, "Helena Wells and Her Family," 38-40; Helena Wells, *Constantia Neville; or, the West Indian*, 2nd ed., 3 vols. (London: T. Cadell, Jr. and W. Davies; and Edinburgh: W. Creech, 1800), I, 5-6.

[37]The preface to the first edition, as given in the second edition, is dated "May the 10th, 1798." The preface to the second edition is dated "Feb. 6, 1799."

[38]Helena Wells, *Constantia Neville; or, the West Indian*, 3 vols. (London: T. Cadell, Jr. and W. Davies; and Edinburgh: W. Creech, 1800), III, 305.

[39]Helena Wells, *Letters*, [iii-iv].

[40]Helena Wells, *Constantia Neville*, I, [iii]-iv.

[41]Ponick, "Helena Wells and Her Family," 32-33; Helena Wells, *Constantia Neville*, 2nd ed., I, [1]-4.

[42]Obituary of Helena Wells, *Gentleman's Magazine*, 94 (Dec. 1824), 569.

[43]Helena Wells, *Letters*, 2nd ed. (London: printed for the author, 1807); *Thoughts* (London: T. N. Longman, 1809). I have not seen *Thoughts*. See Ponick, "Helena Wells and Her Family," 36.

[44]*Ibid*.; *Critical Review*, 17 (May 1809), 109.

[45]See Lillie Deming Loshe, *The Early American Novel, 1789-1830* (New York: Frederick Ungar Publishing Co., 1958), 15; Henri Petter, *The Early American Novel* (Columbus, Ohio: Ohio University Press, 1971), 169-170, 236-237. Petter, 413-414, 457-458, gives convenient plot summaries of Helena Wells's two novels.

[46]For discussions of educational theory and practice in the novels, see, for instance, Helena Wells, *Constantia Neville*, I, 195-199; III, 243-247. The table of contents of Helena Wells, *Letters*, lists many of the same points of instruction as does the table of contents to *Constantia Neville*. *Cf*. Mary Wollstonecraft, *Thoughts on the Education of Daughters with Reflections on Female Conduct, in the More Important Duties of Life* (London: J. Johnson, 1787).

[47]For some of Helena Wells's criticisms of Mary Wollstonecraft see *Constantia Neville*, II, 37-45, 412-420.

[48]*Ibid*., I, iv-v; Helena Wells, *The Step-Mother*, 2nd ed., I, vi-vii.

[49]Helena Wells treats the same level of society in her fiction as does her younger contemporary and fellow novelist of manners Jane Austen. Austen's and Wells's characters are also similarly placed in that society. However, Jane Austen's characters live primarily in the English provinces, while Helena Wells's live primarily in urban centers like Hamburg, Liverpool, and London. Consequently, landed interests form the background to Austen's novels, while mercantile interests form the background to

Wells's.

[50]Louisa Susannah Wells, *Journal*, i; "Petition of
Robert Rowand ...;" Mabel L. Webber, "Records from the
Elliott-Rowand Bible," *South Carolina Historical and
Genealogical Magazine*, 11 (Jan. 1910), 57 *et seq.*

[51]Of the South Carolina subscribers, Gabriel Manigault,
Esq., was active in the Charles Town Library Society when
Robert Wells was. So were Alexander Baron, M.D., and Brian
Cape, whose wife subscribed. See the Committee Minutes and
the Journals of the Proceedings of the Charles Town Library
Society in the Charleston Library Society, Charleston, South
Carolina. Martha Laurens Ramsay was the sister of Robert
Wells's older son's school mate, John Laurens. See "Letters
from Hon. Henry Laurens to His Son John, 1773-1776," *South
Carolina Historical and Genealogical Magazine*, 5 (April
1904), 75. A number of the South Carolina subscribers,
among them Baillie, Wallace, and Ballie, Archibald Campbell,
M.D., Mrs. Elizabeth M'Pherson, and Andrew M'Farlane, had
Scottish names. As the Wellses had been so closely identified with the Scottish community in Charles Town, this is
not surprising.

Four of the 53 subscribers in South Carolina were doctors: Alexander Baron, Archibald Campbell, ---- Chichester,
and Samuel Wilson. And the wives of two other doctors,
James Carson and David Ramsay, also subscribed. This was to
be expected as well, since the Wellses had been associated
with numerous physicians in Charles Town both because many
of the doctors had come from and/or been educated in Scotland, and because doctors played a central role in the cultural life of South Carolina throughout the eighteenth and
much of the nineteenth centuries. See Joseph Ioor Waring,
The History of Medicine in South Carolina, 3 vols. (Columbia,
South Carolina: The South Carolina Medical Association, 1964-
1971), I, 45, 79, 173 *et seq.*; II, 199 *et seq.*

Several South Carolina names also occur in the list of
British subscribers. Among them is Elias Vanderhorst,
American Consul in Bristol. See Jeannie Heyward Register,
"Marriage and Death Notices from the City Gazette," *South
Carolina Historical and Genealogical Magazine*, 27 (Oct.
1926), 222. The George Ogilvies listed may be the loyalist
exiles from South Carolina. See Berkeley and Berkeley,
Alexander Garden, 166, 255-256. The Mrs. G. Roupell listed
may be the wife of George Roupell, who, like Robert Wells,
was a member of the St. Andrew's Society in Charles Town.
See J. Harold Easterby, *History of the St. Andrew's Society*

of Charleston, South Carolina, 1729-1929 (Charleston, South
Carolina: published for the Society, 1929), 52, 54, 57.

[52]William Charles Wells, *Two Essays*, ix. Another of
William Charles Wells's five friends, Matthew Baillie,
M.D. F.R.S., also subscribed.

[53]Names in the British section of the subscription
list to *Constantia Neville* which appear in either Louisa
Susannah Wells, *Journal*, or William Charles Wells, *Two
Essays*, include Baillie, Home, Hume, Hunter, M'Culloch,
Maitland, Ogilvie, Robertson, Roupell, Tunno, Wallace, and
Williams. Several of the subscribers, like the Ogilvies,
lived in Aberdeen, the birthplace of Helena Wells's
brother-in-law, Alexander Aikman. Only one subscriber,
a Mrs. Milligan of Dalskairth, Galloway, gave a south-
west Scotland address, and no one gave a Glasgow address.
This suggests that Helena Wells had not many personal
ties with the birthplaces of her parents. (Glasgow was
her mother's birthplace.) Several of the Campbells,
Frasers, Murrays, and Ogilvies on the list seem to have
been members of single families, and this suggests that
those and other families which subscribed were, for whatever reasons, eager to support Helena Wells's literary
enterprise.

[54]Rosser H. Taylor, *Ante-Bellum South Carolina* (Chapel
Hill, North Carolina: University of North Carolina Press,
1942), 34.

[55]Helena Wells, *The Step-Mother*, II, 240; Helena Wells,
Constantia Neville, I, 61, 76-77; III, 70-71.

[56]Ponick, "Helena Wells and Her Family," 32-33.

[57]Isaiah Thomas, *The History of Printing in America*,
II, 159. See Winton, "The Colonial South Carolina Book
Trade," 80-81.

[58]William Charles Wells, *Two Essays*, liv.

[59]Helena Wells, *Constantia Neville*, I, 134.

[60]Sophia Hume (see note 5 above) and Eliza Lucas
Pinckney (see note 61 below) were of the planter class,
as was Eliza Wilkinson (see the discussion of her by
Edwin Arnold in this volume). They, Helena Wells's sister

Louisa, Mrs. Charles Cotesworth Pinckney, Mrs. David
Ramsay, and Martha Logan (see the discussion by Edwin
Arnold in this volume) are virtually the only eighteenth-
century South Carolina women who left writings, excepting
discrete business and government records, periodical
contributions, and isolated letters, which are known.

[61]See Elise Pinckney, ed., *The Letterbook of Eliza
Lucas Pinckney, 1739-1762* (Chapel Hill, North Carolina:
University of North Carolina Press, 1972), *passim*; Harriott
Horry Ravenel, *Eliza Pinckney* (New York: Charles Scribner's
Sons, 1896), *passim*; Norton, "Eighteenth-Century American
Women in Peace and War," 386, 394-395.

[62]Two parts of Helena Wells's *Letters*, for instance,
which evoked contemporary commentary and may be worth
study are her advice on reading (pp. 13-19) and her
discussion of "improprieties of Language frequently
ocurring [*sic*!] in familiar conversation" (pp. [155]-179).
See Ponick, "Helena Wells and Her Family," 27-30. Helena
Wells's observations on reading and the commentary it
provoked provide suggestive footnotes to Spruill's discussion of women's tastes in reading in *Women's Life and
Work*, 229-230. The commentary on Helena Wells's language
usage guide indicates that she used a mixture of Scottish,
American, and English expressions. If so, her "Lessons
on the Improprieties of Language" may be of interest to
historians as well as historical linguists; her retention
of Scotticisms and Americanisms in her speech may prove
revealing, for instance, of the ways in which she and her
family were assimilated and/or resisted assimilation first
in Charles Town and then in London.

Josephine Pinckney

by

Herbert P. Shippey

Josephine Pinckney, along with Du Bose Heyward, Hervey
Allen, John Bennett, and others, was one of the founders of
the Poetry Society of South Carolina. The organizational
meeting was held in October, 1920, in the South Carolina
Society Hall in Charleston.[1] Miss Pinckney was very much
involved in the activities of the Society throughout its
first decade and regularly contributed poems to its
Year Book.[2] Her first book, *Sea-drinking Cities*,[3] a
collection of verse about the low-country, was published in
1927 and was awarded the Caroline Sinkler Prize by the
Society for 1927-1928.[4] Miss Pinckney continued her association with the organization; but, as it became less
vibrant over the years, she built a literary reputation in
her own right. Evaluating the Society in a 1930 *Sewanee
Review* article, she wrote ". . . the Poetry Society of
South Carolina has not 'produced' a single poet or poem,
nor do I know of any instance of such parthenogenesis
occuring [*sic*] elsewhere. Poets are made by other pro-
cesses, and poetry will out regardless of societies."[5] In
continuing, however, she recognized a valuable function
which it had served: ". . . there can be no question that
those of the Charleston group who may be said to have
achieved some success in the literary world have found it
immensely valuable as a door by which to enter that world;
through it they have passed to fruitful contacts with the
literary gentry and to public recognitions."[6] Miss
Pinckney passed through that door and in the succeeding
years turned her attention to the novel. It is as a

novelist that she achieved her greatest artistic successes, and as a novelist that she should best be remembered. A *New York Herald Tribune* interviewer asked her in 1952 if she still wrote poetry, and she replied: "'No, and I feel badly about it, because I regard it as the highest calling. But one can't go on and on writing pastoral poetry.'"[7]

(1957)

Since her death eighteen years ago, Miss Pinckney's works have received little attention. Apart from reviews and character sketches in newspapers or magazines, occasional mention in such works as Emily Clark's *Innocence Abroad*[8] or Frank Durham's *Du Bose Heyward: The Man Who Wrote Porgy*,[9] and brief biographical summaries placed with her poems which have been anthologized, there has been no study of her life or writings. She does not deserve this neglect, for she wrote at least two or three novels which should still be read. She is a minor writer, but in a few novels she attained a measure of artistic success which should not be forgotten. It is appropriate, therefore, briefly to survey her novels, considering some of their themes and techniques.

Josephine Pinckney was born in Charleston on January 25, 1895; but she did not publish *Hilton Head*, her first novel, until 1941, when she was forty-six. During the remaining years of her life, she published *Three O'Clock Dinner* (1945), *Great Mischief* (1948), and *My Son and Foe* (1952).[10] She died in New York on October 4, 1957.[11] At the time of her death she was working on a fifth novel, which appeared posthumously in 1958 under the title *Splendid in Ashes*. Her novels were widely publicized and overall received favorable critical reviews in such prominent periodicals as the *New York Times,* the *New York Herald Tribune*, and the *Saturday Review of Literature*. *Three O'Clock Dinner* became a best seller and was published in several countries. The Literary Guild made it their October selection for 1945, and Metro-Goldwyn-Mayer paid $125,000, plus royalties, for motion picture rights to the book before it was published.[12]

Although Miss Pinckney's novels, except one, have Charleston settings, they are not simply local color works. Their themes have universal relevance, and the style in which they are written is cosmopolitan. Beneath the surface of sparkling wit and poetic description, they have serious thematic undercurrents concerning family and community relationships, the workings of fate, the play between the comic and the tragic, and the antithesis of change and tradition.

Her first novel, *Hilton Head*,[13] is an historical work developed slowly in a realistic manner. It gradually builds a composite picture of the life and times of Henry Woodward, the first English settler in what is now South Carolina. The novel portrays him realistically as a stubborn man with vanities and foibles, not highly gifted intellectually, sometimes mistrusted by his fellow colonists, yet possessing a special way with Indians, children, and animals. By gradual pen strokes, Miss Pinckney reveals his weaknesses and strengths, slowly delineating him as a credible character who possesses the traits of greatness.

In this work she displays a wide knowledge of the early history of Carolina and the politics of England which determined its course. The Indians are presented sympathetically but realistically. Her knowledge of the various tribes of Carolina, Florida, and the unsettled country to the west is extensive. In the text she includes an edited version of Woodward's actual letter to Lord Ashley describing his trip to the Westo Indian village on the Savannah River in 1674. The accounts of the Creeks on the Chattahoochee and the St. Elena Indians on the Carolina coast provide convincing details of Indian village life.

By developing Woodward's life from his arrival in the New World at Barbados, through his adventures as a resident among the St. Elena Indians, a captive in St. Augustine, a Caribbean privateersman, an original settler in old Charles Town, an Indian trader, the deputy of Lord Ashley, a colonial doctor, and finally as a prosperous sea island planter seeking to expand the extent of Charleston's trade with the Creek Indians, Miss Pinckney provides a panoramic sweep of the early history of Carolina, which assumes epic proportions in its magnitude.

The novel, nevertheless, possesses flaws. It is rather slow moving. At times the action drags as she develops some minor detail. Also, the reader misses a sense of excitement in the events depicted. Sometimes the style seems too reserved and unemotional. But the writing is poetically descriptive without succumbing to sentimentality, and it moves with a steady pace, giving a sense of passing years with the gradual rise of the colony and

the concomitant rise of legend around Woodward's
character.

In the epilogue Miss Pinckney shows the flow of life
continuing after Woodward's death, the colony developing
in part because of what he had accomplished. And it is
this sense of slow, steady movement, the perpetual flux
which repeats the same essential patterns, that permeates
the entire narrative. This philosophy is expressed in the
closing lines of the novel by Shadoo, one of Woodward's
longtime Indian friends, who states to a group of settlers:
"'New water running, always same river' . . . ."[14] The
idea that life moves on, repeating basic patterns, establishing fundamental order in spite of crises and catas-
trophes, is one of the main themes in Josephine Pinckney's
novels.

Three O'Clock Dinner is her most artistically written
work.[15] The book sets forth the idea, central in her
fiction, that character is fate. It presents an antithesis
between traditional values, represented by the old, established Redcliff family, and modern values, represented by
the more recently arrived and less refined Hessenwinkle
family. There is a clear implication that traditional
values will eventually lose. The aristocratic family is
falling apart, since the only surviving son is in revolt
against its values.

Judith Redcliff is one of the most skillfully portrayed characters. She must learn to give up old ways and
accommodate herself to unpleasant realities. She discovers
that her dead husband loved her less than she realized and
that he had fathered an illegitimate child shortly before
his death. At the conclusion of the novel Judith adopts
this child, named Red, though she has strong doubts about
doing so. The final scene reveals her alone with the child
for the first time trying to stop his crying. She finally
shouts at him: "'Shut up, you little fiend! . . . I don't
like you any more than you like me! But I've got to learn
. . . you've got to learn . . . we've just got to learn to
get along; nobody can help us now . . . .'"[37] The closing
words of the novel emphasize her dawning awareness of new
realities which she must confront:

> The lights in the room seemed to go up a little
> as if from some hidden source of candle-power;
> the yellow and gray chintz, she noticed in this

challenging clarity, had worn out its time; it
would have to go, the new furniture covers would
have to be practical, planned (like everything
else in her life) to withstand marauding hands
and feet. Red made himself comfortable against
her and his demand set up a flow from her body
to his as warm and direct as milk.[17]

This passage is an example of Miss Pinckney's direct approach, the way that she avoids being sentimental. The
conflict between stasis and change which it expresses is
found elsewhere in her works. She creates characters who
are resilient enough to adapt to change. Basically her
works express an optimistic viewpoint, though this optimism is also tempered with, and even strengthened by, the
ludicrous and ironic.

Her finest descriptions of Charleston are found in
this novel. Through the mind of Lucian Redcliff, another
well-drawn character who enjoys observing the life about
him with a detached sense of amusement and irony, she provides this portrait of Charleston:

The swampy area on which he had been born, had
lived, and hoped to die was probably in no way
superior to similar acreages . . . but no . . .
that was hardly true . . . some special lucence
bathed this plot of ground, he insisted . . .
this precious stone set in a slightly muddy sea.
For people loved it with extravagance . . . in
spite of its absurdities, its gross failures.
Perhaps because of them . . . . For life was
richest when it was dappled, paradoxical, in
flavorsome layers running counter to each
other.[18]

These last lines could easily be applied to Miss Pinckney's
writing, for a love of paradox and ironic juxtapositions
is perhaps the distinguishing trait of her fiction.

The third novel, *Great Mischief*, is a fantasy painted
in vivid, romantic details.[19] It is a light treatment of
the Faust legend, which tells the story of a Charleston
apothecary of the late nineteenth century who becomes involved in black magic and is willingly enticed to his
destruction by a charming hag. The book combines low-
country folklore and superstitions with realistic details

of Charleston life. In the process it gives a pleasant
account of how hags can sail through keyholes by holding
a cat bone in their mouth, how conjure balls placed in
chimneys can sometimes keep hags away, and how a hag can
slip her skin and leave it behind the door to fly through
the air on nocturnal mischief. At one point the apothecary
meets the devil, and he notes with astonishment that he
looks very much like a Charlestonian.

My Son and Foe[20] shows family conflicts, as does
Three O'Clock Dinner, but in this novel, set on the small
island of St. Finbar, the conflict is between opposing
character types within a single family. The atmosphere of
the novel is darker and more fatalistic. It is tightly
constructed, possessing the kind of inexorable development
of events characteristic of a classical tragedy. The book
is an imaginative *tour de force* with unity of theme and
tone. It recreates in modern terms the old tragic patterns
of brother against brother, parent against child, and man
against the dark workings of fate. Yet, it also has some
of the urbane wit and comic perspective of *Three O'Clock
Dinner* and *Splendid in Ashes*.[21]

The latter work portrays the reaction of Charleston to
a flamboyant native son who achieves success away from home.
Beginning with the news of his death and the return of his
body to Charleston, the story of his successes and failures
unfolds through a flashback technique leading up through
the years to the funeral and the reading of the will. The
central character and his wife are revealed through the
gossip and conversation of Charleston society and through
the anonymous Charlestonian whose narrative voice controls
the story.

Parts of *Splendid in Ashes* are well written, in
particular the beginning and conclusion. But Miss Pinckney
may not have had the chance to polish the work as she
wished before her death. The overall conception of the
work is excellent, but in places the execution drags, the
dialogue at times becoming too matter-of-fact.

The central character, John Augustus Grimshawe, is
reminiscent of some of F. Scott Fitzgerald's male characters, especially Jay Gatsby, Dick Diver, and Monroe Stahr.
He has the same type of meteoric glitter and splendid
failure as these figures. His death is an ironic but
characteristic resolution to the pattern of brilliant

success followed by humiliating failure which he had established earlier in life. He and his wife Carlotta are the cynosure of Charleston eyes, by turns arousing admiration, scorn, and pity. One Charlestonian remarks: "When you consider how long the Grimshawes' affairs had given us blissful diversion from breadwinning, depressions, and taxes . . . We ought to put up a monument to them on the Battery . . . ."[22]

This work has the same kind of ironic conclusion, with its anticlimactic continuance of daily life, found in the other novels of manners. The conclusion has double-edged irony. Grimshawe apparently dies a millionaire, willing handsome sums of money to his family, his retainers, and the community. But his fortune founders after his death, and all the rich legacies turn to ashes, creating a sensation in Charleston. Yet, the last laugh may be on the community, since Grimshawe, knowing the pattern of his earlier failures, may have realized that his bequests would come to naught. Perhaps the final masquerade of wealth and generous gifts is simply his way of exiting in splendor with his usual panache. The richness of irony in the conclusion partially redeems the slow-moving central portion of the novel and the somewhat weak characterizations of other figures.

No one of these five novels can serve as an example of the rest, for they are all different. The variety of subject matter and technique reveals that Miss Pinckney was a versatile writer not content to settle into a niche and produce novels according to a tried pattern. Over the years she explored new methods. She was a careful craftsman and composed her works slowly.

Her novels are imbued with a comic viewpoint. She obviously enjoyed the paradoxes and ironies of life. In her works there are numerous humorous episodes imposed upon a basic comic foundation. Life, as she depicts it, is a kind of social comedy played out in the midst of the tragic realities of the world. These realities break through in her fiction, but they do not overwhelm the comic perspective. Indeed, they may inspire it. After a tragic or disorienting occurrence, there is always a coda, or epilogue, which shows life continuing with its ironies, its absurdities, and its wisdom acquired. The chief characters may be saddened, or even damned, as is Timothy Partridge in *Great Mischief*; but they are never overwhelmed. Something is always salvaged from the wreckage. These epilogues are written in an unsentimental, direct manner. They present ironic resolutions to the tensions and conflicts developed earlier.

At one point Miss Pinckney was considering entitling *Three O'Clock Dinner* "The Laughing Animals: A Comedy of Manners."[23] This proposed title was inspired by the opening passage of William Hazlitt's *Lectures on the English Comic Writers*,[24] which begins as follows: "MAN is the only animal that laughs and weeps; for he is the only animal that is struck with the difference between what things are, and what they ought to be."[25] A few lines further Hazlitt states: "To explain the nature of laughter and tears, is to account for the condition of human life; for it is in a manner compounded of these two! It is a tragedy or a comedy---sad or merry, as it happens."[26] An ironic, tragicomic attitude is also reflected in the title *Splendid in Ashes*. The title is taken from a passage in Sir Thomas Browne's *Hydriotaphia*, or *Urn Burial*, which reads: *"Man is a noble animal, splendid in ashes, and pompous in the grave."*[27] An attempt to probe the condition of life, to account for the laughter and tears, is what Josephine Pinckney's novels are basically about, in spite of their flaws. The mixture of comic and tragic elements is present in all of her fiction.

She is not so skilled in portraying the deepest and most powerful human emotions. Perhaps she even shuns them on purpose to avoid a possible lapse into the sensational or sentimental. But she is adept in painting the lesser passions, the everyday, social being of people. She treats man as a social animal, whose psyche is well worth probing. Her last three volumes are psychological novels as well as comedies of manners with tragic undertones. With her, as with Henry James, even a single gesture can become a telltale event. Paradoxical juxtapositions abound in her narratives. She is a master of the shrewd observation and the urbane, cleverly turned phrase.

Her characters on a first survey may seem rather superficial. A more careful scrutiny, however, reveals that they are complex. Lucian Redcliff in *Three O'Clock Dinner* is such a character. He appears to be unemotional, a kind of social vulture who thrives on other people's clashing emotions. But a further consideration of Lucian reveals that he does indeed have deep emotions and at the same time an ability to step back out of a scene and view himself and others humorously or ironically. He is a well-conceived character creation. He serves in the novel the way a skillful artist does in life, as a spectator who feels deeply but also remains detached intellectually in order to see events truthfully.

Miss Pinckney demonstrates skill in using this kind of character. Such a figure is distant enough from the characters in the center of the conflict to provide some degree of objectivity and to give an embracing view of them, but he is still close enough to become involved at least tangentially. The spectator of other people's misfortunes cannot really remain outside the events which he follows. To watch is to become involved and in turn to influence. The disparity between the apparent detachment and actual involvement is a source of irony which enriches the narrative.

Kirk McAfee in *My Son and Foe* is a character of this nature. Through him the reader obtains some overview of the Metellus family, but accepting his interpretation of characters and events is misleading. He is not a disinterested outsider. He enjoys manipulating the lives of Elsi, her husband Basil, and their son Rikky, as well as James, Elsi's son by a prior marriage. By dabbling in their affairs as if he were a deity, McAfee becomes at least partly responsible for initiating the crisis which leads to Rikky's death by drowning. But because of his emotional shortcomings, he cannot fully appreciate his role as catalyst to the accident. In the last scene of the novel he is preparing to continue his travels and his role as self-detached observer elsewhere as he loads his camera with fresh film.

In all the novels there is an interest in family life. The interactions within the community and family are one of her principal subjects. In *Three O'Clock Dinner*, *My Son and Foe*, and *Splendid in Ashes*, there is a lively interaction among characters. Miss Pinckney selects some person who serves as a source of conflict, and the other characters cluster around this individual, talking and analyzing. These novels display the sensitized probing and mastery of light wit characteristic of a Henry James novel.

As an artist Miss Pinckney is detached from her material; it does not carry her away. Consequently her

works impress one by their reserved style and firm control
of emotional distance from the matter portrayed. She pre-
cludes sentimentality by the use of subtle irony and realistically observed details. Her settings are provincial,
her style is cosmopolitan, and her themes are universal.
Her works do not have the eccentric vitality possessed by
the writings of younger Southern women authors, such as
Flannery O'Connor or Carson McCullers, though she does convey some of the forcefulness of mind which they display.
There are flashes of the comically eccentric, such as
Theodore Grimshawe's mynah bird, which screeches obsceni-
ties and Latin phrases in *Splendid in Ashes*. But on the
whole Miss Pinckney's style is more restrained, more cosmopolitan. Traces of Nathaniel Hawthorne's mixing of fantasy
and the realistic, Henry James's concern for subtle, detached analysis of people, and F. Scott Fitzgerald's love
for resplendent characters who fail grandly can be seen in
her fiction. But she lacks their power and overall artistry. She is a minor writer, but in two or three of her
novels she is a skilled artist. And in her combination of
urbane wit, subtle irony, and paradoxical humor touched
with tragedy, she may be unique among Southern writers.

Notes

[1]For information concerning the founding and organization of The Poetry Society of South Carolina, see the following: *Year Book of The Poetry Society of South Carolina for 1921*, Charleston: Poetry Society of South Carolina, Inc., 1921; Josephine Pinckney, "Charleston's Poetry Society," *Sewanee Review*, 38 (January 1930), 50-56 (hereafter cited as Pinckney, "Charleston's Poetry Society"); Drayton Mayrant [Katherine Drayton Mayrant Simons], "'If Any Man Can Play the Pipes': A Sketch of the Poetry Society of South Carolina," *South Carolina Magazine*, 14 (September 1951), 9, 21-22; James G. Harrison, "South Carolina's Poetry Society: After Thirty Years," *The Georgia Review*, 7 (Summer 1953), 204-209; Frank Durham, *Du Bose Heyward: The Man Who Wrote Porgy*, Columbia: University of South Carolina Press, 1954 (hereafter cited as Durham, *Du Bose Heyward*); _____, "The Rise of Du Bose Heyward and the Rise and Fall of The Poetry Society of South Carolina," *The Mississippi Quarterly*, 19 (Spring 1966), 66-78.

[2]During the first ten years of the Society's existence, Miss Pinckney served as treasurer, first and second vice-president, secretary, and a member of the executive committee. She was also chairman of the editorial committee and served on the dramatic, program, entertainment, Blindman Prize, and Caroline Sinkler Prize committees. She received the Caroline Sinkler Prize (1920-1921) for her poem "In the Barn," the Southern Prize (1926-1927) for "An Island Boy," and the Caroline Sinkler Prize again (1927-1928) for *Sea-drinking Cities*. This information can be found in the year books of the Poetry Society for the years 1921-1933.

[3]Josephine Pinckney, *Sea-drinking Cities*. New York: Harper & Brothers, 1927.

[4]*The Year Book of The Poetry Society of South Carolina* [for 1928] (Charleston: The Poetry Society of South Carolina, 1928), pp. 25, 26.

[5]Pinckney, "Charleston's Poetry Society," p. 54.

[6]Pinckney, "Charleston's Poetry Society," p. 54.

[7]John K. Hutchens, "On the Books: On an Author,"
New York Herald Tribune Book Review, 111 (January 20, 1952),
2.

[8]See: Emily Clark, *Innocence Abroad* (New York:
Alfred A. Knopf, 1931), pp. 10, 228–229, 235.

[9]See: Durham, *Du Bose Heyward*, pp. 27, 107–108.

[10]Stanley J. Kunitz and Vineta Colby, *Twentieth Century
Authors: First Supplement* (New York: The H. W. Wilson
Company, 1955), p. 778.

[11]Charleston *News and Courier*, October 5, 1957, pp. 1-A,
9-A.

[12]Charleston *News and Courier*, August 29, 1945, p. 1;
also, Charleston *News and Courier*, October 5, 1957, p. 1-A.

[13]Josephine Pinckney, *Hilton Head*. New York: Farrar &
Rinehart, Inc., 1941. (Hereafter cited as Pinckney, *Hilton
Head*.)

[14]Pinckney, *Hilton Head*, p. 524.

[15]Josephine Pinckney, *Three O'Clock Dinner*. New York:
The Viking Press, 1945. (Hereafter cited as Pinckney,
Three O'Clock Dinner.)

[16]Pinckney, *Three O'Clock Dinner*, p. 295.

[17]Pinckney, *Three O'Clock Dinner*, p. 296.

[18]Pinckney, *Three O'Clock Dinner*, pp. 157–158.

[19]Josephine Pinckney, *Great Mischief*. New York: The
Viking Press, 1948.

[20]Josephine Pinckney, *My Son and Foe*. New York: The
Viking Press, 1952.

[21]Josephine Pinckney, *Splendid in Ashes*. New York:
The Viking Press, 1958. (Hereafter cited as Pinckney,
Splendid in Ashes.)

[22]Pinckney, *Splendid in Ashes*, p. 153.

[23]Letter, dated May 28, [1945], from Josephine
Pinckney to Pat [Pascal Covici] of The Viking Press. The
Viking Press Archives.

[24]Letter, dated June 4, 1945, from Josephine [Pinckney]
to Pascal Covici of The Viking Press. The Viking Press
Archives.

[25]William Hazlitt, *Lectures on the English Comic
Writers. The Collected Works of William Hazlitt*, A. R.
Waller and Arnold Glover, eds. Vol. 8 (London: J. M. Dent
& Co., 1903), 5. (Hereafter cited as Hazlitt, *Lectures on
the English Comic Writers.*)

[26]Hazlitt, *Lectures on the English Comic Writers*, p. 5.

[27]See quotation at the beginning of Pinckney, *Splendid
in Ashes.*

Session II: Discussion

MISS GREGORY: Mrs. Scafidel, I wondered how you are able
to tell which are her poems in these albums and which
are copied from other sources?

MRS. SCAFIDEL: She indicates the author of her quotation
or the source at the end of the quotation. If it's
from a novel she'll give the title, or sometimes she'll
give a particular author's name. There were a couple
of poems and fragments that I couldn't identify; I believe they're hers, but I didn't want to take the
chance and say so.

MISS GREGORY: How many of her own poems are there, approximately, in the two albums?

MRS. SCAFIDEL: Well, in those two albums, maybe altogether
thirty. But some of them are hardly worth mention.
She wrote a poem when she sent back a book from John
Russell that she had borrowed and kept for a couple of
months, and was apologizing for it. A very few of the
poems are pretty good.

MR. POLK: Mr. Shippey, what kind of a Pinckney archive is
there?

MR. SHIPPEY: The only papers that I know of at the moment
are in the hands of members of her family and one of
her publishers. One of her nieces by marriage, who
lives in Richmond, Virginia, has some manuscript
material from her novels. Viking Press in New York has
a good bit of material, at least seven file folders,
I'm told by an editor, Mr. Marshall Best.

MR. MERIWETHER: I think you might comment on those two
letters you placed on exhibit at the Caroliniana.

MR. SHIPPEY: These are copies of two letters Mr. Best sent
me. They concern the proposed change of title in *Three
O'Clock Dinner*. The letters are very interesting, since
they reveal that she was seriously considering changing
the title to *The Laughing Animals: A Comedy of Manners*.
But the title remained *Three O'Clock Dinner*.

97

MISS RUTLEDGE: Three o'clock dinner is a hangover from
    the 18th century, from the Caribbean, from a semi-
    tropical climate---from planting hours.

MR. INABINETT: Going back to a question that was directed
    to Beverly Scafidel a while ago, about the composition
    of the albums, I believe it was taught in schools.
    I've seen other instances where students made up little
    books. We acquired one very recently as a gift from a
    dealer, and it's absolutely of no importance, but it
    has a mock-up title page with a Charleston imprint. It
    has half a dozen little poems in it, made up into a
    little booklet, and I believe it's a carry-over from a
    school exercise, to do that. How old was she when she
    started the album?

MRS. SCAFIDEL: Seventeen.

MISS ENDRES: Mary Moragné has a scrapbook of newspaper
    clippings with poems in it---

MISS GREGORY: So does Mrs. Chesnut.

MISS ENDRES: ---and they're also unsigned. The only way
    you know that anything in there is by Mary Moragné is
    that she's pencilled in her initials at the bottom,
    apparently claiming her authorship.

MRS. CHILDS: Mrs. Petigru was more or less an invalid and
    I think considered to be an extremely difficult charac-
    ter, staying in bed. She really did nothing in the way
    of being a housekeeper or a mother or a hostess. And I,
    from very scattered reading, I had the impression that
    intellectually Caroline and her father were very close.
    She read, and she was hostess for quite a group that
    came and borrowed Petigru's books and ate dinner there,
    and whenever interesting people were in port they came
    to the Petigrus' for dinner. There was quite a *salon*
    there for a few years when Caroline officiated, and
    after she was married I thought she was probably very
    often separated from her husband too.

MRS. SCAFIDEL: I've not been able to piece together very
    much about her movements, but she does seem to have been
    separated from her husband fairly often. There is a
    letter in which Petigru remarks about Caroline's not
    being at Badwell, one particular summer, and it seems

like a very dreary place to him in her absence.

MISS GREGORY: In Mrs. Chesnut's novel, she's describing
one of the characters, one of the daughters of the
central character, who is a very straightforward girl,
and the narrator says she did not keep scrapbooks and
copy poems as heroines did. And so it seems to go
along with what you're saying, that there might have
been a dominant convention of some sort that they were
both drawing from there.

MRS. SCAFIDEL: There's also an indication in Jane Austen's
Emma about ladies keeping albums in this very fashion.

MR. HAYHOE: Herbert, I'm curious whether there are any
other works by Miss Pinckney that have been published
that you didn't mention, perhaps short fiction.

MR. SHIPPEY: At first she was a poet. She published a
number of poems which have never been collected, in
various periodicals and magazines. As to whether or
not she published short fiction, I do not know. She
published a few essays. I've come across a few of her
published essays, but that's all that I've been able to
find so far.

MR. INABINETT: Herbert, you said that two or three of her
novels should continue to be read, and I wasn't quite
sure which you preferred.

MR. SHIPPEY: I prefer *Three O'Clock Dinner* and *My Son and
Foe*. But I think that *Hilton Head* is a pretty good
historical novel. It is more than just a sentimental
romance with a historical background.

MR. INABINETT: Where does *Great Mischief* come in your
scale?

MR. SHIPPEY: It's a charming and pleasant book, I think,
and very witty. It's an interesting work, because it
presents some of the low country folklore, as well as
an ironic interpretation of the Charleston Earthquake
of 1886.

MR. INABINETT: I think a little explanation at the beginning of *Great Mischief* would have helped. Even I,
who grew up in Charleston, knew nothing about conjurers,

and hags' skins, and cat bones, and things like that.
But I found it difficult reading without having some
sort of explanation at the beginning as to what I was
embarking on. I recognized it immediately as a play
on the Faust legend, but I think I would have enjoyed
it more with some explanation---

MR. MERIWETHER: Does her depiction of the Devil as a
Charleston gentleman represent the vein of irony or
the vein of realism?

MR. SHIPPEY: I'm not quite sure. He's very suave, I
know.

MRS. OLIPHANT: There is a fine story of Samuel Gaillard
Stoney, who came here to the Columbia Club. He waked
up in the night and decided he would exercise up and
down the hall just before day, and one of the maids
took him for the Devil. She let out a screech that the
Devil had come and raised the whole club before day.

MR. MOLTKE-HANSEN: He made a point of pulling his eye-
brows up and combing his goatee every morning.

MR. SHIPPEY: *Splendid in Ashes* has some good points, but
it drags too much in the center. I don't think that
she had time to polish and finish it as much as she
would have if she had lived longer.

MR. INABINETT: I understood that the Josephine Pinckney
papers were turned over to the Historical Society in
Charleston.

MR. SHIPPEY: No; but they have papers concerning the
Poetry Society of South Carolina, the Du Bose Heyward
papers, and the John Bennett papers, and there are
references to her in those materials. People in
Charleston have some of her personal letters, of course.

Susan Petigru King:
An Early South Carolina Realist

by

J. R. Scafidel

Susan Petigru King, the youngest daughter of the
South Carolina statesman, James L. Petigru, was born in
Charleston on October 23, 1824. Described by Petigru as
a "lively" child,[1] Susan spent, according to her testimony, much of her youth reading novels and romances and
avoiding whenever possible dry works of history.[2] After
attending a fashionable school in Philadelphia, she
returned home to marry Henry C. King, a lawyer in Petigru's
firm. Although her career as an author lasted only from
1854 to 1864, she was involved in a few related activities.
She toured parts of the North, giving dramatic readings,[3]
and she once began a project with William Grayson to publish Petigru's letters.[4] Her later years were spent in
Washington, D. C., as the wife of C. C. Bowen, a congressman from South Carolina. Bowen became Sheriff of Charleston in 1872; Susan King Bowen lived there until December,
1875, when she died and was buried next to her father in
St. Michael's Churchyard in Charleston.

The inscription on her gravestone provides a clue
to the personality of King, who became, in George A.
Wauchope's words, "the most distinguished woman novelist
of ante-bellum South Carolina."[5] The inscription describes
her mind as "brilliant" and "gifted with genius," and her
soul as "bruised, not crushed."[6] Brilliant she did seem
to be. She was well known for her wit. Mary Boykin
Chesnut, in her *Diary from Dixie*, describes an evening
gathering with King and others: "Somebody came in . . .

101

with a message from Captain Bacon. He could not come
because he had a sick baby. Sue King found that a very
amusing message. 'Women have babies, men only have children!' Then she added: 'But it is natural, he wants to
save his little Bacon.'"[7] Her first book, *Busy Moments of
an Idle Woman*, published in 1854, was praised lavishly for
its wit and sophistication in two separate issues of *The
Charleston Daily Courier* (Jan. 5 and 7, 1854), and called
a "clever book" by F. A. Porcher in *The Southern Quarterly
Review* 9 (Jan. 1854), 212. King, Porcher wrote, "may
claim a place. . . equal to any in the walks of female
literature." James Petigru had earlier predicted that his
daughter would "turn out a wit";[8] now he was impressed by
the clever dialogue of the stories of *Busy Moments*.
Writing to her in November, 1853, he says of the book,
"I have no doubt you will receive a great deal of praise,
for the dialogue is witty and sparkling, and the descriptions circumstantial and striking. I dare say that if you
were to take to study, you might, in time, attain to the
delineation of the passions and rise to the walk in which
Miss Austen is admired." He goes on to say that her book
"will be remembered longer than anything that any of the
rest of us have done."[9] A few years later he casually
referred to her as a "great writer."[10]

King's brilliance wasn't always admired or appreciated, however, for with it she combined the tendencies to
be over-bearing, rude, moody, and world-weary. She had
been sent to school in Philadelphia at the age of fifteen,
and it is possible that it was there that she developed, or
cultivated, the air of world-weariness that pervades her
fiction. From Philadelphia she wrote home affected letters
in bad French, much to Petigru's irritation. "She affects
to be very unhappy," he once wrote, "but it appears to me
she is very unreasonable."[11] Petigru, who valued self-
control above most other virtues, also disliked his daughter's temper. He was displeased at her tendency to be
rude to servants[12] and warned her that if she didn't mend
her ways her life would be "'lost in quicksands and
shallows.'"[13] In point of fact, Susan King seems to have
irritated or intimidated a number of people with her wit
and boldness. William Henry Trescot, the eminent South
Carolina statesman and diplomat, believed that King was a
"fast" woman. People, he said, liked to talk about her
flirtations but then avoided her because she was "quarrel-
some."[14] Mary Chesnut, who disapproved of King's going
about with her "shoulders, etc., all bare,"[15] once

described a biting comment she made to King and then wrote
in her diary, ". . . yet I am as afraid of her as death!"[16]

King's personality, whatever its true nature, was controversial. A story concerning Sue King, William Makepeace
Thackeray, and the Baxter family of South Carolina, whom
Thackeray visited during his lecture tours in America, is
replete with contradictions and various points of view that
will indicate the extent to which she in one way or another
impressed those with whom she came into contact. The story
begins in March, 1854, shortly after the publication of
Busy Moments. Sally Baxter set out to discover the author
of the book, made investigations in Savannah, and learned
the identity of the "idle woman." She was greatly impressed with King, "a pretty blonde woman rather stout & with
an expression about her of being *some body*." She managed
to get into a bit of embarrassing wordplay with King,
which she seemed to enjoy. Then, upon learning that she
was indeed the author of *Busy Moments*, Miss Baxter became
ecstatic: "I screamed with delight," she wrote, "rose from
my seat, M[rs] King ditto & we fell into each other's
arms--!!--Such a mutual congratulating, such a compliment-
ing, you never neard. . . . Altogether it was the most
amusing scene I ev[e]r witnessed or took part in--"[17]

Thackeray now enters the picture. At a party, apparently in 1853, when Thackeray was delivering lectures in
Charleston, he encountered Susan King, who was not yet a
published author but a well-known wit in Charleston society. Ida Raymond (Mary T. Tardy) in 1870 described the
event very much in King's favor, the witty American getting
the best of the great Thackeray. She reports his saying to
King upon meeting her, "Mrs. King, I am agreeably disap-
pointed in you; I heard you were the fastest woman in
America, and I detest fast women." King answered, "And I
am agreeably surprised in you, Mr. Thackeray; for I heard
you were no gentleman."[18] Charleston tradition corrobo-
rates the story; Charles A. Wauchope in 1910 wrote that
"the celebrated English author. . . undertook a tilt with
[King] and was badly discomfited."[19] The narrator of
Lily, King's novel published in 1855, gives quite a different account of the meeting with Thackeray. She refers
to him as "the greatest living novelist"[20] and to herself
as a person modestly in the background at a social
gathering, listening to Thackeray explain his theory of
realism in fiction: "From my corner," she writes, "I lis-
tened to the great man, drank in his words, and added my

humble approbation and conviction."[21]

Thackeray came to South Carolina again in 1855; this time we get an entirely different picture of Sue King and the English writer. Lucy Baxter, Sally's sister, gives an account of a dinner party in Charleston in which King is presented as an obnoxious pest:

> I went alone with him, my sister not being well, a lady was present [King] who from their first meeting had antagonized Mr. Thackeray. She was clever and rather brilliant, but had written some very trashy novels, whose reputation had certainly not extended beyond her native city. On this and other occasions she seemed determined to attract Mr. Thackeray's attention, to his great annoyance. At last when something was said about the tribulations of authors, the lady leaned across the table, saying in a loud voice, "You and I, Mr. Thackeray, *being in the same boat*, can understand, can we not?" A dead silence fell, a thunder-cloud descended upon the face of Mr. Thackeray, and the pleasure of the entertainment was at an end. . . . This annoyance on the part of the lady was the culmination of numerous attacks, and struck just the wrong chord.[22]

Whether or not Lucy Baxter is fair to King in this report, or is speaking out of jealousy, I don't know. Thackeray's own comment was that though he considered King "vulgar," he rather liked her.[23]

Susan King wrote only four books, all of them now out of print. After *Busy Moments* in 1854, she published her only full-length novel, *Lily* (1855). The first two-thirds of this novel concern a dull, virtuous young girl in school in Philadelphia and in Charleston society. She is described and dealt with realistically; as one reviewer wrote, she is not "one of those misty abstractions," but "a woman who may and does exist."[24] But then as the novel draws to a close, the heroine becomes a kind of symbol for perfect maidenhood, the hero gets bored with her, out of nowhere his part-Negro mistress appears, she poisons Lily and then dies herself. It would be difficult to imagine a more inappropriate ending for such a novel as this one. The book is an artistic failure, but it has its virtues,

descriptions of high society life in Charleston and Philadelphia, summers at Sullivan's Island in the mid-nineteenth
century, and numerous aside comments by the narrator on the
art of fiction and on women novelists of the day.

Sylvia's World, her third book, made up of a novella
published in *The Knickerbocker*, and six stories from
Russell's Magazine, appeared in 1859.[25] The book as a
whole is marred by an inclination toward didacticism, but
it contains some of King's finest fiction. Her only other
published work[26] is "Gerald Gray's Wife," which appeared
in the *Southern Field and Fireside* (Jan. 2-23, 1864). It
describes the gradual and oppressive loss of individuality
in marriage. "Gerald Gray's Wife" is said to have been
printed as a pamphlet,[27] probably one of the *Southern
Field and Fireside* novelettes, but I haven't found any
confirmation of that anywhere. Apparently the serialized
form of the story is the only version now extant.

The clearest vantage point from which to examine these
four books is Lewis Lewisohn's observation that King "made
an earnest attempt to treat life sincerely and vigorously.
And for this attempt she deserves praise. For the writers
of fiction in the various Carolina magazines wrote in
utter oblivion of such a thing as a real world with real
men and women inhabiting it."[28] King's own description
of her approach anticipates the trend of realism in fiction
fostered by William Dean Howells and others a generation
later. "If we undertake to write novels," she says, "bear
this in mind, that heroes and heroines of the present day
must act like men and women of the present day, or else
they are mere *Marionettes*, and show their rags and wood-
work instead of their flesh and blood."[29] Her attempt is
"to paint the thing itself--to sink a shaft in the breast
of my neighbor, and to draw thence a living stream--to
eschew portraits, but to make 'fancy sketches' life-like
enough to induce people to say, 'Ah! that is meant for so
and so.'" She goes on to say, "I do not believe in sudden
reformations, where the 'devil' of the piece is made
instantly good by the death of the 'angel,' or by his
marriage with her, and turns as quickly as you turn the
leaf into an excellent and virtuous character, just as if
excellence was a coat or gown, and virtue a cap or bonnet,
which you purchase or have presented to you, and wear com-
fortably ever after."[30] In the pursuit of what she calls
"everyday tales,"[31] she disdains the mid-nineteenth century trap of sentimentalism. She blamed Dickens for the

barage of sentimental stories about "serious girls" and "prayerful babies" and unnatural heroines who sacrifice their lives for the sake of being good. "Their labors," she writes,

> are superhuman. They bake, wash, and brew—
> educate, and care for their fathers, mothers,
> grandmothers, and grandfathers, to the re-
> motest generation, and *naturally*, after all
> this, die of extreme old age at fifteen or
> thereabouts, leaving behind them reputations
> of unparalleled magnitude. Their conversations
> are of the deepest theological research, though,
> for the most part, a little ungrammatical; and,
> in short, were I capable of portraying such
> monsters. . . my book would always lack one
> important reader—myself.[32]

King concentrates instead on selected realistic, some-times humorous details for her effects. She describes, for instance, a dancing-master as someone "who looked like a dirty-faced grasshopper,"[33] and a lady's costume as "a well-mixed salad."[34] An interesting use of realistic detail for a certain effect occurs in *Lily* as the hero, Clarence, at an opera suddenly sees a woman's hand before him. In this romantic setting, instead of describing the hand as one being placed gently in Clarence's view, King writes, "a woman's hand suddenly fell on the cushioned front of this box, just beneath his eyes."[35] "I do not mean a hand severed from the arm," she continues, "and lying all bloody and terrible, but a living hand, whose owner was concealed behind the curtain." Clarence stares at it: "He dreamily tracked a blue vein which presently struck his gaze, rising like a little stream from a bed of snow, and slowly he followed its course till it buried itself in the white arm."[36] By such attention to realistic detail King attempts to avoid sentimentality in a romantic opera scene.

What gives King's method some depth, however, is a perceptive manipulation of two opposing points of view, the "romantic" and the "practical." This conflict is the vantage point from which a character in a story, male or female, or the narrator herself looks at the evils of apparently simple human relationships. Through this per-spective King articulates her ideas. In "A Man of Honor," for example, the sixth story of "Crimes Which the Law Does

Not Reach," Frank Egerton wins the affection of a scandal-
ized, vulnerable divorcee who is ostracized by society; he
brings her out, then cruelly drops her, explaining to her
that he must give her up: "I am twitted on all sides for
my reckless devotion. Every man I meet alludes to my
romantic and unpractical views for the future."[37] By
giving up what he and society regard as foolish and romantic, affection with marriage, by preferring the "practical"
thing, dropping Mrs. St. Maur, he psychologically demol-
ishes her. The ironic turn here is that in this case what
society regards as foolishly romantic is humane, what is
practical is not.

     Another apparently simple story that is given a simi-
lar turn is "The Best of Friends." At first we are taken
in by the narrator's point of view toward her story.
"Aunt Milly," as she is called, is a plain woman telling
her nieces what appears to be the story of a beautiful and
admirable woman who was ruined by her family and her "best
friends." But if we look closely, we see that Milly is
cynical: "I have long come to the conclusion," she says,
"that the earth would be a fair place to dwell in, if it
were not for the men and women that inhabit it."[38] In her
cynicism, she despises Madge's family for not saving the
"naturally noble and rare creature from the consequences
of her rashness and her misery."[39] She believes that
Madge is a lovely woman hounded and ruined by her selfish
relatives and acquaintances. Yet slowly the evidence
accumulates which suggests another view--Madge's sister
contends that she constantly ignored her family; there is
gossip about Madge which may be justified; in short, there
are a few facts which indicate that perhaps she is not the
pure persecuted heroine that Aunt Milly is describing to
her nieces. Not only does she abruptly leave her husband
and children to pursue an acting career, but fourteen years
later has the audacity to write a letter to her husband
preventing him from re-marrying. Milly looks upon such
actions as "romantic": "To leave her children," she says,
"was a terrible sin; but not on her head should the blame
fall. The crime of this. . . rested on 'the best of
friends.'"[40] Face to face with Madge she calls her "romantic" and "unpractical,"[41] but she loves Madge (her alter
ego) so much that she wears the ring Madge gave her even
in her old age, has memorized her letters, so much that
she shifts the blame entirely upon Madge's friends and
family. What emerges, then, is the fact that this is primarily the story of Milly, an old woman who has lived an

isolated, uneventful, lonely life, who has become a cynic, and who is now corrupting her nieces by telling them the story of Madge through a distorted perspective.

The conflicts that King explores are not just those of romanticism and practicality, however; they are conflicts of attitudes which are either sanctioned or censured by society. Physical attraction, for example, King regards not as a romantic notion, but a realistic fact. Anna Mansfield, in "Marriage of Persuasion," doesn't want to marry Mr. Gordon because she isn't sexually attracted to him. "I should not like to engage myself," she tells her mother, "to pass my life with a man whose attentions would be repulsive to me."[42] Her mother dismisses her romantic view of sex as ridiculous, forces her into a marriage with Gordon, and Anna turns into a kind but "pale and cold"[43] wife. Her marriage is childless, Anna is "scrupulously polite" to Gordon, "but there is not an atom of sympathy between them." Their house and life together are dull and "joyless."[44]

On the other side of the coin, marriage itself, for all its romantic trimmings, King considers a fact of a woman's existence; to avoid it because of its inadequacies is a failure to face the realities of life. One of her most interesting stories has an insipid title, "Old Maidism vs. Marriage," but it illustrates King's interest in presenting a realistic, unsentimental look at one of the institutions of society. The story deals with seven young girls who one evening draw up a document, a pact that they will meet ten years later if single; if married, they will each send a letter describing her marriage. Ten years later, Caroline Bloomfield, the only single woman left, is being pressed by a young man to marry, but she decides to read the others' letters before she agrees. The marriages are all disastrous—boring, sterile, lifeless; women with children pulling hair and spilling ink, and making "chickens and boats"[45] of the document the girls had drawn up years before, dominated wives with no freedom. Miss Bloomfield calls in her sister-in-law for advice and is told unromantically that there is no individuality in marriage, no freedom; one can only "bear and forbear."[46] Yet in society an older single woman has no social position, very little respect, and no value. In the last scene of the story, Caroline decides to marry.

The theme of romanticism vs. practicality comes out
quite clearly in a number of King's strong, hard-hearted
women who become (as perhaps King herself became) cold,
stern, aggressive, and, in many ways, witty and charming.
These are women scarred by the battle of the sexes, by the
conflict of their own natural inclinations and the values
promoted by society. Azzy Dudly, in "A Male Flirt," is a
sweet little bird flushed out by Charles Vernon, who is
looking for fun while his fiancee is away. He toys with
her, breaks off with her, flippantly saying, "Why the
deuce aren't women. . . more like men?"[47] In two years
Azzy becomes a clever, almost majestic woman admired by
all society; yet her heart has been made ugly by the
experience. She self-indulgently accosts Vernon and chas-
tises him, romantically picturing herself as the avenger
for all the innocent women hurt by thoughtless men. She
leaves him with a warning to let her alone: "I have more
power" than other women, she tells him, "because I have
more beauty and the knowledge to use it."[48] Angelica in
Lily is another such woman, a coquette, the foil for the
dull heroine of the novel. Angelica prefers the company
of men to women, flirts a good deal, but "properly"
(allowing no familiarity), a woman aloof, who keeps a
train of admirers to amuse herself, who makes fun of sentimental literature and the "Nell Noodles and Poll Poodles,
the eternal Rose Matildas of [the] weekly journal[s]."[49]

The most extensive and the best portrayal of this
kind of woman is in "Sylvia's World." Like "The Best of
Friends," the story uses a frame device; here Sylvia
Sutherland draws a flighty young girl into her cold and
gloomy world by reading to her a manuscript which depicts
the rite of passage of Helen Latimer. I only have time
enough to suggest some of the richness of this novel,
King's most effective single work. The characters of the
novel each contribute in some way to Helen's maturation.
One is the sophisticated and realistic Bertha St. Clair
who sees life as an "incessant struggle which goes on from
sunrise until sunrise; the constant, eager grasp and
pressing forward to gain a little or a greater prize."[50]
In contrast to Miss St. Clair is Helen's mother, who
vicariously relives an old affair with Harry's father by
promoting his courtship of Helen. She lives romantically
in the past, clings to an illusion and forces it upon
Helen. King symbolically suggests the distorted perspective of Mrs. Latimer by describing a scene on the pictor-
ial wallpaper in her old-fashioned house: a "tender love

scene"[51] is pictured in which a young man is kneeling
before a woman with a child, "pouring out his soul."[52]
But the wallpaper has a seam in it, and the characters are
thrown out of place. The lover seems to be shouting at
the infant who, because of the poor joint in the paper, is
located near the man's heels. The scene graphically depicts the wrongness of the relationship which Mrs. Latimer
is forcing upon her child.

Besides the effective handling of character, King
strengthens this study of a woman's maturation with such
symbols as the house of Oaklevel, which ultimately burns
and upon whose ruins Helen erects her new world, or the
worm and the rose, in a scene in which Helen makes a
flower into a symbol and as a result unwittingly drives
her lover away from her. The symbol she creates is worked
around by King to elucidate Harry's position and further
the degeneration of the relationship of Harry and Helen.

The point of view of the novel is sophisticated.
Most of what we see in "Sylvia's World" is through the
point of view of Helen, the heroine, but we also see Helen
through the eyes of her wiser alter ego, Sylvia, or through
those of the innocent Olivia, who is listening to the
story. And once, in the crucial theater scene, the point
of view shifts to that of Bertha St. Clair. Shortly after
the relationship with Harry ends and Helen has been exposed
to some of the evils of the world, she attends a play in
which Ellen Kean is acting. Bertha watches her, noting
that there are two great actresses in the theater. Helen,
the other, plays her role flawlessly and Bertha looks on
with mixed feelings. She gives us her impression of this
moment in Helen's life when she has to summon up her courage to carry off the social situation:

> Never had Helen Latimer looked so lovely as that
> night; never did she so look again! It was the
> last gleam of her youth and freshness--when "the
> world" again saw her, they saw a different woman.
> The light of hope, of girlhood, was quenched for-
> ever; but this night, it burned with a borrowed
> lustre. . . .[53]

"Sylvia's World" ends realistically. Sylvia does not pine
away and die, nor does her personality shrivel up after
this experience. She later marries, is "admired" and
"sought after," as Olivia says,[54] becomes a strong,

capable, attractive, but very hard woman. Her soul has
become bruised, not crushed. A study of this novel can
reveal much about King's approach to the writing of realistic fiction. It is an "everyday tale" with believable
characters and plausible conflicts; it is a comedy of manners in which King perceptively explores the development
of a woman's personality.

The tradition of realistic or anti romantic fiction
in the ante-bellum South has in recent years begun to
assert itself in literary scholarship, mainly as a result
of interest in this kind of fiction in the twentieth century. Modern scholars have established and are now exam-
ining the strain of strong masculine fiction represented
by such writers as A. B. Longstreet, William Tappan
Thompson, Johnson Jones Hooper, and George Washington
Harris. Yet the kind of fiction written by Susan Petigru
King, psychological realism in comedies of manners, has
been totally ignored, and, I suppose, assumed to be non-
existent in this period. King as a psychological realist
very clearly belongs to the group of writers that includes
William Dean Howells and Henry James, yet today she enjoys
no recognition as such in literature. In this particular
tradition of realism, one that complements that of the
humorists of the Old South, Susan Petigru King does have
a place. As a result of that place, her work stands as a
significant contribution to the fiction of South Carolina.

Notes

[1]James Petigru Carson, *Life, Letters and Speeches of James Louis Petigru* (Washington: W. H. Lowdermilk & Co., 1920), p. 227.

[2]Letter to Adele Allston, Aug. 26 [1849], located in the R. F. W. Allston Papers in the South Carolina Historical Society, Charleston, South Carolina.

[3]Ida Raymond, *Southland Writers* (Philadelphia: Claxton, Remsen & Haffelfinger, 1870), II, 862.

[4]Letter to Emily Elliott, May 16, 1863, located in the Elliott-Gonzales Papers, Southern Historical Collection, University of North Carolina Library.

[5]Wauchope, *The Writers of South Carolina* (Columbia: The State Co., 1910), p. 58.

[6]*Inscriptions on the Tablets and Gravestones in St. Michael's Church and Churchyard, Charleston, S. C.*, arranged by Clare Jervey (Columbia: The State Co., 1906), p. 48.

[7]Chesnut, *A Diary from Dixie*, ed. Ben Ames Williams (Boston: Houghton Mifflin Company, 1949), p. 465.

[8]*Life of Petigru*, p. 204.

[9]*Life of Petigru*, p. 297.

[10]*Life of Petigru*, p. 319.

[11]*Life of Petigru*, p. 204.

[12]*Life of Petigru*, p. 227.

[13]*Life of Petigru*, p. 278.

[14]*Diary*, p. 212.

[15]*Diary*, p. 465.

[16]*Diary*, p. 465.

[17]Letter from Sally Baxter to Mrs. Baxter, March 8, 1854, located in the South Caroliniana Library, University of South Carolina. This letter is used here with the permission of Ann Hampton, who is currently preparing an edition of Sally Baxter's letters, and E. L. Inabinett, Librarian of the South Caroliniana Library.

[18]*Southland Writers*, II, pp. 861-862.

[19]*Writers of South Carolina*, p. 223.

[20][Susan Petigru King], *Lily. A Novel* (New York: Harper & Brothers, 1855), p. 187.

[21]*Lily*, p. 188.

[22]Lucy Baxter, Introduction to *Thackeray's Letters to an American Family* (New York: The Century Co., 1904), pp. 13-14.

[23]Letter from Thackeray to Mrs. Baxter, Feb. 17, 1856, in *American Family*, p. 133.

[24]Review of *Lily*, *The Charleston Mercury*, Nov. 21, 1855.

[25]"Sylvia's World" appeared as "The Heart-History of a Heartless Woman" monthly from August to December, 1859, in *The Knickerbocker*. "Crimes Which the Law Does Not Reach" appeared in *Russell's Magazine* from October, 1857 to March, 1858.

[26]Wauchope, in *Writers of South Carolina*, p. 223, mistakenly ascribes to King a novel entitled *The Actress in High Life*, which was written by Gabriel Manigault. See Ludwig Lewisohn, "The Books We Have Made. A History of Literature in South Carolina," *The News and Courier*, Aug. 30, 1903.

[27]*Southland Writers*, II, p. 861.

[28]"The Books We Have Made," Aug. 30, 1903.

[29]*Lily*, p. 189.

[30]*Lily*, p. 188.

[31]"A Man of Honor," in *Sylvia's World* (New York: Derby and Jackson, 1859), p. 343.

[32]*Lily*, pp. 103-104. King was also critical of the ideal Southern woman in real life. In a letter to her aunt, she wrote, "I am so tired of the stupid, self-sufficient, wearisome style of young ladies, that *we* Southerners consider 'all that they should be.' Women, who have not three ideas, who spoil a little French, who play a little music, & have not a grain of agreeability, are the highest standard with us. True, they are quite fit for what they become, housekeepers & nurses, so after all, it is a wise dispensation of Providence which places no loftier aspirations within them." (Letter to Adele Allston, Aug. 26 [1849], in the Allston Papers at the South Carolina Historical Society.)

[33]*Lily*, p. 81.

[34]*Lily*, p. 85.

[35]*Lily*, p. 168.

[36]*Lily*, p. 169.

[37]*Sylvia's World*, p. 372.

[38]*Sylvia's World*, p. 259.

[39]*Sylvia's World*, p. 272.

[40]*Sylvia's World*, p. 274.

[41]*Sylvia's World*, p. 282.

[42]*Sylvia's World*, p. 215.

[43]*Sylvia's World*, p. 225.

[44]*Sylvia's World*, p. 225.

[45][King], *Busy Moments of an Idle Woman* (New York: D. Appleton & Company, 1854), p. 244.

[46]*Busy Moments*, p. 252.

[47]*Sylvia's World*, p. 246.

[48]*Sylvia's World*, p. 256.

[49]*Lily*, p. 223.

[50]*Sylvia's World*, p. 118.

[51]*Sylvia's World*, p. 33.

[52]*Sylvia's World*, p. 33.

[53]*Sylvia's World*, p. 167.

[54]*Sylvia's World*, p. 9.

Katharine Boling:
The Bigham Story Retold

by

G. Michael Richards

Katharine Boling's literary canon is by no means a
large one. It is, however, a significant one and worthy
of our attention. In 1972, after three years of research,
Mrs. Boling published *A Piece of the Fox's Hide*,[1] an
intensive, indepth biographical study of the infamous
Bigham family of Marion and Florence counties. Mrs.
Boling, a resident of Pamplico, South Carolina, developed
an interest in the Bighams largely through living in the
region that had felt the intense power of three generations of Bighams. In addition to now living on what was
once Bigham land, Mrs. Boling is also linked to the Bigham
era through her husband's great-grandfather George Steele,
who died while on the witness stand testifying against
Edmund Bigham. According to many, Steele was a victim of
the Bigham hex.

Before going further, a brief biographical sketch of
the Bighams is in order, and indeed there is only one
place to begin such a sketch. On January 15, 1921, around
three o'clock in the afternoon, a man named Garrison was
passing the Bigham home when he was flagged down by Louise
Bigham, the eight year old daughter of Edmund Bigham.
Shortly thereafter, a mail carrier named Bostick was also
stopped, this time by Edmund Bigham himself. What Garrison
and Bostick found at the Bigham homeplace was the body of
Edmund's mother, Dora Bigham. Mrs. Bigham's body was lying
in the back yard, and she had been shot twice, in the head
and neck. Bostick then found the body of a small boy who

117

had also been shot. The boy was found lying on the back
porch and was one of the two McCracken boys who had been
adopted by Edmund's sister Marjorie Bigham Black.

Around dark on the fifteenth, a third body, that of
Edmund's sister, Marjorie, was discovered in her upstairs
bedroom. She had been killed by a bullet entering her
left temple. The horrendous discoveries of the evening
were not over, for around eight o'clock a rustling was
heard near a potato hill, and upon investigation the elder
McCracken child was found shot but still alive. He would
not live out the night.

During the afternoon and night of Saturday,
January 15, 1921, Edmund Bigham repeatedly expressed
the belief that his brother Smiley had been responsible
for the four deaths. Edmund's contention was that Smiley
had been suffering from severe mental stress as a result
of financial and legal difficulties. The entire family
was involved in a dispute among themselves over deeds to
certain plots of Bigham land. As a result of Edmund's
suspicions, a search was organized on Sunday morning,
January 16. The search party was unsuccessful until
Edmund, who would not leave the house, told the party
that they were searching in the wrong area and suggested
where Smiley might be found. Smiley was indeed found
there, and he too was dead. The nature of the gunshot
wound in Smiley's temple and the manner in which Smiley
was found holding a pistol gave, superficially at least,
the impression that Smiley had taken his own life, that
he had done so after taking the lives of the other four
members of his family. Edmund Bigham claimed that he and
his wife and two daughters had returned home to find Dora
Bigham standing bloody in the front yard and exclaiming,
"Smiley has killed me."[2]

The issue might have ended here, but it did not.
Charges were ultimately brought against Edmund Bigham for
the deaths of his mother, brother, sister, and his sister's
two adopted sons. If this were the extent of the Bigham
story, if this bizarre and grotesque mass murder were all
there is to tell, there might not be two biographies of the
Bigham family. But this is not the case, for the Bigham
myth, and Bigham legend, was mature long before the eventful afternoon of January 15, 1921. The residents of
Marion and Florence counties had been steeped by events in
the Bigham way of life, the Bigham way of doing things.

William Jackson, a black man, was reportedly killed
by Leonard Bigham, Edmund's grandfather. Leonard was never
convicted of this crime. Leonard Bigham himself reportedly
died of potassium cyanide given him by his son, Smiley,
Sr., who among other things was the first state senator
from the newly formed Florence County. Smiley, Sr., was
never convicted for the death of his father. Smiley, Sr.,
shot and killed the black man Lassus Smith. No conviction
occurred. Smiley, Sr., died at the hands of either his
wife or sister who administered potassium cyanide to him
as he had done to his own father. Again, no conviction.
Another black man, named Arthur Davis,[3] was found dead
from a ten penny nail which had been driven through his
ear canal into his brain. Smiley, Jr., was tried and his
brother Edmund implicated, but no convictions resulted.
Ruth Crisp Bigham, wife of Grover Cleveland Bigham, the
younger brother of Edmund and Smiley, was shot to death
at Murrell's Inlet by William Avant, who was accompanied
by Grover Cleveland Bigham himself. Bigham and Avant were
found guilty not of murder but of manslaughter. A three
year sentence was given each, but Grover Cleveland Bigham
jumped bail and never served the sentence. Finally, a
card playing companion of Edmund's was found dead in a
Georgia swamp after a card game in which it was reported
that Edmund lost a sizeable sum of money; the man's skull
had been crushed. Edmund was quick to accuse the third
member of the card game, and upon his testimony the third
man was convicted of murder. So, on that day in January,
1921, there was much to stir the imaginations *and the fears*
of the residents of Florence and Marion counties. There
was much to be remembered, many crimes yet to be solved,
and many strong prejudices and foregone conclusions concerning the innocence or guilt of Edmund Bigham to be
expressed.

It is under these circumstances that the first biography of the Bighams took shape. The editor of the
Florence *Morning News-Review* at the time of the Bigham
murders and the subsequent trials of Edmund Bigham was
J. A. Zeigler. Zeigler covered these events for his paper
and in 1927 published a book length biographical study
entitled *The Last of the Bighams*.[4] Zeigler began his book
with the prefatory statement that the reader was about to
read the story of "A family who tried to take the majesty
of the law in their own hands and shape it to their own
selfish ends. A family that produced school teachers,
senators, doctors, and everyone of them master criminals."[5]

Zeigler follows in his biography the trials of Edmund
Bigham through to the final trial's conclusion on April 14,
1927. Edmund was found guilty by the Florence jury of his
first trial and sentenced to die in the electric chair.
A. L. King, Edmund's attorney, appealed the decision to
the Supreme Court of the State of South Carolina, which
upheld the lower court's ruling. In June, 1922, as Bigham
returned to the Florence court for re-sentencing, A. L.
King introduced new evidence in the form of letters written
by Smiley to Edmund. These letters were rejected by Judge
Shipp as forgeries, and Edmund was again sentenced to
death. Again Bigham's case was appealed to the Supreme
Court of the State of South Carolina. This time the decision favored Bigham, and he was granted a new trial. A
change of venue was also granted, and the new trial was
held in Horry County in October, 1924. The verdict was
once more guilty, and Edmund Bigham was again sentenced
to death. A. L. King made an appeal, as he had done twice
before, to the Supreme Court of the State of South
Carolina. King won his appeal on the grounds of legal
technicalities, and the final trial began and ended on
April 4, 1927. Bigham's attorneys had made a deal with
the prosecution. Edmund was to be found guilty, and the
jury was to recommend mercy. Edmund was again sentenced,
but this time he was sentenced to life imprisonment.

It is at this point that Zeigler ends his biography.
The final trial of Bigham was labelled a "farce-tragedy"
by the Florence newspaper man.[6] Zeigler wrote in *The Last
of the Bighams*, "Edmund Bigham had cheated the law, he was
triumphant; his every action showed his relief at escaping
beyond the shadow of the electric chair."[7] Zeigler's view
was shared by other newspaper men around the state. The
Greenville News reported, "The agreement of counsel which
resulted in a life sentence for Edmund Bigham is one of
the worst blows at justice that has been struck in South
Carolina's criminal court history."[8] The *Marion Star*
carried this statement, "After six long years of error,
delays, procrastination and futile effort to bring
Edmund D. Bigham to justice on the charges of murdering
five members of his family, the state of South Carolina
'traded' with the attorneys for the defense and 'compro-
mised' on a verdict which gives the cold-blooded murderer
his life."[9] And in the *Calhoun Times*, the following
appeared, "The Bighams have borne a highly unsavory reputation for generations, but it took Ed's case to reflect
most unfortunately upon our criminal court procedures."[10]

With these statements from prominent South Carolina newspapers fresh in our minds, we must turn to Katharine Boling's *A Piece of the Fox's Hide* and ask what is the necessity of this second biography. How is the Boling biography significantly different from the Zeigler study? In her preface to *A Piece of the Fox's Hide*, Mrs. Boling deals with this question. She states, "There will be those, and rightly so, who question the necessity of telling once again the awful story of the Bighams. In justification, it is a good story."[11] This answer is unsatisfactory, for it raises more questions than it answers. The most important of these concerns our stance towards the book. Are we to regard *A Piece of the Fox's Hide* as a biography? If so, it carries none of the scholarly apparatuses peculiar to such works. Are we to view it in light of the new journalism and such a book as Truman Capote's *In Cold Blood*? Or, is *A Piece of the Fox's Hide* a historical novel? These are important questions, for the Bighams have entered the realm of South Carolina's legends and myths. Fact and fiction have often been confused and at times fused in the various tellings of the Bigham story. Any work which allows us to place in a proper perspective the actions of the Bighams and the community's response to them is to be valued. Other works may prove to be entertaining, but they must not be mistaken for what they are not.

In her preface Mrs. Boling addresses the questions concerning what is fact and what is fiction, what is historical and what is hysterical. In answering, however, she shifts the burden to those who experienced the Bigham mystique and terror: "The community neither knew nor cared [what was fact and what fiction]. Once there was an opportunity to be finally rid of the last remaining Bigham, they did so with all haste."[12] With regards to her own book, she states, "As to the morality in the telling, let us, instead, judge the twisted tale according to whether it is well or badly written."[13]

Mrs. Boling's answers to these questions, which must be answered if we are to evaluate the usefulness of her work, seem at best to be equivocal and at worst to be metaphysical. Yet there is a key which will open the way to an appraisal of her work. In 1973, Mrs. Boling brought out a reprint edition of Zeigler's *The Last of the Bighams*.[14] The text was unaltered and accompanied by a preface written by Mrs. Boling. In this preface, she

states, "Another reason for exposing this volume to the
public again is in support of my own private theory that
Edmund, guilty or innocent, was in part convicted by news
coverage which bombarded the reading public with stories,
not only of events not admissible as evidence during the
trials, but of the past history of the family's criminal
behavior. Much of the news of the trials carried by the
state's newspapers was originally written by Mr. Zeigler
and developed in the same vein as *The Last of the
Bighams*. . . . Mr. Zeigler's 'corner' was anything but
neutral."[15]

Katharine Boling's position on the press's influence,
particularly the influence exerted by J. A. Zeigler, in
the outcome of the Edmund Bigham trials is a valid one.
We have already seen the press response to the reduction
of Bigham's sentence from death to life imprisonment.
Zeigler's belief in Edmund Bigham's guilt was still
unflinching as late as 1959. Attempts to secure Bigham's
parole were at their peak at this time, and in support
Eugene Fallon wrote a series of articles for the Florence
Morning News. In these articles, Fallon reintroduced to
the public the ambiguities of the evidence. Zeigler was
quick to respond. In a letter to Fallon, he wrote,
"Mr. Fallon, you were right in your final conclusion that
'a Bigham did it.' You have handled the story brilliantly
considering all this probably happened before you were
born. Remember, fellow newshound, this old scribe 'was
there' and while you may prefer the dead Smiley, I am
forced to let what I know for sure weigh the scales
against the yet living Edmund."[16]

The beauty and value of Katharine Boling's *A Piece of
the Fox's Hide* rest in the book's unbiased, unprejudiced
presentation of the Bigham story. It is not, I think,
going too far to say that *A Piece of the Fox's Hide* gives
Edmund Bigham the fair hearing that he deserved but was so
often denied in the past fifty years. Always aware of her
belief that Bigham was in effect convicted by partisan
news coverage, Boling is careful to avoid any reverse
partisanism in her own chronicle of the Bighams. Whenever
possible her policy is to let the principals of the Bigham
story speak for themselves--through their newspaper articles, their reminiscences and recollections, their letters,
and most importantly through their own testimony as it
appears in the trial transcripts.

A Piece of the Fox's Hide is the most readily available source of documents relating to the Bighams.
Zeigler's *The Last of the Bighams* in no way contains the
documentary material found in Mrs. Boling's work. For
example, Zeigler reproduces only one of the letters introduced as new evidence in 1922. These letters, it must be
remembered, were labelled forgeries by Judge Shipp.
Ultimately, however, they would result in a new trial
for Edmund when the Supreme Court of the State of South
Carolina ordered that the authenticity of the letters
should be determined by a jury and not by a judge.
Thirteen of these letters are reproduced in Boling's
biography.

For those who would track down the original documents,
the road is a rough one. More often than not, my own
attempts at tracking down documents were frustrated.
Issues of the Florence *Morning News-Review* are extremely
rare. Our own South Caroliniana Library has only three
issues of this paper, and they are for dates after the
final Bigham trial. In Florence County, no county documents remain. I was told they had been stolen. In Horry
County, documents pertaining to the Bighams were loaned
several years ago and not returned. In essence, *A Piece
of the Fox's Hide* provides ready access to documents that
can be tracked down only with the greatest difficulty.
In some cases these documents have been misplaced, and in
others they are in the private possession of various indi-
viduals.

Furthermore, *A Piece of the Fox's Hide* contains
extensive excerpts from the trial transcripts. In a conversation with Mrs. Boling, I was told that some felt she
had quoted too extensively from the court transcripts.
This is not the case. To have summarized court testimony
would have assuredly introduced an artificial polemic.
This is in fact what occurs in the Zeigler biography. By
judicious selection and summation, Zeigler advances his
own thesis about the guilt of Edmund Bigham. As a result,
his argument forces him to condemn a judicial system that
fails to inflict its fullest punishment against the defen-
dent.

What is more important than either Boling's or
Zeigler's personal feelings about Edmund Bigham's guilt
or innocence is the polemics that evolved between the
witnesses, the attorneys for the defense, and the

the attorneys for the prosecution. It must be remembered
that all evidence given at the trials was circumstantial
evidence. After the Florence trial, Judge Memminger felt
obligated to explain to the jury the nature and value of
circumstantial evidence. He did so by telling them the
story of Robinson Crusoe, who upon finding a mysterious
foot print on his island is forced to revise his beliefs
about the size of the island's population. As discon-
certing as it may be, we shall never know exactly how
events transpired at the Bigham farm on January 15, 1921.
Those few who knew for certain the sequence of events have
taken their knowledge to the grave with them. The question
of Edmund Bigham's guilt or innocence has become a moot
point, an interesting puzzle to be tinkered with but not
to be solved. We must maintain an understanding that, no
matter how successful our attempts to fit the pieces
together, there will always be a few pieces missing, thus
preventing the reconstruction of the full picture.

One of the most powerful sections of *A Piece of the
Fox's Hide* occurs when Mrs. Boling in consecutive chapters
reconstructs the crime. In the first, we are given the
sequence of events as they were told by Edmund and his
wife and daughters. A convincing case is rendered for the
contention that Smiley killed the four members of his
family and then took his own life. In the second, the
evidence given by other key witnesses is used to construct
a sequence in which Edmund is the murderous villain. Again
a convincing argument for the case can be made from the
reconstructed evidence.

The hard pitch sale found in the Zeigler biography is
lacking in Boling's *A Piece of the Fox's Hide*. The emphasis has been shifted. No longer is the guilt or innocence
of Edmund Bigham the central focus. Attention is now
centered on the handling of the evidence. The jurists,
the judges, and attorneys, the witnesses, the newspaper
men and the residents of Marion and Florence counties
command the significant position in *A Piece of the Fox's
Hide*. For it is their response to the Bighams that ultimately determined the fate of Edmund Bigham. It is their
behavior that can be adequately evaluated and judged. It
is through their own testimony and newspaper articles that
they are presented to us. *A Piece of the Fox's Hide*
presents more than the story of a family; it tells more
than the story of one man; it is the story of a community
of people and their response to those who felt a feeling

of superiority to the laws and moral fabric of the community. Whether innocent or guilty, Edmund upon his
conviction cursed those who testified against him and
compared himself to Christ who was crucified on lies.
The Bigham curse had power in the minds of the South
Carolinians who had lived under the aura of this family,
and there were few who were willing to cross the Bigham
path. In Katharine Boling's *A Piece of the Fox's Hide*,
we have the story of those who dared to cross that path
and of those who saw fit to march clear of the Bighams
and their curse.

Notes

[1]Katharine Boling, *A Piece of the Fox's Hide*, (Columbia, S. C.: Sandlapper Press, 1972).

[2]Boling, p. 244.

[3]J. A. Zeigler in *The Last of the Bighams* (Florence, S. C.: n.p., 1925), p. 50, contradicts Boling (*Fox's Hide*, p. 102), giving Sam Johnson rather than Arthur Davis as the name of the man killed.

[4]J. A. Zeigler, *The Last of the Bighams* (Florence, S. C.: n.p., 1925). Although 1925 is listed on the title page as the date of publication, *The Last of the Bighams* was in fact published in 1927.

[5]Zeigler, p. [5].

[6]Zeigler, p. 214.

[7]Zeigler, p. 222.

[8]Zeigler, p. 222.

[9]Zeigler, p. 223.

[10]Zeigler, p. 225.

[11]Boling, p. vii.

[12]Boling, p. viii.

[13]Boling, p. ix.

[14]J. A. Zeigler, *The Last of the Bighams* (1925; rpt. Florence, S. C.: n.p., 1973). Includes an introduction by Katharine Boling.

[15]Zeigler, (1973 rpt.), p. [vi].

[16]Zeigler, (1973 rpt.), p. [v].

Women Diarists and Letter Writers
of 18th Century South Carolina

by

Edwin T. Arnold, III

From the year 1754 to the year 1781 Mrs. Ann Manigault, wife of a wealthy Charleston merchant, kept a diary. For a period of twenty-seven years Mrs. Manigault recorded the daily events which she witnessed or of which she heard. Her entries were sparse, simple, and direct, yet they managed to include most facets of the society of 18th century Charleston: its sermons and soirees, its births and deaths, its wars and peace. Her journal offers an intriguing mixture of the commonplace and the extraordinary. On June 13, 1754, for example, she noted that Mr. Whitfield--- the Rev. George Whitfield, the revivalist who stirred the entire eastern seaboard into religious enthusiasm---had come to Charleston. On February 28th of the next year, Mrs. Manigault went to hear him preach.[1] On June 20th, she "went to Mrs. Wragg's with Mrs. Stead;"[2] on November 10th, she "went to a Ball;"[3] on March 27, 1756, she recorded, "A child found in a cellar;"[4] on April 5th, "Col. Bird from Virginia dined with us;"[5] on July 12, 1758, "Col. Pinckney died;"[6] on December 10, 1759, "I had a very bad tooth-ache;"[7] on May 4, 1761, "A terrible Storm several vessels lost and several people drowned;"[8] on November 25, 1763, "Went to Mrs. Logan's to buy roots;"[9] on May 14, 1765, "I went to see experiments in Electricity;"[10] on June 19, 1770, "A good many children die of the Hooping-cough;"[11] on January 15, 1778, "A most dreadful Fire in Town, which occasioned great distress;"[12] on February 13, 1780, "We are much afraid of the British, who are on John's Island."[13]

127

Taken individually, Mrs. Manigault's entries are understated, stark, even cryptic---one wonders about the child in that cellar. Yet, cumulatively they begin to outline for us a time, a society, and a people which seem both removed and still surprisingly alive. In its very skeletal form, through its monotonous, almost chanting repetition, her journal displays a muted, yet powerful force of feeling, of what it must have been like to have lived and died in this time. Listen, for example, to this description of her grandson's illness:

> My little Grandson Peter was taken very ill the
> 18th. July in the night. On the 20th he was
> baptised being very ill. 21st very much altered.
> 22d. very ill. 23d. the same 24th. a little
> better. 25th. Better, but has a sore mouth.
> 26th. Still uneasy. From 26th July to Aug. 3d
> very sick. 4th. very ill. 5th. very ill with a
> sore throat. 6th. very ill. 7th. very ill. A
> Blister put on. 8th. Another blister put on.
> We thought him dying. 9th. and 10th. Mending
> very slowly. 13th His blisters very sore and he
> is hoarse again. 14th. not well. 16th. a little
> better. 18th. Not well. 21. He was carried up
> to Mr. Ben. Smith's by my Daughter for a change of
> air. 23d Very ill. 24th. Very ill. 25th. He
> died at 12 oc'clock at night.[14]

I doubt that we today would consider Mrs. Manigault an extraordinary woman, and there is little indication that her contemporaries saw her as more than a wealthy, respectable, and friendly neighbor. Yet, for some reason, Mrs. Manigault took the time and the trouble to record her world, and by some stroke of fate, luck, or what-have-you, her journal survived the years to give the record to us.

Of course, Mrs. Manigault was not the only woman of 18th-century South Carolina to leave us, through her letters, diaries, or journals, a view of her time. The Charleston society was in many ways a writing society. Letters were a chief form of communication, and it was a standard and understandable practice to keep copies of these letters in copybooks. This was also the age of the epistolary novel, and the art of composing such letters was emphasized. Young ladies were encouraged as part of their education to keep thought books or religious devotionals, and diaries were then, as now, a form of private stock-

taking. What makes these writings important to us today is
that they preserved the thoughts and doings of their time
and that they have survived to tell the tale. Some of them,
like the letters of Eliza Lucas Pinckney and the letters
and journal of Martha Ramsay, are marked by a degree of
literary excellence which gives them added importance, but
all remain worthy of our notice.

With one exception, none of the writings I intend to
mention today were published in the 18th century. Many
have remained hidden or largely unknown until quite recently. That one exception, however, proved to be an influential work. It was a collection of letters and extracts
from a journal written by Mrs. Mary Hutson. Mrs. Hutson
was the great-granddaughter of Dr. Henry Woodward, the
first English settler in South Carolina.[15] After the death
of her first husband, Isaac Chardon, she married William
Hutson, a preacher who had come to America in 1740 first as
an actor and who was later converted to the ministry by
George Whitfield. In Charleston, Hutson was employed as a
tutor by Hugh Bryan, an eccentric disciple of Whitfield.[16]
Bryan, as a boy, had been captured and enslaved by Indians;
as an adult he was given to enthusiastic prophesying among
Negro slaves, predicting their eventual revolt against
their masters, which made not a few of these masters cast
an uneasy eye at Mr. Bryan. This is the same Hugh Bryan
mentioned by Eliza Lucas Pinckney in 1741 as one who, like
a minor-league Moses, attempted to divide the waters of a
stream with a stick and who predicted that he would die the
same night after the miracle occurred.[17] Neither of these
events took place as Bryan had predicted, and it was not
until 1753 that he managed to fulfill at least half of his
prophecy. Four years later, in 1757, Mrs. Hutson also
died, and in 1760, the writings of these two worthies---
Bryan and Hutson---were collected by William Hutson, who
had since married Hugh Bryan's widow. They were published
in London under the title *Living Christianity Delineated*.[18]
The book was subsequently published in America in 1809 and
enjoyed wide popularity.

The writings of Mrs. Hutson selected by her husband
reveal a highly devoted Christian woman who alternates between the extremes of rapture and self-abasement. In her
journal she writes, for example, "Last night I was enabled
to pour out my soul sweetly in prayer to my dear
Redeemer. . . . How did I long and pant after holiness,
whilst sin appeared exceeding sinful indeed to me. . . .

and I seemed to have some kind of fellowship with the
blessed angels, and longed much to be with them, and my
dear fellow servants that are gone before me."[19]   On
another occasion she writes, "I am weary of living here, in
this dry and baren land, where I do nothing but sin against
my God."[20]   Perhaps her complete and rather frightening
piety is best illustrated when she writes, "I am afraid to
go out of my chamber, I am afraid of my children, my servants; every object my eye sees; every noise I hear; lest
they should draw me from my God."[21]   The portrait of Mrs.
Hutson we get from these letters apparently was quite
accurate, for we also have Eliza Lucas Pinckney's perceptive description of her in one of her own letters. She
writes of Mrs. Hutson, "She was ever as good as women could
be, but fain would have been an angel before her time and
in the attempt ceased to be rational, and is now inferior
to her own species of which she was so lately an orna-
ment."[22]

A work similar to Mrs. Hutson's collection, yet a
little less celestial, was the *Memoirs of the Life of
Martha Laurens Ramsay*, first published in 1811.[23]   Mrs.
Ramsay was the daughter of Henry Laurens and the third wife
of Dr. David Ramsay, the distinguished South Carolina
historian. After his wife's death in 1811, Dr. Ramsay,
perhaps following the pattern set by the Rev. Hutson, selected from her letters, journals, and private papers those
which he felt would best portray his Christian wife, and to
this collection he added a biography which he had written
of this very interesting woman. The book went through at
least six editions.[24]

Mrs. Ramsay was a very well-educated lady, having been
schooled in Europe, where she had lived for ten years
during the time of the Revolution. Ramsay tells us in his
biography that his wife destroyed most of her writings from
this period, with the exception of a series of "Religious
Exercises," which he included in the book. At the age of
fifteen, Martha Laurens had made a "Self Dedication and
Solemn Covenant with God,"[25] and in these religious writings we find self-castigations similar to those of Mrs.
Hutson. "I am all filth, and guilt, and uncleanness," she
writes as a teenage girl. "My soul is covered with leprosy;
but I know that if thou wilt, thou canst make me clean, and
restore me to peace and comfort."[26]   Yet it would be a mistake to picture Mrs. Ramsay as another Mrs. Hutson. Her
letters reveal that she was much too sensible and practical

and human to attempt to become "an angel before her time."
From one letter, not included in the collection made by her
husband, we learn that as a young woman of 22, while still
in France, she was courted by a middle-aged Frenchman named
DeVerne, of whom her family disapproved. She defended him
in a letter to her father, writing that he was "a gentleman
whose only fault is that he cannot join house to house and
lay field to field." Henry Laurens answered that "his
affections are fixed on 'house & fields' acquired by my
labor, while he has none to add to them, nor does he, nor
means he to labor for any. *You* he would make the vehicle
for conducting him to the possession of those which he
supposes are already provided."[27] Even in those letters
selected, Martha Ramsay comes across as a very real person.
Her grief, for example, in trying to accept the death of
her young daughter Jane is moving and powerful.[28] In other
letters we get the picture of a delightful and practical
lady, who recognizes the value of the secular as well as
the religious. For instance, she encourages another of her
daughters, as part of her education, to read Priestley's
lectures on history, but warns, "Bear always in mind, that
he is a Socinian. . . . Profit by his science, while you
lament his errors in divinity. . . ."[29] And again she
writes this daughter, "I beg you never to make any excuse
for writing badly to me, because the time spent in writing
the excuse would have enabled you to do better."[30] Her
series of letters written toward the end of her life to her
son David, who was attending his first year at Princeton,
confirm this portrait. "I trust you will not be indolent,"
she warns him after his departure, "and that a manly
shame . . .will prevent your adding yourself to the list of
Carolina triflers, whose conduct has brought a college,
such as Princeton, into disrepute."[31] When David writes
that the hundred dollars he has spent on clothes is not
enough, she admonishes, "Your wardrobe must be unnecessari-
ly costly or miserably laid in . . . . With prudence, one
hundred dollars will go a great way; without it, ten times
the sum will be like water put into a sieve."[32] And
finally, when her son suggests that it might do him good to
forget college for awhile and spend a few years in
Charleston, she puts her foot down with a firm "I will
oppose all my influence to so mad a scheme. You should
rather spend them in the Indian country, and learn the
rugged virtues of savages, than in the desultory, dissipated habits of Charleston. I flatter myself your last
letter was written under the transient impression of some
juvenile folly, which is already dissipated, and that your

next letter will be more judicious, better reasoned, and in
every respect more worthy yourself."[33] One must wonder if
memories of her defense of her old French suitor ever
haunted her during this correspondence.

Martha Ramsay's interests were extensive; she was
apparently well-read in science, philosophy, and religion.
Her interests also included horticulture, and her husband
asserts in his *History of South-Carolina* that she and her
father were responsible for the naturalization of the olive
tree in the state.[34] This interest in the "vegetable
world," as Eliza Lucas Pinckney termed it, was a common one
in this time. Of course, Eliza Pinckney, through her extensive and successful experiments with indigo, is perhaps
the best known of these women horticulturalists, but she
was by no means the only one to write of these matters.
One of the earliest surviving letters of 18th-century South
Carolina is from Mrs. Hannah Williams, who was living here
before 1692, to James Petiver, the English botanist and
entomologist. Dated February 6, 1704/5, her letter states:
"These may Informe you thatt I have sent you some of Our
Vipers & several sorts of Snakes Scorpions & Lizzards in a
Bottle & of the Other Insex & I would have sent you a Very
good Collection to y[e] plants if I had any Vollums of brown
paper---butt haveing none Could nott . . . ."[35]

A series of similar letters were sent between another
Charlestonian, Mrs. Martha Daniell Logan, and John Bartram,
the naturalist and father of William Bartram. Despite his
several trips to Charleston, Bartram and Mrs. Logan apparently met just once, and then only for about four minutes.
Yet he later referred to her as "Mistress Logan, my
facinated widow" and so aptly described her when he wrote,
"Her garden is her delight."[36] Martha Logan had indeed
cultivated one of the first gardens in Charleston. After
an attempt at establishing a school in town failed, she
opened what apparently became a successful nursery, the
same mentioned by Mrs. Manigault. Sometime around 1751,
Mrs. Logan also wrote a "Gardners Kalander," which subsequently appeared in several almanacs.

Only a few letters from Mrs. Logan to Bartram, written
between the years 1760-1763, have survived;[37] none of his
letters to her have been found. With her fellow investiga-
tor in Philadelphia, Mrs. Logan carried out a series of
experiments regarding the effects of climate and soil on
various plants. She introduced Bartram to plants indigenous

to the South. Back and forth between the two travelled a
"little silk bag" containing the chosen seeds, often
accompanied by tubs of dirt and roots. These experiments
were sometimes marked by disappointment. In 1760, Mrs.
Logan wrote Bartram that, having put up some roots in a
closet to dry, "the mice Devoured them before I had a
thought of it," and then she made him a proposition: "If
these Seed with you and Canbe Spaire them, I shoulde be
Vastly glade to make the[e] any Return for a fue, Ither
roots or Seeds."[38] Mrs. Logan also had a similar trade
with fellow naturalists in England. Her curiosity remained
great, and at the age of 70 she was still working in and
writing on her "delight," her garden.

Despite these pleasant references to such civilized
goings-on, we should not forget that 18th-century South
Carolina was still often a violent and dangerous place to
live. From Mrs. Manigault alone we get a clear indication
of the ravage of disease, but there were other, more human
threats with which these early Carolinians had to contend.
Up through the 1750's, the fear of Indian wars was never
far from people's minds. In the second half of the century, the major event was, of course, the American Revolution. The War in South Carolina was an extremely bloody
and savage affair. The colony became occupied territory,
bands of marauders ravaged the country, and, as Mrs.
Manigault wrote, everyone was "very much afraid of the
British."

One of the best accounts of this time is found in the
letters of Eliza Wilkinson, which give what appear to be a
contemporary view of the invasion and capture of Charleston
by the British in 1779. In a series of twelve letters, Mrs.
Wilkinson describes the landing of the British and their
movement toward Charleston, the anticipated arrival of
General Benjamin Lincoln, and the eventual defeat of the
Americans near Stono Ferry. The last few letters give a
picture of Charleston under British rule and include a
visit to a prison ship and the joy experienced at
Cornwallis' surrender.

Although these letters are dated 1781-1782, they were
first published in the *Rose Bud* (which became the *Southern
Rose Bud* in August, 1833) from 1832-1835, and were not published in book form until 1839,[39] at which time they were,
according to the title page, "Arranged From the Original
Manuscripts" by Caroline Gilman. They are, as published,

the most consciously "literary" of any of the works I have
mentioned. The letters are marked by such common fictional
devices as the developing protagonist, extended dialogue,
and rather elaborate character description, and contain
such plot devices as mistaken identity, extended suspense,
and last minute reversals. Each letter is centered around
a main event and together they have a continuity similar to
that found in the typical epistolary novel of the day.

I have, so far, been unable to find any record of Mrs.
Wilkinson except in connection with these letters, and she
has been, in all references, a very shadowy figure.[40] It
seems to me, at this point, that Mrs. Wilkinson, in writing
these letters, or Mrs. Gilman, in "arranging" them, allowed
her creative hand rather free rein, and that what we have
here is something much closer to an epistolary novel than
simply a collection of letters. However, whether they be
works of fiction, or genuine, or a combination of the two,
the letters do give a believable account of the Revolution
in and around Charleston.

The types of situations and incidents described in
Mrs. Wilkinson's letters are more or less confirmed by
other letters written during the war of whose authenticity
we are more assured. The few letters we have of Mary Lucia
Bull,[41] for example, deal with some of the same events, and
the similarity between them is striking. Mary Bull was the
great-granddaughter of one of the early cassiques of South
Carolina and a grand-niece of the first Lieutenant Governor.
One of her letters tells of the British invasion. "It is
impossible for me to describe to you what I felt, while the
British Army was on this side [of the] Ashley-Ferry," she
writes: "we never went in to our beds at night, had Candles
constantly burning & were alarmed at every noise that we
heard." When the British do break in and begin to plunder
their home, she explains, "for my part, I expected nothing
but death, & indeed, at that moment it was indifferent to
me whether I lived or died. . . . One of the British
Colonels came to the House, we told him we were very uneasy
about the Indians & common Soldiers, he was sorry they dis-
turbed us, (he said), but we had better fee him to stay
with us, for he had good spirits, cou'd sing a good Song &
had a deal of chitty-chatty. . . ."[42]

Two other views of the Revolution can be gathered from
the letters of Mrs. Alice DeLancy Izard, wife of Ralph
Izard, and from the journal of Louisa Susannah Wells Aikman.

Mrs. Izard viewed the war from Europe, where her husband
had been sent by Congress as Commissioner to the Court of
Tuscany.[43] After he returned in 1780, Mrs. Izard remained
in Paris until the war was well over, in 1783. In her
letters she mentions her meeting with LaFayette, gives a
French account of the battle of Eutaw Springs, a notice of
Benedict Arnold, who, she says, is "in high life in
London,"[44] and a description of her husband's dining, under
pressure, with Cornwallis after the latter's defeat at
Yorktown, but notes that Mr. Izard absolutely refused to
speak to the British general throughout the meal.

Susannah Wells Aikman, on the other hand, gives us the
loyalist's view of the Revolution. She was the daughter of
Robert Wells, the prominent Charleston publisher, and the
sister of Helena Wells, of whom we have already been informed by Mr. Moltke-Hansen. In 1778, following her
father's example, Susannah left Charleston for London, and
in the next year, 1779, wrote from memory her account of
the journey, which was not published until 1906.[45] Because
the ship on which she sailed was seized by mistake by the
British navy and was taken into New York harbor, where it
was trapped by the French blockade, Mrs. Aikman was able to
represent the life in British occupied New York as well as
Charleston, before describing the voyage to England. Her
journal is a witty, entertaining, and informative work.

One last traveller deserves to be mentioned among
these diarists and letter writers. This is Mrs. Mary Stead
Pinckney, the wife of Charles Cotesworth Pinckney. After
the Revolution, Pinckney was prevailed upon by Washington
to become United States Minister to France, to replace
James Monroe. Mrs. Pinckney accompanied him reluctantly,
and her fears proved to be well-founded, for the mission to
France ended pretty much as a fiasco. Although Pinckney
acted with great honor and dignity, the relationship between the United States and France was so strained that the
Pinckneys were asked to leave the country only a few months
after arriving.[46] Mrs. Pinckney kept a letter book of this
journey, which began on November 14, 1796, as they were
preparing to land at Bordeaux in the midst of both a storm
and a mutiny. They end on August 29, 1797, after the
mission had failed. These letters were published in
1946;[47] they are lively, intelligent, and perceptive, and
in their view of foreign diplomacy offer a fitting conclusion to a century which witnessed the evolution of the
United States from a collection of colonies into a nation.

Throughout this paper I have mentioned Eliza Lucas Pinckney without actually discussion her own accomplishments as a writer. There are two reasons for this. First, the publication of her letterbook by the University of North Carolina Press in 1972 makes her the most easily accessible of any of the writers I have mentioned today. Secondly, she deserves more space than I could possibly give her here. Suffice it to say that her letters and journal mark the highest achievement of any 18th-century South Carolina writer. She represents the fulfillment of what is hinted at in these other works.

Notes

[1]"Extracts From the Journal of Mrs. Ann Manigault: 1754-1781," with notes by Mabel L. Webber, *South Carolina Historical and Genealogical Magazine*, XX (January, 1919), 59.

[2]*SCHGM*, 60.

[3]*SCHGM*, 60.

[4]*SCHGM*, 61.

[5]*SCHGM*, 61.

[6]*SCHGM*, XX (April, 1919), 130.

[7]*SCHGM*, 133.

[8]*SCHGM*, 136.

[9]*SCHGM*, XX (July, 1919), 205.

[10]*SCHGM*, 208.

[11]*SCHGM*, XXI (January, 1920), 18.

[12]*SCHGM*, XXI (July, 1920), 115.

[13]*SCHGM*, 119.

[14]*SCHGM*, XX (July, 1919), 210-11.

[15]See Joseph W. Barnwell, "Dr. Henry Woodward, the First English Settler in South Carolina, and Some of His Descendants," *SCHGM*, VIII (January, 1907), 29-41.

[16]See William Maine Hutson, "The Hutson Family of South Carolina," *SCHGM*, IX (July, 1908), 127-40.

[17]*The Letterbook of Eliza Lucas Pinckney, 1739-1762*, ed. Elise Pinckney (Chapel Hill: The University of North Carolina Press, 1972), pp. 27-30.

[18]Mr. Hugh Bryan and Mrs. Mary Hutson, *Living Christianity Delineated, in the Diaries and Letters of Two Eminently Pious Persons Lately Deceased* (London: J. Buckland, 1760). Also (Boston: Hastings, Etheridge and Bliss, 1809).

[19]Hutson, p. 128.

[20]Hutson, p. 130.

[21]Hutson, p. 138.

[22]*Letterbook*, p. 46.

[23](Philadelphia: James Maxwell, Printer, 1811). I have not seen a copy of the 1811 edition. The information is taken from Robert J. Turnbull, *Bibliography of South Carolina* (Charlottesville, Va.: University of Virginia Press, 1956), I, 477.

[24]I have seen the following: (Charleston: Samuel Etheridge, Jun'r, 1812); (Boston: Samuel T. Armstrong, 1812 and 1814); (Lexington, Kentucky: Thomas T. Skillman, 1813); (London: Burton & Briggs, 1815); (Philadelphia: American Sunday School Union, 1845). Turnbull lists other editions (I, 486–487).

[25]Ramsay, 2nd edition (Charleston: Samuel Etheridge, Jun'r, 1812), p. 64.

[26]Ramsay, p. 101.

[27]Quoted in David Duncan Wallace, *The Life of Henry Laurens* (New York: G. P. Putnam's Sons, 1915), p. 414.

[28]Ramsay, pp. 166–171.

[29]Ramsay, pp. 204–205.

[30]Ramsay, p. 202.

[31]Ramsay, p. 244.

[32]Ramsay, pp. 262–263.

[33]Ramsay, p. 264.

[34]David Ramsay, *History of South-Carolina: 1670-1808*, II (Charleston: David Longworth, 1809), p. 221.

[35]"Early Letters From South Carolina Upon Natural History," *SCHGM*, XXI (January, 1920), 5.

[36]Quoted in Buckner Hollingsworth, "Martha Logan," *Her Garden Was Her Delight* (New York: The Macmillan Company, 1962), p. 18.

[37]"Letters of Martha Logan to John Bartram, 1760-1763," ed. Mary Barbot Prior, *SCHGM*, LIX (January, 1958), 38-46.

[38]*SCHGM*, 41.

[39]*Letters of Eliza Wilkinson*, arranged from the original manuscripts by Caroline Gilman (New York: Published by Samuel Colman, 1839).

[40]In the discussion following the presentation of this paper, Mr. E. L. Inabinett, Director of the South Caroliniana Library at the University of South Carolina, pointed out that I had overlooked an important source: George Wauchope's *The Writers of South Carolina* (Columbia, S. C., 1910). Wauchope gives Mrs. Wilkinson's birth as February 7, 1757. She was the daughter of Francis Yonge and Sarah Clifford. After the death of her first husband, she married Peter Porcher, Sr., of St. Peter's Parish. Wauchope also mentions some thirteen other letters written after the Revolution; in reality there are fifteen other letters and one poem which have remained unpublished. Transcriptions of all of Mrs. Wilkinson's letters may be found at the South Caroliniana Library. I do not know the whereabouts of the manuscript letters. The *Library of Southern Literature* also lists Mrs. Wilkinson, but incorrectly gives her date of birth as 1857.

[41]Mary Lucia Bull, "A Woman's Letters in 1779 and 1782," *SCHGM*, X (April, 1909), 125-30.

[42]*SCHGM*, 126.

[43]"Letters From Mrs. Ralph Izard to Mrs. William Lee," *The Virginia Magazine of History and Biography*, VIII (July, 1900), 16-28.

[44]*Virginia Magazine*, 23.

[45]Louisa Susannah Wells, *The Journal of a Voyage From Charleston, S. C., to London* (New York: Printed for the New York Historical Society, 1906).

[46]See Marvin R. Zahniser, "The First Pinckney Mission to France," *SCHGM*, LXVI (1965), 205-17.

[47]Mary Stead Pinckney, *Letter-book of Mary Stead Pinckney*, ed. Charles F. McCombs (New York: The Grolier Club, 1946).

Session III: Discussion

MR. INABINETT: Mike, would you explain the title of Mrs. Boling's book to me?

MR. RICHARDS: It comes, I believe, from a quote found in Plutarch. If I may paraphrase very freely: when there's not enough of the lion's skin, you have to substitute a piece of the fox's hide. And that accounts for the strange behavior of this notable family, which did produce a senator, a doctor, schoolteachers, all within one generation. She attributes it to that strange piece of the fox hide which was fitted in to make up the total covering.

UNIDENTIFIED SPEAKER: You asked the question, "Is it biography? Is it new journalism?" and you did speak of the Boling biography. Is that your conclusion?

MR. RICHARDS: It's a guarded conclusion, and there are several specific reasons. If you simply look at *A Piece of the Fox's Hide* and do not know her preface, or do not know the Zeigler biography, it's almost impossible to determine what kind of book this is. I was very confused. Part of the reason for my confusion is simply that she avoids scholarly techniques. All of the section from the transcripts, which comprises maybe one-fourth to one-third of the book, is put in as dialogue. From the appearance of the dialogue, she might have simply made this up. In fact, she didn't. It comes straight from the transcripts. She was very interested, she told me, in allowing the reader to make up his own mind. She gives three kinds of information: reminiscences that she has received from those still living, letters and newspapers articles, and this court testimony. The letters and the newspaper articles are set off in block quotes, but that's the only identification we have for them, and you have to spend some time tracing these things down to see if they are fact or fiction. And I was unsure, actually, until I spoke to her, and she gave me leads to follow up, and I found then that they were accurate. Most of her book is nonfiction, and I would consider it a biography, although it lacks all the usual trappings of a biography.

141

MR. MERIWETHER: But your conclusion still depends, Mike, on external evidence. You're defining this work on the basis of evidence from outside of the work itself, which brings up a problem that you and I have discussed before. Is a book an autobiography if you can prove it's factual, and is exactly the same work a first person novel if you can't prove it is factual? In either case, you're always at the mercy of secondary materials which can be changed with further research.

MR. RICHARDS: Yes, I think we have to come to the same conclusion that she---that was made at the time, about Edmund Bigham, and that is, the evidence that she presents is circumstantial. That's all the evidence we have. Dr. Meriwether is absolutely correct. If someone would turn up further information, then it could amend my position on this biography.

MR. MERIWETHER: If all of her facts were wrong, would that then make it a novel? [Laughter]

MR. RICHARDS: My contention is, so much of her book is not her own; in other words, it's merely a reproduction of those three different sources---

MR. INABINETT: She should have described herself as a compiler and editor, then, perhaps--- What percentage of the book would be, actually, a verbatim transcript of letters and testimony? Fifty percent?

MR. RICHARDS: Yes. The latter half is almost totally transcript material. She told me that there had been some complaint about this. I feel that it was the best thing that could be done in respect to the fact that the Bigham situation is so controversial, still. In fifty years it has become legend, myth. The high percentage of material coming from the period, transcribed exactly, helped to avoid the polemic that I think existed in the Zeigler biography. I think it is the best handling, and I think it is a Rogerian type of approach, where the biographer makes no attempt to pass judgment. Certainly Zeigler did that. Boling simply wants to present the information and allow the reader to come to his own conclusions.

MR. INABINETT: What was your conclusion? Was it Smiley, or Edmund?

MR. RICHARDS: I think my conclusion---and I'm not copping
out on this---my conclusion is it's a moot point. The
evidence can be arranged either way. If we ever have a
Reynolds Conference on South Carolina criminals, I'll be
back.

MR. INABINETT: You probably read it more carefully than I
did, but Edmund came out as the guilty party in the
book, to me. I mean, I don't think it was that unbiased
myself.

MR. RICHARDS: That's an interesting conclusion, because if
I were to talk about Mrs. Boling's prejudices, they would
have to be in favor of Smiley, I think. Or, maybe not
so much in favor of Smiley as in favor of saying that
Edmund Bigham was, in fact, tried in the papers, and un-
justly so, and that we need to re-evaluate this evidence.

MR. INABINETT: Which do you think was the better literary
work, *The Last of the Bighams* or *A Piece of the Fox's
Hide?*

MR. RICHARDS: I'm in favor of *A Piece of the Fox's Hide*.
Zeigler's *The Last of the Bighams* is a totally personal
account. It's opinionated throughout. Very few facts
are given, as I mentioned, and only when they support
Zeigler's position. It's the most biased of the two
books. Boling's worked very hard to keep her book unbiased. Edmund lived until 1962. He spent from 1927,
his final trial, to 1960, when he was paroled, in the
state penitentiary. Mrs. Boling tells us, incidental-
ly---if there is a bias, this is it---that the entire
time Edmund was in prison he was a model prisoner, with
one exception: he became violent when confronted with
a copy of Zeigler's book.

MR. INABINETT: *The Last of the Bighams* is a rarity. It
was printed on the cheapest kind of paper, and I understand only a few copies have survived.

MRS. CHILDS: I wanted to ask Mr. Scafidel, did Mrs. King
do much in the way of journalism?

MR. SCAFIDEL: None at all that I know of.

MRS. CHILDS: Did she ever write under the name of Bowen?

MR. SCAFIDEL: Well, actually, she usually didn't sign her books. She only signed a few of her stories.

MRS. CHILDS: I've heard some rumor that she gave a play-by-play description of the St. Cecilia that wasn't much appreciated.

MR. SCAFIDEL: I don't know anything about that.

MISS RUTLEDGE: Did she divorce King, or did he die?

MR. SCAFIDEL: He died in 1862.

MISS RUTLEDGE: Did she ever marry Bowen?

MR. SCAFIDEL: Yes, I think she married Bowen, although I can't find a record of it.

MR. MERIWETHER: Mrs. Childs, where was that reputed account of the St. Cecilia published?

MRS. CHILDS: Well, I read it so long ago, I can't, I don't remember.

UNIDENTIFIED SPEAKER: Have any of her books been reprinted?

MR. SCAFIDEL: No. I doubt if there are very many in existence. All of them are over in the Caroliniana, though. And there's one novel published as a serial in *The Southern Field and Fireside* in Augusta, in 1864.

MR. INABINETT: There's really not much, not enough titles to draw any conclusion, but you know, they all have sort of a modern ring to them, as though she were in advance of her time in that respect, too. Is there any evidence that she consciously veered from the norm to come up with these titles?

MR. SCAFIDEL: About the titles, I don't know. The reviewer in the *Charleston Courier* was fascinated with the title, *Busy Moments of An Idle Woman*, and the other reviewers who did allude to the book, whether they liked it or not, were entranced by the title, but I have read nothing by her about her titles.

MISS RUTLEDGE: Who wrote the inscription on her tombstone? Was it her sister Caroline, who did that, or her father?

MR. SCAFIDEL: I don't know. She may have done it. That inscription is———I only quoted part of it. Wish I had quoted the rest of it, but it was very chaotic.[1]

MR. INABINETT: Why was Mrs. Chesnut afraid of her?

MR. SCAFIDEL: Most everybody seemed to be.

MR. INABINETT: Was there a risk that they would appear in an unfavorable light in one of the novels?

MR. SCAFIDEL: Yes, but I think Mary Chesnut resented her comments, resented the way she conducted herself. She flirted, although she was married, and I don't think Mrs. Chesnut approved of that, and she apparently had a good deal of self confidence and was at least a little intimidating.

MRS. HAMPTON: Brassy.

MISS ENDRES: I think either you or Beverly Scafidel talked about the relationship between the two sisters. Do you have any further information on that? Did Caroline support Susan in her literary efforts?

MR. SCAFIDEL: The only information about that is the dedication to *Busy Moments*. She dedicates it to her sister Caroline, and in that dedication she mentions that Caroline was responsible for encouraging her to publish those stories.

MR. INABINETT: Did she get that type of encouragement from her father? Most of what you said seemed to be critical of her.

MR. SCAFIDEL: Well, he didn't know that she was writing until she published the first book. He evidently got a copy of it, and Caroline told him who the author was, and he suggested that they keep it a secret from their mother.

MRS. SCAFIDEL: In answer to Mr. Inabinett's question, in one of the William Elliott letters, Elliot has just read *Sylvia's World* and writes back to his wife that it's just awful, and he thinks that she must be giving vent to her rage at every snub that she ever experienced. So it looks as if her acquaintances had good reason to be afraid they might wind up as characters in her novels.

MR. SCAFIDEL: Which would account for Lucy Baxter's term, "trashy novel."

MR. HAYHOE: Chip, you mentioned in your paper that most of the material you dealt with had not been published until this century, or at least till well into the nineteenth century. Do the manuscripts of most of those ladies still exist?

MR. ARNOLD: I would say for most of them, yes. I don't know about the Martha Ramsay letters, though, and they're among the more interesting. I would like to know where they are. The Eliza Wilkinson letters apparently don't exist.

MR. INABINETT: Chip, did you mean to say that Eliza Wilkinson did not exist as a person, but was only a character created by Mrs. Gilman?

MR. ARNOLD: What I'm suggesting is, that I think Mrs. Gilman might have made them a little better in the actual publication.

MR. INABINETT: You could even conclude that from the Wauchope biographical sketch, in which he states that the thirteen other letters are of considerably less literary value.

MR. ARNOLD: Well, I think it goes further than that. I think that, and this is just again an idea, but you have pages and pages of dialogue in the letters. They read like a novel, and I think that either Eliza Wilkinson wrote it---of course she wrote it, but I mean rewrote it as a novel, or Caroline Gilman fixed the letters up, still putting them under Eliza Wilkinson's name. I don't know.

---

[1]The epitaph is quoted in Clare Jervey (compiler), *Inscriptions on the Tablets and Gravestones in St. Michael's Church and Churchyard, Charleston, S. C.* (Columbia: The State Company, 1906), p. 48: "In Memory / of / SUSAN PETIGRU, / Beloved wife of /

Christopher C. Bowen. / Youngest daughter of / Hon.
James L. Petigru. / Born Octr. 23rd. 1824, / Died
Decr. 11th. 1875. / Gifted with Genius, versatile,--
Inherited; / The OBSERVED of Circles chosen,--brilliant;
/ Disciplin'd in vicissitudes of eventful times, / Her
Soul,--bruised, not crushed--Undismayed, / Won a
crowning Grace-- / Brave--Trusting--Unshaken-- /
WIFE-HOOD. / Peace to her memory. / 'Glittering Tissues
bear imblaz'd / Holy Memorials, acts of Zeale and Love
/ Recorded, eminent.'"

Sally Baxter Hampton

by

Ann Fripp Hampton

Among South Carolina's women writers, Sally Baxter
Hampton is certainly not widely known. Her literary work
consists only of her letters, and only enough of them survive to make one slim volume. Yet even those few are significant enough to establish her as one of the important
letter-writers of her place and time. They reveal not only
a capable reporter recording events with clarity and
personal conviction in a momentous period of history, but
also an appealing, lively, witty and charming woman who
died tragically young yet remained fascinated with life to
the end of her final illness.

She was a native of New York, born there in 1833, who
married into South Carolina's Hampton family in 1855 and
lived near Columbia during the years immediately preceding
the Civil War.[1] She was a contemporary of Mary Boykin
Chesnut, who mentions her in the *Diary From Dixie*,[2] and of
Susan Petigru King, whose meeting with Sally in Charleston
was the subject of an enthusiastic letter from Sally to her
mother.[3] She was a friend of Thackeray's, whom she met in
New York on his 1852 visit to this country,[4] and exchanged
many letters with him. A large number of his letters to
her and her family have been published, though often in
highly edited and abbreviated form, and nine original manuscripts are now in the Caroliniana Library.[5] Unfortunately,
only two of her letters to him have been found,[6] as
Thackeray's daughters destroyed the others after his
death;[7] and Sally's own papers were undoubtedly lost when

149

the Hampton homes near Columbia were burned by Sherman's army in 1865.[8]

So, what little correspondence we have was preserved by her family in New York. Her sister Lucy Baxter, who lived to be nearly ninety years of age, apparently passed the carefully kept letters to her niece and namesake Lucy Hampton, Sally's daughter who had made her home with the Baxters for awhile after her parents' death. This Lucy Hampton in turn passed the letters down to her niece and namesake Lucy Hampton, later Mrs. Hagood Bostick.[9] From the depths of an old leather trunk in the Bostick attic, the letters came to light a few years ago, tattered and faded but for the most part perfectly legible.

She was born Sarah Strong Baxter, the eldest child of George Baxter of New York City and his wife Anna Smith Strong.[10] Her father was a prosperous warehouse owner who suffered some financial reverses when Sally was about twenty.[11] His people had been Bostonians[12] and were connected somehow in the past with the illustrious Adams family of Quincy;[13] a friendship existed between the George Baxters and the family of Charles Francis Adams, although the distant relationship is never mentioned.[14] In her mother's family the men for the most part were respected professional men in banking, law, or government.[15] The Baxters' social position was quite good, although not in the highest echelon, and among their friends and acquaintances were some of the prominent New Yorkers of the day.[16] Sally grew up with a younger sister Lucy and two younger brothers, Wyllys and George, in a family that encouraged amateur theatricals and literary efforts of all sorts, and where books were read and discussed critically.[17]

Into this setting the English novelist William Makepeace Thackeray was introduced in the fall of 1852, when he came to America for his first lecture tour. Presented to the Baxters by a mutual friend, he soon found himself very much at home in their brownstone house on Second Avenue; throughout his stay in this country he often retreated there for a quiet evening with the family. He became attached to them all, including Mrs. Baxter's sister Mrs. Snelling, her brother Oliver Strong, and his daughter Libby, but his special attraction was to Sally. She was nineteen then and a belle of the season; three days after meeting her he wrote to his mother that he was in love.[18] He was forty-one years old and looked even older; but Sally was undoubtedly charmed by his attentions, and they apparently enjoyed a brief flirtation which ripened into a lasting friendship. He had finished writing *Henry Esmond* before coming to the States and found in Sally the personification of its heroine Beatrix; Mrs. Baxter he likened to Lady Castlewood and often referred to her by this name.[19] Although married, Thackeray was essentially a widower, for his wife had been insane for years and required institutional care. He had her housed with a family who lived in the country and reared their two daughters himself.[20] He was a sentimental man who freely admitted that he loved women. A letter to Sally written on July 26, 1853, after his return to England, shows something of his feeling for her. The original, which is in the Caroliniana Library, was found in the Bostick attic along with Sally's letters, and varies considerably from the previously published version.

Here is the published version, from *Thackeray's Letters to an American Family*, p. 85:

The fourth of July landed a little letter which has been 3 weeks on its way since, before it found the person to whom it was addressed -- I got it at Lausanne the day before yesterday -- a glum little letter.... What for do you reproach me?... Haven't I written you 3 letters for one?...

And here is the original:

The fourth of July landed a little letter w$^{\underline{h}}$ has been 3 weeks on its way since, before it found the person to whom it was addressed -- I got it at Lausanne the day before yesterday -- a glum little letter, hinting reproaches and ennui and disquiet. What for do you reproach me? How can you say you are indifferent to me? Haven't I written you 3 letters for one? Except one person, and my own girls whom do I care for if not for you? -- Sometimes I think not for any one, person and girls and you included. Not being allowed that w$^{\underline{h}}$ my heart would have, it seems as if it's dead & buried. These complaints ought not to be trusted to pen and ink however; as you formulise your sentimental griefs you increase them -- And at my age they become ridiculous -- I'm old enough to be a grandfather and am I to go on puling because I cant get ever a female partner of my loves & woes?

You stupid old fool, get to your books; give up
your laziness, don't spend your great stupid time
hankering after women. Leave that to young people.
My dear Sarah though I shall never forgive you keeping me waiting those 3 times and writing me those
little bits of letters when I went to the South, and
so slaying the elderly cupid within me -- yet he was
so absurd and untimely a little brute that Death was
the best thing w^h could happen to him. He was
ludicrous, being born at my time of life, as Jacob
was no I mean Isaac, when your Biblical namesake
laughed at the idea of his appearance in the world.
Theres a time for all things: for brilliant young
Sarah Baxters; bright eyes and coquetry and triumphs
and passions and filial duties -- for old folks like
me; art and ambition and money-getting and parental
cares.

One must read between the lines of Thackeray's letters
to Sally to devine her feelings for him; certainly she
sought his advice about her marriage as she wavered inde-
cisively between suitors. Then a few months after the
above-quoted letter she suffered a serious illness and the
following February departed on a Southern tour to regain
her health. After visiting Savannah and Charleston, she
and her father reached Columbia, planning to go on to Aiken
after a quiet stay here, but to her great surprise she
found herself happily busy in Columbia. She had a letter
of introduction to the renowned professor Francis Lieber
and became good friends with him and his family. She met
and was entertained by much of Columbia society, including
the Prestons, Louisa Cheves McCord, and young Frank Hampton.
He was the son of Wade Hampton II who at that time was one
of the richest planters in the country.[21] The following
spring, Sally returned to South Carolina to visit Mrs.
McCord at her plantation and by September was engaged to
marry Frank Hampton.

The wedding took place in New York on December 12,
1855. Thackeray was again in this country, but declined to
come down from Boston for the occasion claiming that he was
ill.[22] He later admitted to Mr. Baxter that he would as
soon have witnessed the ceremony as seen one of his children
have a tooth extracted.[23] However, when he met Frank in
Charleston several months later he expressed his approval

and sent them a silver tea set as a wedding gift.[24]

Sally and Frank settled down initially at Millwood, the home of his father, and later established themselves at nearby Woodlands, which had been the plantation home of Wade Hampton I of Revolutionary fame. Four children were born to them between 1856 and 1861, while Sally's health declined. Finally it was known that she suffered from tuberculosis and although they travelled to climates thought to be beneficial, nothing stopped the progress of her disease and she died on September 10, 1862, four months before her 30th birthday.[25]

Frank had remained in South Carolina during her final illness, travelling from his post with the army at Charleston to be with her whenever he could. After her death he joined his brother Wade's command in Virginia, the Hampton Legion, and was killed in battle the following June.[26] His sister Caroline, who had nursed Sally so tenderly, was named guardian of the four children:[27] Franky, almost 7; Georgianna, aged 5; Lucy, 4; and Caroline, a year and a half. Little Frank and the infant Caroline remained in the care of their Hampton aunts while the two little girls went to live for awhile with their Baxter grandparents and Aunt Lucy; there Georgie died early in 1865.[28] The other three children grew up to marry, but only Franky had children and they are the Hampton men known in Columbia today.

As an articulate and well-read person, Sally was able in her letters to her family to give them a real picture of her South Carolina life. One particularly interesting letter tells of Christmas preparations on their plantation and contrasts her life here with that of a Northern counterpart.

SBH to George Baxter, December 22, 1860:

Your letter found me in the midst of my Christmas preparations... here you know Xmas is the Negroes peculiar festival -- it is then they harvest & take to market their crops -- for three or four days the plantation is theirs - the horses - mules & wagons are all given up to their use & they haul into town & sell their little crop of cotton or corn, or potatoes, or whatever it may chance to be. This year however their master has bought all their

corn as his crop fell short & as we are quar-
antined from Columbia on account of Small Pox,
they are to have a festival at home. A barrel
of whiskey - a Hogshead of molasses - & oxen for
a Barbecue are their master's contributions & I
am to go down on Monday & give out Sugar - Coffee
- Rice & Flour to all that want- But some of them
are well to do in this world & supply themselves
with those little luxuries- In these hard times
the raising of money is no easy matter but the
Negroes will be paid the $500 or so that their
crop amount to, on Christmas whether money is
tight or easy....

What I wonder would my many & beloved friends in
New York say if they could turn from their luxuri-
ous & well-trained northern households & their
Christmas preparations - which consist of an order
to the butcher & confectioner - & "so many to
dinner Cook" -- to me in the store room, in the
pantry - presiding over first the boiling of hops
& making of yeast for the necessary Xmas loaves, &
afterwards the selection of fat poultry, the cutting
of a saddle of mutton - the proper picking of game -
the making & baking of cakes & pies & confections
ordinary and extraordinary- And these are all
necessary duties of a Southern housekeeper...

As the Civil War approached her interest in the
politics of the day exceeded that of many women of the time
and she wrote to friends North and South urging moderation
and conciliation.

She wrote the following letter early in 1861 to Samuel
B. Ruggles, an influential New Yorker who was active in
many public fields:

You remember asking me in New York, what man we had
in South Carolina "a head & shoulders above all
other men, who could retain the state in the position
she had assumed as leader" -- I have looked about
me earnestly since I have been here & honestly I
tell you *there is no man here*. The spirit which
prevails in South Carolina is wholly & entirely a
military one. She can fight & *will* to the last,
desperately & enduringly, but for a head to govern
& a hand to lead she must look elsewhere.... It

is useless to say that the South has been rash or
precipitate - what she has done has been a posi-
tively essential precaution - it was a question
of existence, & self-preservation is the first
instinct of humanity. These matters have been
quite sufficiently discussed by far wiser heads,
but it may not be useless that I - a Northern
born & bred woman, living on a plantation in the
midst of three hundred Negroes, knowing them &
their nature as well as five years careful study
& keen observation could teach knowledge -- seeing
constantly the Southern people of every age, condition & grade - mixing with them freely & inti-
mately on all occasions, it may not be in vain
that I speak when I speak to a man like you....
Have people with you thoroughly envisaged the
difficulties & dangers of their position -- do
they realize what a civil war must be to this
country & above to their section of the country.
In God's name I conjure you, place the matter
clearly before them & endeavor to have it left to
the voice of the people whether they will lend
their hands to a crime that will bring home its
curses - or whether they will leave that sect of
fanatics who have been so far such "blind guides"
& assume the place which will be gladly conceded
to them in a fraternity with their Southern sister
states.

Even in her despair over the impending secession of
South Carolina she shows an understanding for her adopted
home and its people. She wrote the following letter to her
family in December of 1860, shortly before South Carolina
was to secede:

After this you may not hear from me again or I
from you, for on the 18th the state will be out
of the Union - Oh! I cannot - cannot say it
without bitter tears - which break out whenever
I realize - which I do now - where we stand. I
am no Southerner heaven knows & at heart if not
abolition at least anti-slavery but I must concede
that the tone at the South has been most firm -
calm - manly and decided. They act with a strong
feeling of patriotism & desire of justice to their
country but at heart with as ardent a regret for
the dissolution of the Union as I have or you or

anyone I know. It is quite useless for me to
attempt composure or indifference - I should have
lived & died unknowing that I had a spark of
patriotism or pride of nationality but this - the
destruction of all that made one's home - one's
country - one's life brings all the latent enthusiasm & devotion into action....

The important men of the day were often guests in her
home and she could report on events and opinions with a
first-hand knowledge. The following letter was also
written to her family in early December of 1860:

I had to spend Sunday with me - M͞r͞ Char͞s͞ Lowndes
... a member of the house & M͞r͞ Wagner - of the
Senate.... M͞r͞ Lowndes says he has been "Union"
to the last moment - & now yields only partially
to the current. He deprecates their haste, he
laments the urgency of the occasion, but he feels
deeply in the cause of the South & strongly as a
slaveholder- As belonging to a family of Revolutionary memory & attached in many ways both to the
North & South his opinions are valuable & he says
it is *inevitable*. There is no doubt a very strong
tide of public opinion here which drives all the
legislators *on on* more rapidly than their own
judgments would allow- Wagner said "no man would
dare to postpone the day of secession - *even a
month*." They feel & say that it will not do to
allow the impulse to grow cold. The party to which
M͞r͞ Lowndes - the Prestons - Manning - Wade Hampton
- Memminger - Orr - & Pettigrew belong, advocate
secession but at a later date & greater moderation
in all movements. They would like to hear what the
North will have to say or to do....

I have much & exciting talk with all I see - it
is a crisis that absorbs everything....

It is interesting that she was sympathetic to South
Carolina's course despite her Northern family and friends,
and one can see that her optimism over possible re-union
was at least partially a reflection of the sentiments she
had heard among her Southern family and friends. The
following letter was written probably to her mother, early
in 1861 (January 11):

... my own private opinion is that the men
[in Charleston] enjoy beyond all measure the
excitement of a life which wakes them out of
their "bovine" torpor – & which is such an utter
change from the quiet of a planters existence.

I apprehend seriously however that the enthusiasm
& excitement of so many unoccupied men will get
beyond control & so I think do many of the cooler
heads in Charleston. Wade Hampton for instance
reprobates most strongly the firing on the "Star
of the West" & is entirely disgusted with the
manner in which matters are conducted down there....

Yesterday at dinner my heart rose at hearing for
the first time the word "*re-union*" Surely it was
significant! Men's minds are all acted on alike
in times like these – there is no individuality
& what one man says you may be sure is said by
all men in one way or another – ...

The last letter to her family which we have, was
written five months before her death and went from Charleston through the blockade. After giving them news of mutual
friends, she reveals herself resigned to the disease which
was gradually taking her life. This was dated April 1,
1862:

I have another chance tonight for a letter – by a
Captain who has run the blockade 31 times– I am
never certain if my letters have gone or not &
should repeat each time I suppose – but I have
little strength for writing & must do what I can.
I have been very sick again – after my last
hemorrhage ... I was taken with ... a kind of
dysentery– I have been in Charleston five weeks
& have only left my room twice – ... I do not
get any better & tho' the D^r says I shall improve
... I do not expect ever to be any materially
better.... I am still at the Mills House – intended
to take a house but I am not well enough to undertake the trouble – then I am alone much of the
time & feel safer in a Hotel. Caroline H. is here
now with me ... & Frank comes as often as he can
... so you need not fret about my being alone ...
for Caroline ... is an excellent nurse ... Of the
kindness of Charlestonians I can't say enough –

they vie with each other to treat me in the
warmest & most friendly way - ... I fare much
better here than at Woodlands - & then I am near
Frank-...

This is the 3$^{\underline{rd}}$ letter thro' the blockade - one
by Nashville - one by Catawba - & this by the
Economist-

Her last letter to Thackeray must have gone through
the blockade also, but we have no record of how it came to
be preserved.[29] The horrors of a divided country pitting
kinsmen against each other become more vivid as she tells
him of their former friends. This was written in April of
1862, also, a few days after the preceding one. Writing to
Thackeray of their mutual friends, she says:

Where are they all now?...

That slender youth, with the close cut black
mustache and big melancholy eyes, that gave such
emphasis to his social nothings, he, the petted
darling of society for all these years, is dead
on a sand-bar, of a fever, in sight of the country
he had come to devastate, if he could. The mother
who weeps for him at home was born on that very
shore, her home in youth might have been perhaps
his first prize, - her brother is in waiting behind that distant earthwork to welcome the in-
vaders, "with bloody hands, etc." among his sister's
sons. Another - "the little gentleman" you called
him - he has married since, and carried to the
snows of New York a girl nurtured on Carolina
Jessamine and sunshine. He has left her now among
the icicles, to bring fire and sword to the house
where she was born, and where their first born
lies buried.... This shows you the sorrows among
which we live, and against which we must struggle -
none are exempt, for to those who have no divided
hearts, comes the dread division of Death, the
widow and orphan mourn their dead, and the destitute
the happy homes now in ruins, or the camp-ground
of the enemy. Upon the fertile smiling islands
are marauding bands of runaways who have spurned
the old masters, and, in turn, refuse the new. In
every swamp and thicket are fugitives, fleeing
from they know not what, - dreading like death the

"Yankee soger," yet seeking to leave the master
they love, and the home they have *adored*, in a
vague and nameless terror. The more simple, and
guileless and mild, the greater the fear and dread
and apprehension, - this is what philantrophy
does for the negro, and abolition for the slave,
and civil war for the white man.

This is her last known letter. Thackeray's reply, if
there was one, may not have gotten through the blockade; or
if it did, may not have survived the burning of Columbia.
Sally herself did not live to witness this destruction of
her Carolina home.

Apart from their literary merit and value as historical evidence, what emerges most clearly from these letters
is their author -- a person of courage, charm, wit, and
wisdom. In her debutante days she had captivated the
worldly Thackeray and inspired his devotion and life-long
affection. In early womanhood she had won the heart of
Frank Hampton, young, handsome sportsman-planter, and accepted a total change of environment with a maturity beyond
her years. Through Thackeray's characters Beatrix and
Ethel we can see her as a tall, slender girl with dark hair
and eyes, fair skin and vivid coloring, spirited and viva-
cious. Through her own words we can make out a tender and
careful mother, a loyal and loving wife, a devoted daughter
and sister.

Removed from a life of city comforts, she assumed her
role of plantation mistress with grace and energy. Placed
in a position of divided loyalties, she supported what was
finest on both sides and worked with compassion and intelli-
gence to promote harmony and discourage division. At the
end, in the midst of intense personal suffering, she remained devoid of self-pity and continued to be keenly
interested in people and events around her, almost to the
day of her death. Her depth and strength of character,
observing eye, and keen intellect gave us some of the
finest letters written in ante-bellum and Civil War South
Carolina.

Notes

[1]Benjamin W. Dwight, *The History of the Descendants of Elder John Strong of Northampton, Mass.*, 2 vols., (Albany, N. Y.:   Joel Munsell, 1871), I, p. 627.   Her place of death is said here to be Asheville, N. C., but the Hampton plantation home "Millwood" is cited by other authors, including Gordon N. Ray in his biography, *Thackeray: The Age of Wisdom 1847-1863* (New York: McGraw-Hill, 1958), p. 319.

[2]Mary Boykin Chesnut, *A Diary from Dixie*, ed. Ben Ames Williams (Boston: Houghton Mifflin, 1949), pp. 39, 40, 41, 125.

[3]Sally Baxter to Anna Baxter, March 8, 1854.   Sarah Strong Baxter Hampton Papers, South Caroliniana Library, University of South Carolina.

[4]Gordon N. Ray, ed., *The Letters and Private Papers of William Makepeace Thackeray*, 4 vols. (Cambridge, Mass.: Harvard University Press, 1945), III, p. 149.

[5]Lucy D. Baxter, ed., *Thackeray's Letters to an American Family* (New York: Century Co., 1904).   Many of these letters were edited extensively and can be compared with original manuscripts among the Hampton papers in the South Caroliniana Library.   A larger collection of Thackeray's letters has been edited by Gordon N. Ray and published in *The Letters and Private Papers of William Makepeace Thackeray* (see Note 4); most of his letters to the Baxter family appear in Volume III and a few in Volume IV.

[6]Her letter written in February 1853, which is unpublished, belongs to Gordon N. Ray, who has very graciously sent us a photostatic copy of it.   Her letter of April 5, 1862, quoted from a transcript by Dr. Ray in *The Age of Wisdom*, pp. 317-319, belongs to Thackeray's granddaughter, Mrs. Richard Fuller.

[7]Ray, *Letters*, IV, p. 298.

[8]Charles E. Cauthen, ed., *Family Letters of the Three Wade Hamptons 1782-1901* (Columbia, S. C.: University of South Carolina Press, 1953), p. xvii. Harry R. E. Hampton in "Hampton Homes" (unpublished) mentions specifically the burning of the Frank Hampton residence "Woodlands."

[9]Notes from interviews with Ambrose G. Hampton, Sr., grandson of Sally Baxter Hampton.

[10]Dwight, I, p. 627.

[11]Ray, *Letters*, I, p. lxxxvii. Sally Baxter to William Makepeace Thackeray, February, 1853 (see Note 6).

[12]Dwight, I, p. 627.

[13]Notes from interviews with Gertrude Hampton Barringer, granddaughter of Sally Baxter Hampton.

[14]Several references to the Adams family appear in Sally's letters, for instance her letter to her mother written circa April 1, 1854. There are also letters from George Baxter to Charles Francis Adams, Mrs. Baxter to Mrs. Adams, and Henry Adams to Lucy Baxter in the Hampton Papers, South Caroliniana Library.

[15]Dwight, I, pp. 619, 625, and others. Allan Nevins and Milton Halsey Thomas, ed., *The Diary of George Templeton Strong*, 4 vols. (New York: MacMillan Co., 1952). The author was a cousin of Mrs. Baxter and identifies a number of men of the Strong family and their professions. See III, pp. v, xii, and 63; IV, p. 459.

[16]Mentioned with familiarity in her letters are members of the Cutting, Viele, Ruggles and Dix families.

[17]Sally Baxter's letters to her mother of March 8 and April 1, 1854, include some discussion of books she was reading or wanted to have sent to her; her letter of January 18, 1861, to her sister Lucy mentions an amateur theatrical group she is organizing and indicates that Lucy has written some plays which they may use.

[18]Ray, *Age of Wisdom*, pp. 206-209. The letter to his mother appears in *Letters*, III, p. 148.

[19]Lida Mayo, "Thackeray in Love," *The American Heritage*, XIII, no. 3 (April, 1962), p. 51

[20]Ray, *Letters*, I, pp. clxiv, clxv.

[21]Mayo, p. 105.

[22]Ray, *Letters*, III, p. 516.

[23]*Ibid.*, p. 521.

[24]*Ibid.*, pp. 556, 557, 561, 568, and 569. The silver tea set described by Thackeray (p. 603) is now a part of the furnishings on display at the Hampton-Preston Mansion in Columbia, South Carolina.

[25]She is buried in Trinity Episcopal Churchyard, Columbia, South Carolina.

[26]In *Family Letters of the Three Wade Hamptons* (see Note 8), there are several letters from Wade Hampton, III, to his sister, Mary Fisher Hampton, which indicate that up to June 3, 1862, at least, their brother, Frank, had remained in South Carolina (pp. 83, 86, 89, 90 and 91). Sally's letter of April 1, 1862, tells her family that Frank is near enough to Charleston, where she was then staying, to come for the night. His death is recounted by Edward L. Wells in *Hampton and His Calvary in '64* (Charleston, S. C. and Richmond, Va.: B. F. Johnson Co., 1899), pp. 68-71, and by U. R. Brooks in *Butler and His Calvary in the War of Secession 1861-1865* (Columbia, S. C.: The State Company, 1909), pp. 149 ff. and 165 ff.

[27]No will has been found for Frank Hampton. Papers of administration dated June 29, 1863, name his brother, Christopher F. Hampton, administrator of the estate and his sister, Caroline Hampton, guardian of the children. His plantation was sold to George A. Trenholm for $301,384; included in the estate were 98 slaves.

[28]Ambrose G. Hampton, Sr. (see Note 9) remembers these family details, which are supported by letters from Anne Thackeray to Mrs. Baxter (Ray, *Letters*, IV, p. 303) and from Bishop Horatio Potter to Lucy Baxter (unpublished letter dated January 15, 1865).

[29]See Note 6.

Scarlet Sister Julia:
The Rise and Fall of a Literary Reputation

by

Thomas H. Landess

Time, which can make a diamond or reduce bone to
powder, disposes of literary reputations with the same
sovereign finality. Thus F. Scott Fitzgerald, forgotten
at the time of his death, is now remembered by millions,
while the once-famous Sarah Josepha Hale is known only to
meticulous literary scholars and their most submissive
graduate students. In a few years, of course the relative
renown of these novelists *may* be altered---even reversed.
But somehow I doubt it. For what has made Fitzgerald's
work durable is not the veneer of polite "radicalism" which
may have brought him a portion of his initial readership
in the Twenties. Nor has Sarah Josepha Hale's nineteenth-
century piety redeemed her from oblivion. The only thing
that endures, it seems, is a genuine artistic rendition of
what is true in human nature; and as much as critics like
Lionel Trilling might protest the idea, I am convinced that
most readers of fiction are not primarily interested in
moral postures, social philosophy, or historical verisimilitude. They are interested in stories and people. They
do not read *Moby Dick* as a catechism or as a chronicle of
the short-lived whaling industry, nor would they study
Uncle Tom's Cabin solely as a treatise on the evils of
slavery if they had not been trained to do so by confused
English teachers. The critic who measures works of fiction
against the dogma of some regnant piety in order to determine their ultimate worth is bound to fail, just as a
doctor is bound to fail who determines the relative health
of his patients exclusively on the basis of their views on
the current economy.

163

Obviously this truth is not as self-evident to others as it is to me. Indeed as vital evidence to the contrary, ideologues of all stripes, armed with their own well-honed fragments of truth, continue to hack away at literary reputations, the great as well as the modest. Thus a commentator in *Partisan Review* calls the narrator of *Moby Dick* a white racist honky, while his opposite number in *National Review* convicts William Faulkner of being a "liberal" (the ultimate crime, I would conclude, in that particular court). And poor Henry James, who writes of heroic self-sacrifice in the grand epic tradition, is condemned in both *National Review* and *Partisan Review* for being a deviate of one sort or the other, a sinner against the discrete and contradictory theologies which each faction defends against the onslaught of the infidel.

Melville, Faulkner, and James are obviously impervious to such attack, but the reputation of Julia Peterkin has suffered severely at the hands of ideological critics, both early and late. At the beginning of her career she was denounced by Old South apologist and Fundamentalist preachers, to say nothing of cousins and aunts nervous for the preservation of family status. These adversaries seemed to believe that she was impious toward the local gods; and still unsure of her talent, she was shaken by their abuse, as her early letters reveal.

Fortunately, the initial response from literary circles was friendly, even laudatory, though conditioned to some extent by the social and cultural climate of the day. We must remember that in 1924, when *Green Thursday* was published, the revived Ku Klux Klan was a significant political power, particularly in the Midwest; Al Jolson was at the height of his Broadway career, performing in blackface as the happy, singing "good-old-white-folks' darky." And Jim Crow, after two or three decades, had become the custom as well as the law throughout the South.

Needless to say, literary depictions of black characters were usually reflective of this general atmosphere, and as a consequence, Mrs. Peterkin's work was welcomed by self-styled liberals for what it was———an honest portrait of true-to-life blacks rather than some fictional recreation of Mr. Bones. Joel Spingarn, the scholarly president of the NAACP, wrote of *Green Thursday*, "Nothing so stark, taut, poignant, has come out of the white South in fifty year."[1] W. E. B. DuBois, reviewing the book in *Crisis* (the

NAACP house organ), said of Mrs. Peterkin, "She is a
Southern white woman but she has the eye and the ear to see
beauty and know truth."[2]   Charles Puckette in the *Saturday
Review of Literature* wrote that *Black April* "must stand as
the most genuinely successful attempt yet made to capture
the soul of these people. This book is put down with the
feeling that one stands nearer to truth than one has stood
before, in a field of fiction the surface of which has been
often scratched, and the rich depths seldom upturned....
Other fiction of negro life seems false in the light of
Mrs. Peterkin's achievement."[3]   An anonymous reviewer in
the *Nation* speculated that *Black April* was "the finest work
produced thus far dealing with the American Negro."[4]
Robert Merrick in the *New Republic* said approximately the
same thing: "possibly the most convincing presentation of
the Negro that has yet been made by a white person."[5]

    I cite these passages not only to illustrate the un-
qualified praise with which her early works were greeted in
so-called "liberal circles," but also to make a more important point. As favorable as these comments may seem to
admirers of Mrs. Peterkin's fiction, they all derive from
an assumption, either stated or unstated, that the importance of her achievement is to be measured by the relative
verisimilitude with which she renders black characters. No
one in this group bothers to distinguish between her virtues as a sociologist and her virtues as a novelist.

    In 1924 the failure to make such a distinction proved
harmless enough, and by 1929, after Mrs. Peterkin had won a
Pulitzer Prize for *Scarlet Sister Mary*, her reputation as a
significant American writer seemed to be permanently se-
cured. Yet the political climate began to change rapidly
during the Thirties, and after World War II a new civil
rights movement rendered an earlier sociology obsolete.
Without delving too deeply into the question, I would
suggest that dramatic events in the Fifties and Sixties
produced as a by-product a rigid orthodoxy in "black
fiction" which was designed to serve the specific objective
of reordering society. The enveloping action of this fiction was, by prescription, a white-dominated community of
economic and social exploitation. While important examples
of such fiction had been published in an earlier era, the
piety of the "New Revolution" would no longer tolerate a
realism which did not serve as a means to political ends.
Realism outside the framework of the power struggle was regarded as a form of reaction, and this attitude led to the

swift erosion of the fragile ground upon which Mrs.
Peterkin's reputation rested, for she was no longer a good
sociologist, and no one had ever laid a foundation for her
reputation as a literary artist. Thus at present she is
largely ignored in the pages of critical and scholarly
journals, even those primarily devoted to the study of
Southern literature; and when she is mentioned, it is as a
portrayer of blacks, and invariably she is dismissed with
condescension or outright hostility. As examples of the
current attitude toward her work, I would cite two passages,
one from Willard Thorp's *American Writing in the Twentieth
Century*, the other from John M. Bradbury's *Renaissance in
the South*.

Mr. Thorp, in contrasting Mrs. Peterkin's work with
that of DuBose Heyward, writes:

> Heyward's pages are spotted with purple prose but
> Negro critics agree that his understanding of
> Negro life was remarkable. They are less enthusi-
> astic about Julia Peterkin whose best-known work,
> *Scarlet Sister Mary* (1928), won a Pulitzer Prize.
> As the wife of a plantation manager, Mrs.
> Peterkin knew the Negroes of her region well, but
> in her later work she condescends to them and falls
> back on the legend of the happy, childlike Negro,
> content with a clean cabin and plenty of fat-back
> and pot-liquor.[6]

First, it is interesting to note the sharp contrast between Mr. Thorp's assessment of Mrs. Peterkin's work and
the opinions voiced by her earlier critics. It is difficult to believe that he is discussing the same novelist.
And who are the "Negro critics" whom he cites but will not
name? What do these critics have to say about the unquali-
fied approval of black activists such as DuBois, Walter
White, and Paul Robeson? Were these commentators of the
1920's simply imperceptive or does truth live precariously
in the shifting shadow of the left wing? Whatever the
answers to these questions, I detect one area of agreement
common to the two generations of critics: again, both view
Mrs. Peterkin almost solely in terms of her sociological
significance.

I am puzzled, however, by Mr. Thorp's emphasis on her
"later work" as exemplary of condescension. As a matter of
fact, it is in *Bright Skin*, her last novel, that Mrs.

Peterkin departs from her familiar pastoral mode to explore
in detail the conflict between the stability of an old
agrarian order and the lure of urban life. Cricket, the
"bright skin" or mulatto of the title, is of all the
author's major characters the farthest from being "content
with a clean cabin and plenty of fat-back and pot-liquor."
To the contrary, she is a rebel against the plantation
community from the time she is a child. Her first lover is
a stranger from the outside world, and his chief asset is
an automobile, that basic symbol of change and modernity.
Though he is murdered, Cricket is never again satisfied to
remain among the plantation folk, whom she regards as her
inferiors. In the climax of the novel she leaves them all
behind and flees to New York with a lover and her black
supremacist grandfather, the leader of a separatist movement in Harlem. Her first husband, Blue, who chooses to
remain in the stable plantation community, is, throughout
the novel, too troubled and love-stricken to find true con-
tentment anywhere. And in addition to the major characters,
Mrs. Peterkin introduces some new and disturbing elements
into her familiar world, among them an old man whose keen-
ing lament for his lost childhood in Africa is among the
most disturbing of all her scenes. In this novel no one is
happy; no one spoons pot-liquor; no one's cabin is gratify-
ingly clean.

The same general assessment could be made of *Roll,
Jordon, Roll*, Mrs. Peterkin's final work, which is a collection of early sketches, supplemented by a few tough-
minded additions and several informal essays which touch
on such matters as the degradation inherent in slavery, the
hard discipline necessary for survival in the struggle with
nature, and the customs and beliefs which govern the conduct of the blacks on Lang Syne plantation, a world Mrs.
Peterkin knew better than any of her critics, early or
late, black or white. With one or two minor lapses, I can
think of no book less likely to fit Mr. Thorp's description
than this hard-boiled vision of the spare but dignified
life some blacks lead as a result of historical circum-
stance. Clearly he has read both of these books careless-
ly, if indeed he has read them at all.

Perhaps the more revealing of these later evaluations,
however, is that of John M. Bradbury, which appeared in his
exhaustive study of modern Southern literature published in
1963. Mr. Bradbury is frank in admitting that one of the
purposes in writing his book is to "redress the critical

imbalance" caused by the South's New Critics, who have
ignored "a strong and wide-spread liberal wing," whose
"problem novels," he says, "have proliferated." Presumably
because of sheer bulk they deserve mentioning. Or is it
because of their piety? Mr. Bradbury is unclear, but the
tone of his comments on Mrs. Peterkin is unmistakably
hostile.

> Mrs. Peterkin's novels, all of them Negro-
> bound, display an old Southern weakness, despite
> their basis in intimate observation; her Negroes
> are represented as curious phenomena with sensa-
> tionally odd characters. The fundamental traits
> she exploits are moral irresponsibility and savage
> superstition. *Scarlet Sister Mary* gained wide
> popularity for its lurid mixture of sexual prom-
> iscuity, religion, and superstition, with authen-
> ticity guaranteed by its author's position as
> mistress of a large South Carolina plantation.
> But this novel in particular lacks conviction---
> *Black April* is perhaps her best. In none of her
> four books of fiction do basic economic and social
> problems figure, and white owners appear only as
> vague beneficent deities.[7]

This passage poses greater difficulties than Mr.
Thorp's, in part because Mr. Bradbury's rhetoric is harsher,
laced with contempt rather than with mild distaste. It is
difficult to counter allegations concerning the reasons for
the success of *Scarlet Sister Mary*, but perhaps one can go
to the contemporary reviewers for the best insights on the
question. Herschel Brickell, in *The Saturday Review*, said
the book "firmly establishes its author as an interpreter
of negro character; but more than this, it leaves no room
for doubt that she is a novelist whose work has enduring
quality."[8] Robert Herrick in *The New Republic* said that
the book was "something more than a novel--the revelation
of a race, which has lived with the whites for hundreds of
years, without becoming known beneath the skin."[9] Ben
Wasson, in *Outlook and Independent*, recognized Mrs.
Peterkin's departure from the use of stereotypes. "Mrs.
Peterkin escapes such things; she is above them. Her book
is real because she realizes that people, be they black or
white, are fundamentally alike."[10] And Joseph Warren Beach
found the novel "entirely free. . .from any flavoring of
patronage, sentimentality, apology, defense."[11] Mr.
Bradbury is entitled to his opinion, of course, but there

is sufficient internal evidence in his commentary to suggest that he has an axe to grind.

His reference to *Scarlet Sister Mary's* "lurid mixture of sexual promiscuity, religion, and superstition" provides us with some clues to the nature of his bias, particularly in his telling use of the coordinate conjunction. Obviously sexual promiscuity bothers him when linked with religion and superstition. He does not, for example, find anything "lurid" in the incestuous sexuality and suicide of *Lie Down in Darkness*. Nor is he bothered by what he describes as Charles Curtis Munz's "liberal indictment of white sharecropping practices." Note his tolerance when he writes, "Munz's novel does pile on its rapes and other violences, but it retains a fundamental integrity and rigidly excludes propagandistic author intrusions."[12] Presumably Mr. Munz has been careful to avoid mitigating his sexual assaults with any "lurid" concern for Christian redemption. Neither Mrs. Peterkin nor Dostoevski is so prudent.

Indeed there is a striking resemblance between Mary Pinesett and Sonia Marmeladov of *Crime and Punishment*. Both out of a kind of necessity indulge in sexual intercourse, the former because of her naturally loving nature, the latter to feed her family. Mary takes on a series of lovers, one at a time, and no bedroom scenes exploit the occasions for Mrs. Peterkin's readership. Meanwhile, Mary is a force for good in the plantation community, muting the harsh Phariseeism of church deacons by teaching them, both by advice and by example, to be kind and forgiving to one another and to question the rigid application of church law in cases where penitent sinners are concerned. In the end Mary has a religious vision following the poignant death of her favorite child, and in a scene as "lurid" as anything found in *Elsie Dinsmore* she is rebaptized into the church, the comic heroine in her moment of reintegration.

Superstition does play some role in the narrative, just as it undoubtedly played a role in the black community of Lang Syne plantation. Would Mr. Bradbury have the novelist ignore fact or truth? He is happy enough when the ignorance and bigotry of white characters are held up to the light for examination, though to give him his due, he objects to outright diatribes. Can he not see the historical and sociological implications of superstition in the black community? Mrs. Peterkin is hard on both superstition

and some aspects of religious primitivism. Why does Mr.
Bradbury not understand the sympathetic burden of her
fiction?

An answer to this question may be implicit in the
structure of Mr. Bradbury's argument and in its last sentence. First, I note a similarity in organization between
Mr. Thorp's paragraph and Mr. Bradbury's. Each begins with
a reference to the portrayal of "Negro life," each moves to
a discussion of *Scarlet Sister Mary* and to the question of
Mrs. Peterkin's authority as the mistress of a plantation,
each ends with the suggestion that the author is exploiting
old stereotypes, though Bradbury carries the matter further
by writing, "In none of her four books of fiction do basic
economic and social problems figure, and white owners
appear only as vague beneficent deities."[13] Has Mr.
Bradbury derived his opinion of Mrs. Peterkin from Mr.
Thorp, or are both simply following a natural course in
discussing Mrs. Peterkin's work from a retrospective point
of view? Mr. Bradbury does not cite Mr. Thorp in his
index, so perhaps the latter explanation of these similarities is more logical.

Yet one fact cannot be ignored: White owners do *not*
appear in Mrs. Peterkin's four works of fiction as vague,
beneficent deities. Indeed, they do not appear *at all*.
The author deliberately excluded them from her works because, as she wrote to Emily Clark early in her career, she
intended to avoid the pros and cons of racial controversy,
refusing to subordinate the humanity of her characters to
the "basic economic and social problems" which Mr. Bradbury
demands. Is this attitude "an old Southern weakness"?

To answer that question, let us turn to the two most
successful black novelists of our time, Ralph Ellison and
James Baldwin. Mr. Ellison maintains that the black experience in American fiction has been "distorted through
the overemphasis of the sociological approach" and that
those people who advocate or practice such a literature
destroy the values in black culture "which are beyond any
question of segregation, economics, or previous condition
of servitude."[14] Mr. Baldwin makes essentially the same
point when he writes that "The failure of the protest novel
lies in its rejection of life, the human being, the denial
of his beauty, dread, power, in its insistence that it is
his categorization alone which is real and which cannot be
transcended."[15]

I can think of no better paraphrase of what Mrs.
Peterkin herself believed about the nature of such sociological fiction.   But let us leave these commentators and
turn to Mrs. Peterkin herself.   For if interest in her work
is to be revived---as I think it should be---then we must
at least know what she herself was attempting to accomplish
in her literary career.

We already see that she objects to what Mr. Baldwin
calls "the protest novel."   To this issue I would add only
the observation that in her fiction she quietly trans-
planted her fictional Gullahs from Fort Motte to the Sea
Islands, where there had long been a verifiable tradition
of absentee landlords, thus making her imaginary world consistent with the facts of South Carolina history.   Had she
wished to show the beneficence of white paternalism, she
would surely have included idealized owners in her narratives.

But we have her own written opinion on the subject of
such sentimental portraits.   In a review of Lyle Saxon's
Children of Strangers she launches a more eloquent attack
on old-fashioned stereotypes than either Mr. Thorp or Mr.
Bradbury.   She classifies them into three types:

> The most popular one showed loyal, grateful slaves,
> or ex-slaves who were devoted to the families of
> their present owners and eager to sacrifice them-
> selves for their white friends.   Another prized
> portrayal presented the Negro characters as amiable,
> care-free comic figures, full of easy laughter and
> always ready with a gay song or nimble dance
> step.   A third well-known presentation showed the
> Negro as a drinking, gambling, worthless creature
> who was such a menace to white civilization that
> he spent most of his days on the chain-gang until
> he was finally lynched by a mob of white citizens
> resolved to protect white society from injury at
> his hands.

> These patterns of Negro conduct were empha-
> sized in literary productions so persistently
> that they were accepted as authentic.   And not
> until comparatively recent years have our dark-
> skinned neighbors been treated as individuals, as
> human beings whose position in the social scale
> is complicated by problems and difficulties not

found in the lives of their white contemporaries.[16]

It was against such stylized and unimaginative por-
trayals of the Negro that Mrs. Peterkin was reacting when
she began to write her own sketches in the early 1920's.
To a great extent it was her attempt to render the South
Carolina Gullah in purely realistic terms that led to her
fame as a novelist. Indeed in Mrs. Peterkin's fiction the
stereotypes are present only by implication, hovering on
the brink of possibility like gray ghosts to provide a contrast with the colorful flesh-and-blood characters she
creates. April, with all his arrogance and nobility, is
set in bold relief by the shade of Thomas Nelson Page's
obsequious servant; Budda Ben's bitterness is grimmer because of the frantic good humor of Mr. Bones; and Scarlet
Sister Mary's virtue is at least partially defined by
antithesis in the inflammatory rhetoric of the revived Ku
Klux Klan. That Mr. Bradbury, Mr. Thorp, and others fail
or refuse to recognize this truth seems a pity, for it is
on their authority that present-day students of Southern
literature have ignored Mrs. Peterkin's achievement. I
must admit it is difficult for me not to suspect that most
of these latter day critics have derived their opinions of
her work from rumor and hearsay.

In order to revitalize her literary reputation, I
would suggest that readers and critics approach her on her
own terms, not as a portrayer of "*The* Black" (who, after
all, does not exist in the real world), but as a serious
artist who attempted to render those blacks she knew as
human beings caught up in ancient struggles with the land,
with others, and with themselves, their blackness only one
individual characteristic that places them at a particular
time and a particular moment and place in their unique witness to the timeless truth of the human condition.

Like Mr. Bradbury, I have some grave reservations
about the limitations of the New Criticism, but I believe
such an approach applied to Mrs. Peterkin's fiction would
yield abundant fruit and begin to reclaim her from her
present oblivion. There is enough conscious artistry in
her work---enough irony, paradox, and allusion---to satisfy
any incipient Cleanth Brooks who might care to choose her
work as a major project for investigation. And the essential structure of such novels as *Black April* and *Scarlet
Sister Mary* can be discussed in terms as sophisticated and
"Aristotelian" as those used by Northrop Frye. Indeed at

this particular moment in the evolution of a criticism of
Southern literature, there is more of value still to be
said about her works than about those of Flannery O'Connor,
concerning whom so much has been written.

Finally, it is too much to hope that literary critics
will ever cease to be subverted from their proper task by
ideological concerns. They never have, even in the best of
times; and at present we live in an age that has been
politicized to an almost intolerable degree. More and
more, in our zeal for the abstraction, we are tempted to
superimpose our opinions and will on being, as well as on
the literary works which mirror, recreate, or define being.
We must, however, try to do better, whatever our mode of
approaching the word or the reality.

Notes

[1]Letter from Joel Spingarn to Julia Peterkin, quoted in Emily Clark, *Innocence Abroad* (New York, 1931), p. 224.

[2]W. E. B. DuBois, "The Browsing Reader," *Crisis*, XXIX (December, 1924), 81.

[3]Charles M. Puckette, "On a South Carolina Plantation," *The Saturday Review of Literature*, III (March 19, 1927), 660.

[4]*The Nation*, CXXIV (June 8, 1927), 649.

[5]Robert Herrick, "A Study in Black," *The New Republic*, LVII (December 26, 1928), 172.

[6]Willard Thorp, *American Writing in the Twentieth Century* (Cambridge, 1960), 259.

[7]John M. Bradbury, *Renaissance in the South: A Critical History of the Literature, 1920-1960* (Chapel Hill, 1963), 83.

[8]Herschel Brickell, "A Pagan Heroine," *The Saturday Review of Literature*, V (November 3, 1928), 318.

[9]Herrick, *loc. cit.*

[10]Ben Wasson, *Outlook and Independent*, CL (November 21, 1928), 1212.

[11]Joseph Warren Beach, *The Twentieth Century Novel* (New York, 1932), 232.

[12]Bradbury, pp. 151, 152.

[13]Bradbury, p. 87.

[14]Ralph Ellison, "That Same Pain, That Same Pleasure: An Interview," *Shadow and Act* (New York, 1964), 23.

[15]James Baldwin, "Everybody's Protest Novel," *Partisan Review*, XVI (Spring, 1949), 585.

[16]Julia Peterkin, "One Southern View-point," *North American Review*, CCXLIV (December, 1937), 397-398.

Julia Peterkin's *Green Thursday*

by

Noel Polk

Over the decade or so of my relationship with South
Carolina and South Carolinians I've managed to get a lot
of mileage out of the fact that I'm a native Mississippian. I've seldom missed an opportunity, I believe
Professor Mcriwether will verify, to call attention to the
rich literary heritage of my own state, and to look from a
very high vantage point straight down my nose upon South
Carolina's literary fulminations. Come I now to confess
I've been wrong: the light is beginning to dawn. Maybe I
don't need to confess to *this* audience that the light
first showed itself when I finally got around to *reading*
some South Carolina writers. This conference has forced
that light to grow steadily brighter---and it may well be
that I stand, right now, as the *only* Mississippian to have
seen that light---or at least to have admitted it---at
least in public. I don't mean that I shall discontinue
sighting along my Mississippi nose at South Carolina
literature---only that I will now have to raise it parallel with the floor, and so look *across* it, rather than
down.

Compared to the other writers mentioned here today
and yesterday, Julia Peterkin has been rather extensively
studied---at least two dissertations have been written on
her in the past ten years,[1] and in 1970 the University of
South Carolina Press published a collection of her short
stories.[2] Even so, she has not received the treatment she
deserves, and her neglect over the past forty years is in

177

stark contrast to her lionization by the literary community and her notoriety in her own native South Carolina
during the relatively few years of her career. Mrs.
Peterkin is easily the most prominent of the women writers
of South Carolina, at least in the public eye, by virtue
of the fact that she alone among South Carolina writers
has received a Pulitzer Prize---whatever value you might
ascribe to that---and by the fact that she, a Southern
lady, wrote starkly realistic stories about Negro life,
stories dealing straightforwardly with, to put it bluntly,
sex and violence. This pleases me very much, since as a
card-carrying student of Southern literature, Sex and
Violence are naturally my primary interests. I've even
found some traces of the Gothic in her work: not many it
is true, but enough to prove beyond any shadow of doubt
that she was indeed a Southern Writer.

Mrs. Peterkin was a shrewd, witty, fiery, and gentle
and compassionate woman; but she was also supremely com-
petent---she had to be in order to run a plantation the
size of Lang Syne---toughminded and hardnosed and realistic about people and money and above all about her art:
she was dead serious about her writing. To be sure, her
talent was limited when weighed in the scales of a Eudora
Welty, but it was genuine, and in the course of a brief
career she published five books,[3] two of which, *Scarlet
Sister Mary* and *Green Thursday*, I do not hesitate to call
minor miracles of fiction. And sometimes I'm not so sure
that the adjective "minor" applies: these two books certainly are, in my opinion, much better than most of the
books which have received the blessings, and the spilled
ink, of the academic literary establishment; I certainly
concur with Professor Landess that she is superior to
Flannery O'Connor. And so I believe her to be a writer
of national consequence, and not just of regional interest.

In particular this morning I would like to talk about
Mrs. Peterkin's first book, *Green Thursday*, which was published by Alfred A. Knopf in 1924, though much of the
material for it had been written earlier in the decade.
Green Thursday is a collection of twelve related short
stories depicting the life of Killdee Pinesett and his
family over a period of an indeterminate number of years,
probably close to a decade. The resulting narrative has
the cumulative effect of a novel, but the book is clearly,
it seems to me, not a novel but a collection of stories

built around a single major character, each of which deve-
lops the story line, and each of which adds both meaning
and resonance to the others. Historically, this makes
Green Thursday a descendant of Sherwood Anderson's
Winesburg, Ohio, published in 1918, and an ancestor of
Hemingway's *In Our Time* in 1925 and Eudora Welty's *The
Golden Apples* in 1949.

   Green Thursday, however, is very much unlike *In Our
Time*, and for reasons which may very well point to a real
artistic independence even in this, her first book. It
is, I think, a workable generalization that the dominating
forces in American literature of the first half of the
century, and particularly in the 1920's, were World War I
and the poetry of T. S. Eliot. Indeed, American literature of the period was overwhelmed by the devastation
caused by the War, and it is filled with psychically and
physically crippled ex-soldiers trying to cope with a
wasteland of a world in which, after the War, neither
life nor death have meaning. Perhaps it is not too much
to suggest that the archetypal character in the years
following the War was J. Alfred Prufrock---a weak, inde-
cisive man who, if not in fact sexually incapable, like
Hemingway's Jake Barnes, *is* sexually very passive, a
frustrated man afraid of confronting the world's overwhelming questions, afraid of asserting himself against
the forces of the world which are aggressively inimical
to man---a man, in short, afraid of life: a man who
retreats from human relationships of any kind in order,
like Hemingway's Nick Adams, to escape consequences.

   Contraposed to this is *Green Thursday*, which depicts
not a Waste Land, but a fertile farming land. Indeed, it
is the very over-fecundity of the land, the fast-growing
weeds, which forces Killdee to make the mistake of plowing
on Green Thursday (Ascension Day) in order to save his
crop, and thus precipitate, thematically, the series of
disasters which form the narrative line of the book.
Killdee is not even remotely related to Prufrock, except
by contrast; he is very virile, tough, assertive, unafraid
of anything, including God. He is a man of tremendous
physical and spiritual strength, dedicated completely to
his family, and capable of any sacrifice for their well-
being. He is not afraid to act, not afraid to gamble, and
he does so willingly, consciously acknowledging to himself
and to the world that he is ready to bear the consequences
of his gamble, win or lose. In the title story, for

example, he plows on Ascension Day, Green Thursday, deliberately risking the wrath of God in order to gain a necessary day in his plowing; and in "Teaching Jim," one of the
most moving stories in the book, he consciously betrays
his infant son's love and complete trust by putting a hot
coal in his hand, gambling that by doing so Jim will learn
a lesson necessary to his survival, that he shouldn't play
near the fire. It is a hard lesson; and on no one is it
harder than on Killdee.

I do not mean that Mrs. Peterkin had missed World
War I, or that she had not read T. S. Eliot. Nor do I
mean that Killdee has no frustration, that he is free from
fear and anxiety, or that he does not agonize over his
problems, over his failures: of course he does. But he
doesn't let his fear and anxiety incapacitate him, he
doesn't let them keep him from confronting the world on
its own terms, from asserting his own spiritual and physical toughness against anything the world can dish out.
He does not, in short, like Prufrock, let his fears of
life keep him from living. Mrs. Peterkin's world, then,
is more classical than modern, and *Green Thursday* has more
in common with classical tragedy than with modern literature. Hers is a world, simply and grandly, in which life
and death *do* have meaning, in which strong men are brought
low by choices deliberately and consciously made. Her
relatively isolated plantation community, I would suggest,
is not so much a different world she is looking at as it
is a different way of looking at the same modern world;
and it is a vision which insists that impotence and
despair are not the only human problems.

I realize the risk I'm taking by talking about manhood and masculinity at this conference---but that, I
submit, is what *Green Thursday* is about.

Green Thursday begins with the story entitled
"Ashes," which serves as a prologue. It is only indirectly related to the main plot; Killdee and Rose, his wife,
are mentioned only in passing. In this story Maum Hannah,
an aged Negro grande dame, finds herself coolly notified
one morning that she will have to vacate the cabin in
which she has lived her entire life---told this by a po
buckra (her phrase) who has just bought the land on which
her cabin sits, and on which he builds a "big house."
Maum literally has no place to go. Survival at stake,
she prays for a sign from heaven, which comes in the form

of ashes spilled from her pipe. Like Killdee throughout
the book, she acts immediately: she turns arsonist, burns
the newly-built mansion to the ground. Also like Killdee,
she is ready to pay the consequences for her act, and so
walks into town, to confess everything to the sheriff.
The sheriff, however, is understanding and sympathetic.
He feeds her, then drives her home. A couple of inquiries
determine that the new house was completely covered by
insurance, that no one was injured, that no one suspects
foul play, that the family has decided the ground is
cursed and so will not try to build again. The kind-
hearted sheriff admonishes Maum Hannah to silence, and
sends her back to her own cabin: this is, he obviously
assumes, a more humane alternative than sending her to
jail.

It is a rather frail story, the weakest in the book,
which is more successful in its characterization than in
its plot. But it does accomplish two things. It removes
from the book any racial overtones: by acknowledging here
at the beginning the fact that there are both good and bad
white people in the outside world, Mrs. Peterkin simply
dismisses the problem of racial conflict and moves directly
to her treatment of the problems of the human heart which,
in this case, happens to beat in a Negro breast. The
second thing "Ashes" does is to establish the pattern,
recurring throughout the other stories in various forms,
of the willing acceptance of the consequences of a deliberate act. Maum Hannah's consequences, however, are far
happier than Killdee's are to be.

The title story, following "Ashes," introduces Killdee
and his wife Rose, the principal characters, between whom
the central human conflict in the book will develop: Rose,
a church member, is worried because Killdee, a Sinner, is
flouting God by plowing on Green Thursday, the day Jesus
went back to God. Killdee thinks it necessary, but is
somewhat anxious and not at all certain much good can come
of it: "All [his] life he had heard that to stir the earth
on Green Thursday was a deadly sin. Fields plowed or even
hoed to-day would be struck by lightning and killed so
they couldn't bear life again. God would send fire down
from heaven to punish men who didn't respect this day.
Yet here he and Mike [the mule] were plowing. Risking the
wrath of the great I-Am" (pp. 28-29). This leads him into
a meditation over his status as a Sinner, in terms which
state directly some of his deepest convictions about

himself as a man and about his relationship with the community and with God. It is, therefore, an articulation of
one of the book's central themes:

> Preachers say sinners are like goats and Christians
> are like sheep. He'd a lot rather be a goat than
> a sheep. Goats have sense.
>   One Bill yonder went home to sleep with the
> other goats at night. He was afraid of the dark.
> But in the daytime he ran around by himself and
> went where he liked and ate what he pleased and
> had a good time. He was too smart to huddle
> with others of his kind. Bill was a sinner
> maybe, but he was better off than the foolish,
> scary sheep that stayed in a flock all the time....
> He was no poor fool of a sheep. No. He was a
> man. He'd plow to-day and not be afraid. If
> God was, He was fair. Kind. God would like a
> man better if He saw him doing his best. [pp.
> 31-32, 34]

Killdee has much occasion later to question God's fairness.

From this point in the story the action moves swiftly
and mercilessly: in the afternoon while Killdee is nursing
old Mike through a severe case of the colic, a terrible
thunderstorm comes up, a large and powerful electric storm
that frightens even Killdee, who nevertheless continues
his vigil with the ailing Mike. The noise of the storm is
suddenly pierced by a scream; Rose runs out of the cabin
holding Baby Rose, their infant daughter, who has just
been fatally burned. Killdee takes the baby from her and
runs to Maum Hannah's house in the rain. In his agony he
believes this to be the divine punishment he feared. But
Mrs. Peterkin leaves unanswered the question of whether it
is in fact God's punishment, and substitutes an ambiguity
which adds complexities to the relationship between Rose
and Killdee, and intensifies the conflict between Killdee
and God, whom Christians claim to be merciful and just.

After the baby dies, Rose is quite understandably
hysterical, and she reproaches God for the death: "God was
hard. Unfair. Killdee had done wrong. He had stirred
the earth on a holy day. He should suffer. Not her.
Not her child" (p. 45). Killdee of course agrees that it
is unfair of God, but it is not quite that simple. For it
is soon discovered that Rose doesn't actually know how the

baby caught fire, whether it was because she was playing
in the fireplace or because she was struck by lightning;
she doesn't know because she, the Christian, professing to
have faith in God's promise to protect his children, had
been so frightened of the storm that she had gotten in the
bed and covered her eyes in order not to see the lightning.
And in doing this she had irresponsibly left Baby Rose
crawling around on the floor, completely unwatched. Killdee thus blames Rose for the disaster, but he is sure that
God's hand is in it.

> Keen, blasting grief wrung him to the core.
> Resentment heated his blood like a fever. Burnt
> the marrow in his skull. Emboldened him. With
> set lips and rigid muscles, he glared at the
> overhead darkness. He was helpless. Yes. He
> had to take whatever came. There was nothing
> else to do. Nothing! He could fight men. Settle
> with them. But God---Ha!---that was a different
> matter. God kept out of reach. Yes. He did his
> worst. He cut men at the very roots. Blighted
> them. He burned tender girl-children. And nobody
> could ever get even with Him. Up there in the
> sky, He had the whole world in His coldblooded
> reach. [p. 47]

This is a powerful passage, beautifully articulated by
Mrs. Peterkin, which clearly defines Killdee's attitude
toward himself and God, and points the direction which his
struggle with life is to take: the distance between himself and God is firmly established, and the wedge between
himself and his wife is pushed deeper and more firmly in.
The story ends with the birth of Jim, emphasizing the
cyclical nature of life, but it is a birth heavily over-
shadowed by Baby Rose's death: the bitter final image in
the story is that of Killdee's eyes, "fixed on a small
cloth doll that had fallen out of its cigar-box wagon and
that lay face down on the floor" (p. 49).

The next four stories shift away from Killdee and
focus primarily upon Rose and her relationships within and
among the church members. "Missie," the first of the four,
introduces the young girl Missie and her flea-ridden dog
Son. Missie is a waif who appears at Rose's door one
afternoon, and whom Killdee and Rose adopt---a practice
which seems to have been common among Mrs. Peterkin's
Negroes, at least in her fiction. Missie and Killdee

discover an immediate and spontaneous rapport with each
other which even if it is not at this point specifically
sexual, is at least potentially so; Rose, at any rate,
senses their attraction, and views Missie, perhaps not
even consciously yet, as a potential rival for Killdee's
affection. Throughout the book the relationship between
Killdee and Missie steadily grows, while that between
Killdee and Rose just as steadily deteriorates.

    In "Meeting" and "Mount Pleasant" Rose takes Missie
to religious services, where she is introduced to the
wonders and terrors of God at the same time that Rose is
introduced to the Reverend Felder, a visiting preacher who
is ultimately to be the catalyst of the book's final
action. Missie sees Reverend Felder as a "finelooking"
man, but feels he suffers in comparison with Killdee;
Rose feels it is Killdee who suffers. Here also Missie
begins to be aware of the differences between Rose and
Killdee---Killdee, the sinner, who will burn in hell (so
she learns at church and from Rose), is so much more
gentle and kind and loving than the Christian Rose, who
frequently beats her, upon the slightest provocation.
"What a strange man God must be!" she concludes (p. 93).
In "Finding Peace," the next story in this quartet, Missie
breaks with Rose and sides with Killdee in the matter of
religion. The action of the story is simple: Missie,
following the tradition of her people, goes seeking for
a vision which will announce to her and which will con-
vince the church elders that she has received salvation.
When she begins to tell Maum Hannah about her vision, however, she realizes that the face of the kindly man in her
vision who tells her that her sins are forgiven is that of
Killdee, a sinner. She knows that if she tells this to
the deacons they will say her vision was from Satan and
not from God, and so she will be denied entrance into the
Christian community. With Killdee's approval, then, she
decides against further seeking: "After all, what difference did it make if she found peace or not? Killdee was
a sinner. She'd just stay a sinner with him. Sinners
seemed better than Christians, anyway...." (p. 101).

    The next three stories turn the focus back to Killdee
and his trials. In the brilliant "The Red Rooster," a
hungry rooster, mistaking it for a seed, pecks out the eye
of Killdee's and Rose's newest baby girl. In "Teaching
Jim," as I've already said, Killdee deliberately causes
his son a lot of pain, in order to teach him how to avoid

a lot more pain. And, finally, in "Catfish" Killdee runs
afoul of his own ambition: having heard that fish-scrap
makes excellent fertilizer, he mistakenly concludes that
therefore whole fish must be at least as good or better;
so he fertilizes with fresh-caught, whole fish. The dogs,
of course, dig them up, and in doing so completely destroy
his crop. Rose tries to console him with religion, but
Killdee is merely confirmed in his conviction that God is
unfair:

> Killdee raised his weary eyes to her face.
> A sneering smile came to his lips. His bared
> teeth gleamed in a savage way that made her
> shiver. He laughed boisterously.
> "Rose all de time talk de same fool way.
> Trus' who?"
> He laughed again. "Who?" he repeated,
> mirthlessly. [pp. 130-131]

With "Son" the book begins to move swiftly and
directly toward its climax, and the sexual element, heretofore only implied, is made specific. "Son" opens when
Killdee is awakened by the dog's anguished scratching of
his fleas. He pities the poor dog his miseries, but contends that what he needs in the face of this kind of
problem is self-control:

> Fleas had to be. Dogs always had them.
> Son ought to know that and keep quiet. He
> kept himself from sleeping with all this
> uneasy, impatient fidgeting. Son ought to
> learn to rule himself. To hold steady.
> [p. 132]

The fleas, of course, very soon become a metaphor for Son's
(and Killdee's) sexual impulses---it is, as it were, an
itch he must keep scratching---and Killdee contemplates
the force, the urge, that drives Son to search far and
wide, often at his peril, for female companionship: his
thoughts force him to confront, once again, the old Primal
Injustice at the root of things:

> Son couldn't help wanting to go courting last
> night. Something inside him compelled him.
> Drove him. Son wasn't to blame.
> Son wasn't to blame that he wan't strong
> enough to fight other dogs away, without getting

himself beat almost to death.
        Who was to blame? What? Why couldn't
things be fair to dogs?---And to men---and
women? [pp. 136-137]

Killdee's thoughts turn from this directly to Missie,
and he realizes that that "something" which compels Son is
also urging him: his attraction to, his affection for,
Missie is finally made explicitly sexual. But it is a
painful thing for him to admit, because he can envision a
variety of consequences. Killdee knows that his own
sexual drive is every bit as strong as Son's; but he also
knows that he is a man and not an animal, a man with a
strong will, and that, unlike Son, he will not be ruled
by his urges: he will learn to rule himself, to hold
steady, to let the fleas be: "[Missie] was so tender--so
trustful. Could he ruin her because she was what he loved
best? Love was a disease....that would change her clean
freshness to shame" (p. 137).

The longest and most complex story in *Green Thursday*
is "A Sunday," which on a literal level is about Killdee's
handling of a situation caused by his wife's infidelity.
On a more complex level it is about how Killdee learns to
take the advice he had offered Son, to rule himself, to
"hold steady." When he is confronted with Rose's unfaith-
fulness with Reverend Felder, it is not the infidelity
itself which engulfs him---their differences are large
enough by now that he is probably indifferent to her per-
sonally. He does care, however, a great deal about the
fact that she now represents a chink in his social armor,
and that, according to his informant, he is being laughed
at. He is outraged; but he is also humiliated, and he
falls into the kind of despair that only a proud man can
know. He goes to see Daddy Cudjoe, an old conjure doctor,
who makes him see that his troubles are caused by fear:
"Mebbe you's right, Daddy," Killdee admits. "Mebbe I's
'f'aid. Mebbe I's 'f'aid o' dem niggers laughin'"
(p. 163). Daddy Cudjoe reminds him what he has known all
along about the difference between sheep and goats:
"Lemme tell you dis one t'ing befo' you go. Dese preacher,
dese member, all dese Christian, dey is 'f'aid, too! You
'member dat! You mus'n' be 'f'aid dem! Not no mo'"
(p. 163).

This is well and good. Killdee's self-confidence is
restored. But the issue continues to press itself upon

him when he learns that Rose's infidelity is to be made
public, is to be discussed in church the following Sunday
by the deacons, who will probably turn out from the church
both Rose and Felder. With great deliberation and dignity
he rises on Sunday morning, bathes, puts on the best
clothes he has, and goes to church for the first time in
years. The ensuing scene is perhaps the finest in the
entire book: Killdee walks into the church building, to
the great consternation of all the members, and stands

> before them with a cool smile on his face. His
> words were cool. Quiet. He did not lift his
> voice one bit.
>
> "I reckon you-all is surprise' to see me
> heah to-day," he said pleasantly, looking at
> each deacon, then at the congregation. Sheep.
> Scary sheep all running together. Flustered
> now. Addled. Andrew cleared his throat. The
> other deacons moved uncomfortably in their
> chairs. None of them seemed ready to answer,
> although Killdee gave them opportunity.
>
> "I ain' gwine tek up much o' you' time.
> I got to hurry on back home, bein's my wife
> don' feel so well to-day."
>
> He stepped forward a little and put his
> hand on the Bible. Some of the congregation
> took in sharp breaths. What did he mean?
> Putting his hand on the Word of God like that!
> Killdee was a good enough man, but everybody
> knew he was a sinner. He didn't pretend to be
> anything else. Then why did he come here? It
> was too much. Too brazen. The deacons ought
> to make him get down. A wonder God didn't
> strike him dead for blasphemy!
>
> The deacons themselves seemed confounded.
> They sat staring. Dumb. Open-mouthed.
>
> Killdee's voice was a little tense when
> he began, but his words soon flowed distinctly.
> They were emphatic. Explicit, too. But quiet.
>
> "I know why yinner come to chu'ch to-day,"
> he said. "I know all yinner been talkin'. You
> been talkin' 'bout Rose. My wife. I ain' fool
> ez I look," he added.
>
> A smile broke over his face as he looked
> at the congregation. His eyes twinkled at the
> deacons. They seemed, somehow, bewildered.
> Killdee continued:

"I come heah fo' say des' one t'ing. One!
Yinner listen good. I ain' gwine say em but one
time. You listen. It's dis---"
    Killdee laid his hand right on the Bible.
It was as if he swore to something. He leaned
forward. His words snipped off short. His
lips flored and bared his strong teeth.
    "De fus' nigger eber call my wife name een
dis chu'ch is got to deal wid me! Me! Killdee
Pinesett! Da's all."
    Killdee took his hand off the Bible. He
smiled pleasantly at them. Surprise numbed
the tense faces. Taut muscles held still.
    "I'll say good day to yinner now. I see
you-all done heah me good." [pp. 167-169]

The result, of course, is that Killdee wins the day. The
deacons turn Reverend Felder out, but nobody calls Rose's
name.

Having effectively dealt with the public aspects of
the situation, Killdee then proceeds to deal just as
efficiently with the private aspects. He locates Felder,
the violator of his home, and castrates him--an act both
vengeful and appropriately symbolic. Mrs. Peterkin is
delicate and indirect about this, however; in true Greek
fashion the violence takes place off stage, and we simply
extrapolate the facts from the subtle and subdued final
paragraph of the story, in which she writes that "news
came that the preacher was dead. Dead with lockjaw. It
was whispered that the lockjaw was caused by a wound. A
strange wound. Somewhere in his leg. But nobody ever said
how he got it" (p. 169).

"A Sunday" is, I suggest, a magnificent short story,
in which Killdee moves by an act of his own tremendous will
from courage's nadir to its apex. But the events of "A
Sunday," being the culmination, as they are, of years of
increasing dissatisfaction with Rose, do take their toll
on him, and in "Plum Blossoms," the final story of the
collection, Killdee makes the break with Rose when he
sides with Missie in an argument the two women are having.
The open conflict, heretofore only covert, forces him to
choose between them; and, as in all instances throughout
the book, he summons his courage and chooses. The book
ends with his decision, then, to forsake the wife and
family he has worked so hard for, been so dedicated to.

It is not, however, an easy decision to make, and, thematically, at any rate, the complicating factor is that
Killdee is not, like Son, driven by an uncontrollable rut:
he has proven, in "A Sunday," that he is in control of
himself. His is a conscious, deliberate, and premeditated
<u>choice</u> to leave Rose, a choice based upon his weighing of
all the factors: "I'm gwine take one joy whilst I kin" he
says, as the book ends (p. 188).

　　Thus *Green Thursday* closes as it opened, with a human
being in a moral crisis which demands of him a choice
between one of two or more equally difficult alternatives.
And there is no reason to believe that the consequences of
<u>this</u> decision will be any happier than any of his others;
indeed, the portents are ominous: even Killdee recognizes,
in his deliberations, that "Joy can' las' always needer"
(p. 188). But it is to Killdee the measure of his manhood,
of his freedom, to be able to make that choice. He may be
somewhat bloody and slightly bowed by his struggles with
God and Rose and the land over the last decade, but he is
still strong and determined, unwilling to be cowed by
forces he can't control, even if he knows that he can't
beat them. He goes out as he came in, with his eyes wide
open, making his own way.

　　Green Thursday is a much more complex book, a book
much more filled with subtlety and nuance, fine details
of description and characterization, than I've been able
to suggest in this rather tedious plot summary. But I
hope I have been able to convey at least some of the
book's riches. My own opinion is that *Green Thursday* is
a very good book indeed, a masterpiece, in fact, which
gives pleasure in practically every way a work of art can
give pleasure. And it is difficult to overemphasize the
masterful creation of Killdee Pinesett, who has to be one
of the most moving, one of the most admirable, characters
in modern fiction. In 1924 Mrs. Peterkin wrote to H. L.
Mencken that she was finally ready to send the typescript
of *Green Thursday* to him: "I love my black people in it,"
she wrote. "In Killdee I did a better job than God-
Almighty does often. He's a peach of a fellow, I think."
I think so too.

Notes

[1]Louis Henry, "Julia Peterkin: A Biographical and Critical Study," Florida State University, 1965; and Thomas H. Landess, "Julia Peterkin: A Critical Study," University of South Carolina, 1972.

[2]*The Collected Short Stories of Julia Peterkin*, ed. Frank Durham. Columbia: University of South Carolina Press, 1970.

[3]*Green Thursday* (New York: Alfred A. Knopf, 1924); *Black April* (Indianapolis: Bobbs-Merrill, 1927); *Scarlet Sister Mary* (Indianapolis: Bobbs-Merrill, 1928); *Bright Skin* (Indianapolis: Bobbs-Merrill, 1932); *Roll, Jordan, Roll* (New York: Robert Ballou, 1933). Also issued separately was a short piece, *A Plantation Christmas* (Boston: Houghton Mifflin, 1934).

Session IV: Discussion

MR. RICHARDS: How many of Mrs. Peterkin's novels are currently in print?

MR. POLK: The Berg Press in Dunwoody, Georgia, has recently reissued them. I don't know whether they are still in print.

MR. INABINETT: That situation certainly bears out Professor Landess's judgment of contemporary critics. Of the hundreds of titles that have been reprinted in the name of black history, Julia Peterkin's works are conspicuously absent.

MR. POLK: And also, it seems paradoxical that here you've got in one writer somebody who would fit right in the current emphases on black and feminist studies.

MR. INABINETT: This Georgia firm is the only publisher that has shown any interest in Mrs. Peterkin's works, and their edition has certainly not been widely advertised or sold.

MRS. CHILDS: I had some idea that she grew up at Brookgreen, near Georgetown, and then her father moved. He was manager for the people who owned Brookgreen, I think, and the Negroes that she knew really well were those of Georgetown County, of old, more than those she knew later on when she lived in the upcountry.

MRS. OLIPHANT: She was born in Laurens and then moved to the little town of Summerton. I think her house is still standing there. I know my brother-in-law was courting her as a young girl there in Summerton. I know that much. I wonder if anybody knows who was in the group, that met in the back of Mr. Gittman's book store, Mr. Gittman being the leader, that included Julia Peterkin. Dr. James W. Babcock was a member. And I think Alex Salley belonged to it. He lived nearby, was born in St. Matthews. But, of course, she was an upcountry girl, that moved into the middle country, then moved farther down on to the plantation. That's interesting to me, that she had the whole South Carolina experience.

MR. POLK: They maintained a house at Murrell's Inlet for most of her adult life.   I didn't know about the Summerton.

MRS. OLIPHANT: Whether that house is still standing or not, I don't know.   It would be nice to mark it if it is.   I'll ask about that.   But I wish we could remember who belonged to that group in Columbia.   It met regularly, in Mr. Gittman's little office.   He was the leader of the group and a great admirer of Julia Peterkin.

MR. INABINETT: It was called the Coffee Club, wasn't it?

MRS. OLIPHANT: I knew her just one weekend, and that was at a conference at Coker College, where she spoke and where there was a series of parties, and I remember that scintillating wit, bright, charming.

UNIDENTIFIED SPEAKER: Why is it that she stopped writing after 1933?

MR. POLK: Your guess is as good as mine.   As I said, there's a great deal of repetition of material, and it may simply be that she was realistic enough to recognize that she had done what she could do, and stopped. But------

MISS COKER: The reason she stopped was on account of family tragedies.   And I would also like to reply to Mrs. Oliphant's remark about her Coker College appearance.   She had been asked to speak there the year before, and we all gathered in the auditorium and Julia never appeared.   And then a week later Julia came in at 11 o'clock.   She had gotten her dates mixed up.

What Is The Chesnut Diary?

by

C. Vann Woodward

Among the surviving papers of Mary Boykin Chesnut, the greater part of which are now fortunately in the care of the South Caroliniana Library, are numerous manuscripts that might answer to the description, "diary." Included in this loose category are some 5,300 manuscript pages amounting to an estimated 760,000 words. Two editions, both highly selective, have already been published, each under the title "A Diary from Dixie." There is no evidence that Mrs. Chesnut herself ever used that title. Indeed she preferred to call what she wrote a "journal," or "notes," rather than a "diary." The first of the two editions, that published in 1905,[1] contained approximately 141,000 words; the second, published in 1949,[2] contained some 246,000 words. While each of the published editions contains but a fraction of the 760,000 words in the manuscripts, no editor could reasonably be expected to publish them all. A brief description of what I shall call "the journal manuscripts" will indicate some of the reasons.

For most of the more than four years covered by the journals, February, 1861, to July, 1865, there exist more than one manuscript version. For nearly all the period covered, except the months from August, 1862, to the end of 1863, there are at least two versions; for six months of 1861 and more than three months in the period between January 1, 1864, and February 25, 1865, there are at least three versions; for five months of 1861 and two weeks of January, 1864, there are four versions, and for twelve days of January, 1864, there are five versions. While none of these versions is the same as any of the others, there is of course a great deal of repetition.

The solution of the previous editors was to rely almost entirely on what I call Version III. This is the longest and nearest complete version of the journals. Internal evidence indicates that Version III was all written late in the author's life, that at least a fourth and probably much more was written after 1881, and that she was still working on this version near the time of her death in 1886. In writing all this long version of 2,500 pages, save for the part covering the period from August, 1862, to the end of 1863, she appears to have had before her some earlier version of the journal. The most interesting and revealing of these is what I call Version I, which consists of those parts of the journal manuscripts believed to be the original version actually written on or near the dates of the entries made. The part of Version I that survives consists of more than a thousand pages, about 146,000 words, covering the period from February 18 to December 6, 1861, September 21 to December 8, 1864, February 4 to 25, 1865, and May 7 to June 26, 1865. There is reason to believe that more of the original journal once existed and may still exist, but this is all that has been recovered.[3]

Version II is of a very different character and purpose. Consisting of some 1,700 pages written in pencil on loose sheets or scratch pads, it is in effect a rough draft of large parts of Version III. The great bulk of this version, some 1200 pages covering January 1, 1864, to April 15, 1865, is easily dated since the scratch pads bear the printed copyright date 1881 on the covers. It contains some details and identifications not in Version III, but the latter is essentially an elaboration and polishing of the rough draft and, apart from adding to and rounding out abbreviations in the draft, rarely departs in any important way from it. It is, of course, my assumption that at least this part of Version III was written after Version II. Versions IV and V, less than 43,000 words, are more polished versions of entries from March to August, 1861, and twelve days in January, 1864.

The decision of previous editors to confine their work to Version III as the basic text greatly simplified their task but did not define the extent of their selectivity. The earlier of the two editions printed little more than a third of that version. The second editor, who says in his

Introduction that by "various eliminations" the "Diary" had
been "reduced in length approximately one fourth," actually
printed little more than a half. The principles governing
previous editors in their choice of what to print may only
be surmised. Some light is shed on the first edition by a
letter from the principal editor to a publisher. "There is
so much however that is personal in the journal that I
could not allow it to go into any one's hands but my own
and it will be entirely re-written. This will involve a
great deal of labor.... Of course I am quite ready to ...
omit parts of the MS [at] your inspection if you do
desire."[4] The extent of the rewriting undertaken is only
partially suggested by comparison of her transcription that
immediately follows the facsimile of a page of the manuscript reproduced in her own edition.[5] The editor of the
second edition also takes extensive liberties of rewriting
and deleting. In neither edition are the editorial changes
or omissions indicated in the text.

In undertaking a third edition of the journals, my
first impulse was to use Version I, the original journal,
as the basic text, supplementing it with later versions
only in periods not covered by the original. There was
much to be said in favor of this plan from the historian's
point of view. After all, the original and immediate reaction is what the historian values, impressions uninflu-
enced by hindsight or by altered points of view, and changing politics, and unclouded by fading memory. Two decades
or more had elapsed between the original and the writing of
Version III. Furthermore, the original version was
generally more candid, personal, spicy, and fresh. The
sounds and smells and blood and tears pour out of its pages
with the shock of immediate experience. It is perfectly
evident from the content that much of the original was intended for no eyes but her own, not even those of her
husband. Extensive passages have been erased, scratched
out, or cut out either by the author or someone else.
Those cut out are, of course, beyond recovery, but much of
the scratched out parts and virtually all of the erasures
have been recovered by one means or another. Mrs. Chesnut
frequently refers to friends who read parts of her journal
and once to a breach of security by her maid that placed
the manuscript in unfriendly hands. But all these references save the last are found in later versions, not in the
original. The ongoing original was normally kept under
lock and key.

The initial decision for Version I as the basic text, however, was soon abandoned. The change was largely influenced by a growing respect for Mrs. Chesnut as editor of her own writing. Self-critical and intelligent in her perception of what was trivial or ephemeral, she proved sound in most of her choices for deletion and preservation of the original, and what she added was usually worth preserving. As a substantial check on the reliability of her transcriptions and elaborations in Versions II and III, there were available large parts of Version I for much of the whole. The comparison was generally reassuring about the author's integrity and trustworthiness. She did, however, make many deletions, additions, and changes---sometimes changes in her original meaning.

In view of these estimates and circumstances, I returned to Version III as the basic text, but with no commitment or sense of obligation to confine the edition to it. Whatever could be identified as part of the journal manuscripts in whatever version, would be regarded as subject to editorial use or inclusion. If another version were clearer, better written, or more informative than its counterpart in Version III, it would be substituted for that part. If something were omitted that seems significant or interesting it would be inserted. If missing identifications or illuminating details were discovered in other versions, they would be supplied. If two accounts of the same event were contradictory or irreconcilable, they would be placed in parallel columns. In all such departures from Version III, the source of the variation would be noted.[6]

The expansion of editorial responsibility to embrace the entire corpus of the journal manuscripts complicated the editor's task at the same time it enhanced the intellectual rewards and fascinations of the enterprise. New dimensions and meanings were thereby added to the conventional day-to-day diary entries which Mary Chesnut eventually adopted or converted into a genre of her own, a kind of art form to embody her experience of the greatest historical drama of her time---her involvement in it, her perception of it, her reflections on its meaning, its tragedy, and its horror. This work was based in considerable part on what might legitimately be called a diary, but it became more and less than that. Less in so far as it abandoned the Latin meaning of *diarium*, with its implied denial of knowledge of the future. It became more in so

far as she later fleshed out meaning and implication of
event and tapped memory for the maze of interconnection
between events. It became a creative literary exercise
when she consciously or unconsciously used symbol and myth
to convey her feeling and perception of experience and more
or less consciously employed experience and reality as
metaphor to embody myth and convey meaning. To discover
how literal diary evolved into literary product through the
passing of time, the tapping of memory, and conscious revision is one of the rewards of the enlarged editorial
concept.

     As pure diarist Mary Chesnut shared the ambiguity of
motive characteristic of the classic diaries of our literature. The purposes and the intended readers of diarists
always pose questions. The diarist himself, often unclear
or undecided about his own intentions and motives, rarely
gives a clear or consistent answer and often evades the
question. Mary Chesnut herself gave contradictory answers.
"I write daily for my own distraction," she once declared,
and then in the next sentences professed a public purpose:
that what she wrote "may some future day afford dates,
facts, and prove useful to more important people than I
am."[7] At one point she says that her dear and much admired
friend John S. Preston "urged me to begin this journal and
keep it regularly."[8] About secrecy and security she was
equally inconsistent in what she said. "Everybody reads my
journal," she once wrote; and again, "everybody reads my
journal as it lies on the table in my room," but that was
in Version III,[9] and in Version II, the rough draft of the
same passage, she writes, "I usually lock up my book as
soon as I cease to write."[10] And then, slipping into the
past tense that would seem to indicate a reference to the
original diary, she adds that, "I intended in my frantic
candor that no eye save mine should rest upon this page."[11]

     The range and degree of candor she often permits her-
self in Version III, presumably revised for wider reading,
is rather remarkable. There, she says, her rule was, "The
things I cannot tell exactly as they are I do not intend
to tell at all."[12] Later she adds, "I do not wish to do
any harm, or to hurt anyone. If any scandalous stories
creep in, they are easily burned. It is hard, in such a
hurry as things are in, to separate wheat from chaff."[13]
The separation, in so far as it was made, presumably came
with the cutting out of parts of numerous pages of Version
III. In Version I many passages, as mentioned earlier,

have been erased, and from the evidence recovered from
these erasures as well as from numerous pages untouched by
eraser, it is quite obvious that the author had no intention of passing that version around. Her frankness, her
self-revealing confessions, and her ruthless ventures in
self-analysis are enough to preclude that possibility, not
to mention her frankness about her husband and her relations with him, and about her relatives, her friends, and
her politics.

For unintentional inaccuracies she had no apologies.
"Now remember," she says, "I write down all I hear, and the
next day if I hear that it is not so, then I write down the
contradiction too."[14] And at another time: "'Why do you
write in your diary at all,' someone said to me, 'if as you
say, you have to contradict every day what you wrote
yesterday.' Because, I tell the tale as it is told me. I
write current rumor. I do not vouch for anything."[15]
Actually, she was less than fair to herself in her dis-
claimers. She was no idle gossip monger. She normally ex-
hibited an astute skepticism about what she heard,
especially favorable military news and inflated claims and
flattering stories of politicians and military officers
with whom she constantly associated. She recorded, sometimes with gratification, flattery of herself and of her
personal charms. And of that, as pleasing as she often
found it, she was most skeptical of all. She knew very
well that her husband was in a position to dispense favors
and promotions and so were many of her daily associates,
from the President and cabinet members on down. She was
therefore quite apt to ask herself about any flatterer,
what office or promotion he may be seeking at the moment.

Living in daily communion for a long time with such a
vigorous skeptic and such an independent mind, an editor
tends to build up a fund of respect and confidence. She
was unsparing of her own vanity. On the margin of an entry
of March, 1861, in Version I she wrote the date "1875" and
added, "Reading this journal I find I was a vain and
foolish old woman to record silly flattery to myself---in
short an old idiot."[16] Actually she was only thirty-seven
at the time of the recording, and men pursued her regularly
from more elemental motives than quest of court favor.
Being a perfectly normal woman in many ways, she enjoyed
male attention and gallantry at the same time she scoffed
at female vanity and male obtuseness. A resolute feminist
herself, she was nevertheless as ruthless in her gibes at

women as she was at men.

Mary Chesnut did not suffer fools gladly. When she was bored she showed it. "When you are bored by people," her husband admonished, "you are absent minded, sad and weary of aspect, sometimes you groan and often frown and fidget. I wonder you can do so."[17] Others wondered too, particularly women who feared her tongue and avoided her company. She worried about her uncontrollable scorn. "I sometimes fear," she admitted, that "I am so vain, so conceited, think myself so clever and my neighbors such geese that pride comes before a fall. I pray I may be spared."[18] She tried, but in the face of human folly, pretense, pomposity, and charlatanry, the consummate Puck in her got the upper hand. Once she was coerced into evening prayers by a non-conformist chaplain she despised who, she records, "prayed *for me* most palpably. There I was down on my knees, red hot with rage and fury." But, she adds, "Afterwards the fun of it struck me, and I found it difficult to keep from shaking with laughter."[19] It was, in fact, what she called "the fun of it" and the laughter that purged much of the dross of arrogance in her. She said of a sermon she once heard, "It made me cry, and I have no gift that way. Laughing is my forte."[20]

Of faults other than her personal vanity, conceit, and arrogance, she seemed less concerned, if not blindly unconscious. Yet she bristled with class consciousness and family pride and her snobbery could be colossal. She was capable of snubbing the most inoffensive folk, particularly westerners or North Carolinians, who were not, in her habitual phrase, *"comme il faut."* Should such folk aspire to high position, to cabinet rank or a general's stars, or should they or their wives seek to impose their company upon their betters, her snobbery could turn contemptuous and cruel. Her ambition was more covert yet no less colossal. It could, of necessity, be fully expressed only through advancement of her husband, and for him she craved highest advancement, but particularly the mission to England or France. Yet she was frustrated mainly by her husband himself. The complete aristocrat, James Chesnut, as Mrs. Davis told Mary, was "too high South Carolina" to turn a hand in his own behalf. Her frustration was one of the chief causes of her domestic unhappiness. It also condemned her to frequent rustication in Camden and Mulberry, which she could hardly abide, while yearning for the glories of London or Paris or the excitement of Richmond.

In her role as diarist she registered all the usual
complaints and frustrations common to the breed. "The
times when I have most to write I am too busy and too
tired," she confessed, "so the really interesting things
escape, unrecorded."[21] She would neglect her self-imposed
discipline for days and weeks and admonish herself for
negligence. "I must regain the habit of regular writing,"
she scolds, "or my journal will be worthless, for I forget
everything if I neglect it a day. I do not remember
Wednesday at all."[22] She begrudged the time and chafed at
the sacrifice of her leisure for reading which journal
keeping entailed. "I think this journal will be disadvan-
tageous for me, for I spend the time now like a spider
spinning my own entrails instead of reading as my habit was
at all spare moments."[23] By her own account she nevertheless indulged in sprees of omnivorous reading, especially
French fiction. Then she would be swept up in the drama of
events and declare that "no book can interest me ... fiction
is so flat comparatively."[24]

At such times as, in her words, "the scribbling mania
is strong in me,"[25] she would scribble away furiously,
often filling in large gaps in her journal and covering the
events of several days at a sitting. In such circumstances
the dates heading the entries she made are of dubious relevance. It is not always clear, for one thing, whether they
indicate the date of writing or the date of events recorded.
Happening and recording get confused in time, and the sequence of events appears to get jumbled in her memory. In
the parts of Version III for which there are no surviving
counterparts from the original version, especially in the
early months of 1862 and in most of 1864, she writes as if
she had an original version or notes before her. She may
have had for some of it, but there is reason to suspect
that in much of Version III for those periods she was only
pretending she had, and that she was really relying on her
extensive collection of newspaper clippings, many of which
she pasted on verso pages, or drawing upon her memory. Her
writing then becomes a diary *als ob*, a literary form. The
tone and style become less personal and the writing sometimes less vivid.

After August 1, 1862, she abandoned all pretense of
diary form and did not return to it until late in 1863.
What she wrote of the intervening period is frankly a
memoir, an effort as she said, "to fill up the gap from
memory."[26] She explained that, "In Stonemans raid I burned

my journal proper." The raid, which came to the very out-
skirts of Richmond, occurred on May 1-2, 1863. "It was
Molly," her maid, she related, "who constantly told me,
'Missus, listen to the guns. Burn up everything....
they'll put in their newspapers whatever you write here
every day.' The guns did sound very near. And when Mr
C[hesnut] rode up and told me if Mrs Davis left Richmond I
must go with her, I confess I lost my head."[27] Elsewhere
she noted, "I destroyed all my notes and journals, from the
time I arrived at Flat Rock," North Carolina.[28] That would
have been from May, 1863. How much of the journal and notes
she destroyed covering the period prior to and the period
after that date is unclear. In a surviving fragment of her
original diary, on February 23, 1865, she wrote while she
is in flight from Sherman's army, "I have been busily engaged, reading 16 volumes of memoirs of the times I have
written.... still I write on, for if I have to burn, and
here lie my treasures ready for the blazing hearth, still
they have served already to while away for days of agony."
Whether all or part were then committed to the blaze she
does not say, but she adds under the same date, "Today I
was burning papers all day---expecting a Yankee raid." At
any rate, none of the original version between December 6,
1861, and September 21, 1864, appears to have survived,
though she continues to write in diary form for Version III
until the date August 1, 1862.

After that there are no dated entries with one exception (September 20, 1863) until one headed "Bloomsbury,"
one of the Chesnut houses in Camden, September 23, 1863.
This she begins with the statement, "So this is no longer a
journal, but a narrative of all I cannot [sic] bear in mind,
which has occurred since August, 1862." In this memoir
form she continued her narrative with a few dates presumably indicating the date of writing, in the fall of 1863.
At the end of a long entry dated merely October, 1863, she
writes "Dates once more, and not a jumble of scraps and
letters." Not until December, however, do regular dated
entries in apparent diary form pick up again, and that with
no clear demarcation between this form and that of the
memoir narrative.[29] She wrote elsewhere that, "during the
year '63 I burned so much, lost so much, that there are few
scraps left me, and I find it hard to arrange them."[30]
Thereafter until the final entry, July 26, 1865, the diary
form is consistently maintained. For nearly five of those
twenty months there exist original journals, which she undoubtedly used, in composing Version III, and indications

are that there were more that are no longer available.

What happened in the transformation of the original
journal into Version III is difficult to describe and easy
to misrepresent. Much was suppressed, but more was added.
Of that which she suppressed, much was wisely deleted as
trivial or ephemeral or no longer readily intelligible.
Other deletions seem motivated by the desire to spare the
feelings of others. Typically a scandalous anecdote would
be transcribed minus identification of the parties concerned, often without loss to the essential value of the
story. But other suppressions were clearly self-protective
or self-serving. These included embarrassing self-revela-
tions, quarrels with her husband, her thoughts about male
admirers and suitors, and her flirtations, conquests, and
social triumphs, unflattering revelations about and
quarrels with her friends, her family, or her husband's
numerous relatives. Most of these suppressions seem perfectly natural and acceptable.

As an illustration of disparities between Version I
and Version III, Mrs. Chesnut quite bluntly writes in the
latter that she prefers public life to private life. "My
experience does not coincide with the general idea of
public life," she writes in Version III. "I mean the life
of a politician or statesman. Peace, comfort, quiet,
happiness, I have found away from home. Only your own
family, those nearest and dearest can hurt you." She is
thinking specifically about village and plantation life
around Camden, where she says, "Everybody knows exactly
where to put the knife." Now that alone would rank her
high for candor among diarists. But in the original version we find the specific reasons for these gloomy reflections, reasons she omits in Version III. James Chesnut has
just told her that John Slidell got the coveted appointment
as Minister to France. Hopes of Paris have collapsed and
those for London have gone aglimmering. "'All my pretty
chickens at one fell swoop,'" she exclaims. She is, of
course, quoting Macduff, but in a mood more reminiscent of
Lady Macbeth. On top of that, James has refused to turn a
hand to gain reelection to the Confederate Senate and she
sees even the poorer compensations of Richmond also slipping from her grasp. "Now," she reflects, as if in some
Elizabethan tragic monologue, "Now if we are not reelected
to the Senate! ... now as James Chesnut's genius does not
lie in the military, I suppose Camden is my dark fate ...
but I will harbour so dark a thought against my own peace

of mind. Pride must have a fall--perhaps I have not bourne
my honours meekly."[32] We may forgive Mary Chesnut for de-
priving us of that dramatic monologue for a century, but we
could never forgive a responsible editor for perpetuating
the suppression.

More serious in the transition from Version I to
Version III, are the distortions of political history and
the diarist's personal involvement in them. They concern
mainly her relations with Mrs. Jefferson Davis and her
husband and with Mrs. Louis Wigfall and Mrs. Joseph E.
Johnston and their husbands in the Davis-Johnston feud. In
the beginning months of Confederate independence Mrs.
Chesnut was more intimate and friendly with Mrs. Wigfall
and Mrs. Johnston than she was with Mrs. Davis and the
President. Her account of her relations with the anti-
Davis dissidents reflects her sympathy with them. She is
capable of adopting Wigfall's slurring nickname for Mrs.
Davis, "the Empress Eugenie," even while she is dining
daily at the President's table and accepting his favors.
She confided in Mrs. Wigfall, of whom James was quite fond,
that the two ladies were mismatched, that Mary should have
married Louis "the Stormy Petrel" as she called him, and
Mrs. Wigfall the "cool, quiet, poised Colonel." But later
as the anti-Davis movement intensifies and after James had
become aide-de-camp to President Davis, Mary Chesnut makes
a firm, explicit, realistic, and, for that matter, quite
patriotic vow. Hereafter she will be an all-out supporter
of the President, the only one the cause had, come what may.
She never departed from that vow. Thereafter, to the
bitter end, her relations with both Mr. and Mrs. Davis and
their family were unwaveringly loyal, devoted, intimate,
and affectionate. All this comes out in Version I, but in
Version III her earlier deviations were suppressed, or the
account of them was altered.

All of this is of minor importance in the transformation of Version I into Version III---minor, that is, in
comparison with the alteration which converted a more-or-
less bona fide journal or diary into a more-or-less conscious work of literary art. How conscious and calculated
the process was it is difficult to say, but the evidence is
unavoidable---the skilled and effective use of symbol and
myth and metaphor, the shaping of them from real-life experience, and their manipulation with dramatic effect that
is at times powerful.

The mystery and puzzlement of the problem, especially that of conscious purpose, is Mary Chesnut's inveterate habit of self-dramatization. She seems to experience life directly in terms of myth and metaphor. In Version III, in writing of the sectional crisis on March 14 she says, "we separated because of incompatability of temper. We are divorced North from South because we hated each other so. If we could only separate---a *'separation a l'agreable'* as the French say it, and not a horrid fight for divorce."[33] That was while she was in Montgomery, and we read, or recover from erasures in her original diary, omitted in the other version, a running contemporaneous account of what she then believed at the time would be an irreconcilable breakup of her own marriage. She had written there of tempestuous quarrels, and that she had "refused to accept overtures for peace and forgiveness.... I did so hope for peace and tranquil domestic happiness and there is none for me in this world. 'The peace this world cannot give, which passeth all understanding.'" Then in the very next sentence, same paragraph of the original: "Today the papers say peace again. Yesterday the telegraph and Herald were warlike to a frightful degree." And in the following paragraph: "I wonder if other women shed as bitter tears as I---they scald my cheeks and blister my heart."[34]

Back in Charleston in the weeks awaiting the guns of Sumter she throws herself into a flagrant flirtation with ex-Governor John Manning that scandalizes her friends and infuriates her husband. There had been other flirtations at Montgomery. She takes perverse delight in his jealousy. "Is it not too funny, and he so prosy."[35] Domestic crisis and national crisis mount toward climax simultaneously. How much is art and how much nature is hard to say. Her spirited accounts of the franticly gay social whirl in Charleston on the eve of Fort Sumter---never were men so gallant and charming, nor women so beautiful and desirable ---is self-conscious enough to be sure: Lord Byron the eve of Waterloo---though no doubt nature was busy faithfully imitating art. Just as Mary was, and nature was, at Richmond in the desperately gay social season in the winter of 1864, described with variations in no less than five extant versions of that endlessly perfectable "diary."

This nature-art ambiguity is doubtless not all that rare in the history of literary criticism, but there would seem to have been an unusual thickness of confusion in this instance. In one place Mary describes herself pacing the

portico of the Capitol in Richmond, hair windtorn, with a
grief-crazed friend. The two women have come there alone
to view the body of Mary's dear friend, young Frank Hampton.
They weep uncontrollably, recall the boy's wedding, his
bride, and many departed friends. She writes, "It is only
a few years, but nearly all that company are dead, and our
world, the only world we cared for, literally kicked to
pieces."[36] The thing is that the Graeco-Roman portico was
not a stage prop. This was not Medea or Antigone striding
the stage and making speeches. It was not tomato catsup
on the boy's face, but a sabre cut that laid his head open
at the battle of Brandy Station, and "utterly disfigured"
him, she says. It was, in fact, all for real. And an excellent view of a world in the process of being kicked to
pieces was afforded at the moment from Thomas Jefferson's
antique temple, set on its hill nearly a century before.

The Buck Preston-Sam Hood romance that so captivated
the imagination of Edmund Wilson as a metaphor for the rise
and fall of the Confederate cause deserves another look in
the light of new information about the Chesnut "diary" that
Wilson did not have. Here she undoubtedly had the advan-
tage of hindsight in the shaping of Version III of the
romance. No doubt she used it, too. How consciously the
metaphor was shaped as art is another matter. She never
identified it as such, any more than Hawthorne did the
Reverend Dimmesdale and Hester Prynne or Melville did
Captain Ahab and the white whale. The difficulty is that
Version I, and her private correspondence as well, bear her
out. She did not make it up. She almost seems to have
seen experience as metaphor from the start. Just where art
starts is hard to say, but there can be no doubt it is
there.

Another insight of Wilson's deserves comment. I have
in mind particularly his remark that "This household of the
old-world Chesnuts reminds one of the Bolkonskys of *War and
Peace*." He goes on to compare old James Chesnut *pere* with
Bolkonsky *pere*, James, Jr., with Prince Andre, his sister
with Princess Marie---character for character, fiction with
real life, and adds, parenthetically, "comparisons with
Russia seem inevitable when one is writing about the old
South."[37] Mrs. Chesnut herself says James, Sr., was "as
absolute a tyrant as the Tsar of Russia." It is quite
certain that Mary Chesnut never read *War and Peace*, and
there is no evidence that she ever read *Anna Karenina*,
which evokes her spirit even more vividly. Nor is there

any indication of her familiarity with Chekhov or
Dostoievski, or Turgeniev. Once in the fall of 1864, however, after reading Dumas' *Maitre d'Arms*, she noted,
"Russia ought to sympathize with us. We are not as barba-
rous as this even if Mrs. Stowe's word be taken. Brutal
men with unlimited power are the same the world over."[38]

"It is a way you have," scolded the Preston girls when
Mary left them behind once and they missed an enviable
spectacle. "You always stumble in upon the real show."[39]
To be sure, she did have a way of turning up where the
action was: Washington, Montgomery, Charleston, Richmond,
Columbia, and at just the right time. Even at Camden things
seemed to happen when she was around: the Witherspoon
murder, for example. And, after all, a world *was* literally
being kicked to pieces before her eyes, and she watched the
spectacle from a seat in the royal box, so to speak. But
it was not all coincidence, or "nature" for that matter.
And again it is hard to say how much art there was in it
all. Many others saw and recorded the same events. What
gave her account a special quality was, among other things,
a keen pair of eyes and an ingrained sense of irony. She
told once of observing people who "even like the excitement
of seeing people suffer. I speak now of what I have
watched with horror and amazement." And she added, "You
see I can not rise very high. I can only judge by what I
see."[40] And so she recorded it, as she said, "with horror
and amazement," and surely not without some measure of art.

[October 1978: Some of the views here expressed
are subject to revision as the result of additional study of the manuscripts since this paper
was originally delivered. C.V.W.]

Notes

[1]Isabella D. Martin and Myrta Lockett Avery (eds.), *A Diary from Dixie, as Written by Mary Boykin Chesnut, Wife of James Chesnut, Jr., United States Senator from South Carolina, 1859-1861, and afterward an Aide to Jefferson Davis and a Brigadier-General in the Confederate Army* (New York: D. Appleton and Co., 1905).

[2]Ben Ames Williams (ed.), *A Diary from Dixie* (Boston: Houghton Mifflin Co., 1948).

[3]For example, in returning the journal manuscripts to their owners in 1905 after publishing her edition, Isabella D. Martin wrote: "Unaccountably two or three of the numbers have got mislaid. I think considering all their journeyings and handlings it is well there are not more." (Isabella D. Martin to David Williams, March 27, 1905, in possession of Catherine Hill, Columbia, S. C.). Since all the 48 numbered volumes of Version III were returned, the missing volumes were probably from Version I.

[4]Isabella D. Martin to Francis W. Dawson, July 23, 1887, Dawson Papers, Duke University Library. Copied by Eileen Gregory.

[5]Martin and Avery, *Diary from Dixie*, cf. facsimile opposite p. XXII with p. 1. The page in facsimile is now missing from the manuscript journals.

[6]All deletions and editorial intrusions save those listed as silent corrections in punctuation, spelling, and capitalization will, of course, also be noted.

[7]Version III, March 10, 1862, Chesnut Journal Manuscripts, South Caroliniana Library, University of South Carolina. Hereafter citations of the journals will be indicated by version number and date, or if undated, by MS volume number and page.

[8]Version III, undated entry. Vol. 22, p. 35.

[9]Version III, December 13, 1861, November 12, 1861.

[10]Version II, December 13, 1861.

[11]Version III, December 13, 1861.

[12]Version III, December 13, 1861.

[13]Version III, March 10, 1862.

[14]Version III, June 4, 1862.

[15]Version III, August 26, 1861.

[16]Version I, March 6, 1861.

[17]Version II, September 8, 1864.

[18]Version I, September 17, 1861.

[19]Version III, September 23, 1863.

[20]Version III, May 8, 1864.

[21]Version I, October 7, 1864.

[22]Version I, February 4, 1865

[23]Version I, March 11, 1861.

[24]Version III, June 3, 1862.

[25]Version I, October 3, 1861

[26]Version III, August 1, 1863.

[27]Version III, undated (Vol. 21, p. 46).

[28]Version III, undated (Vol. 21, pp. 39-40).

[29]Under the date October 27, 1863, Ben Ames Williams has Mrs. Chesnut write, "I resume my journal." (*Diary from Dixie*, p. 318.) Like numerous other passages in this edition, there is no authority for this one in the manuscript journals.

[30]Version III, undated (Vol. 22, p. 35).

[31]Version III, August 29, 1861.

[32]Version I, August 29, 1861.

[33]Version III, March 14, 1861.

[34]Version I, March 18, 1861.

[35]Version I, March 28, 1861.

[36]Version III, undated (Vol. 21, pp. 41-42).

[37]Edmund Wilson, *Patriotic Gore: Studies in the Literature of the American Civil War* (New York, 1962), 288.

[38]Version III, September 1, 1864.

[39]Version V, January 8, 1864.

[40]Version III, March 13, 1862.

Mary Boykin Chesnut's Journal:
Visions and Revisions

by

George F. Hayhoe

Mary Boykin Miller Chesnut is usually considered as a
commentator on Confederate history and society, not as a
writer of literature. Yet Mrs. Chesnut's only published
work, a journal known as *A Diary from Dixie*, is a first-
rate piece of non-fiction. Edmund Wilson has called it
"an extraordinary document--in its informal department, a
masterpiece; . . . Not only is [Mrs. Chesnut] fully aware
of the world-wide importance of the national crisis at one
of the foci of which she finds herself; she has also . . .
a decided sense of the literary possibilities of her
subject."[1] There thus seems to be no reason why Mrs.
Chesnut and her journal should be considered the sole
province of the historian.

It is the result of Mrs. Chesnut's awareness of "the
literary possibilities of her subject" which I would like
to consider this morning. As Professor Woodward has
already pointed out, one must be wary of basing any conclusions on the 1905 and 1949 editions of *A Diary from
Dixie*, as Edmund Wilson did. These texts have been so
heavily edited and rewritten that many sections bear only
a nominal resemblance to what Mary Chesnut actually wrote.
One must therefore determine how much of the literary
quality of the published editions of the diary has been
imposed on it by the editors.

An examination of the Chesnut manuscripts on deposit
at the South Caroliniana Library of the University of South

Carolina reveals that Mrs. Chesnut's editors have, collectively, omitted more than half of her material; they have
combined and consolidated sentences, paragraphs, and entire
entries; they have changed her somewhat eccentric system of
punctuation, and brought her writing into conformity with
modern English grammar; and they have even occasionally
added material which the manuscripts do not contain. And
yet, when the cosmetics applied by the editors are removed,
one is amazed at the degree of literary genius which Mary
Chesnut's manuscripts exhibit.

Mrs. Chesnut's interest in literature is apparent from
her diary. Here she makes frequent mention of her current
reading, and often quotes from it at length, using the
journal as a commonplace book. Moreover, as Professor
Gregory will point out this afternoon, Mary Chesnut also
wrote several works of fiction. Among her papers are a
draft of a novel, "The Captain and the Colonel," the
characters of which are apparently based on several of
her relatives and acquaintances, and fragments of a fictionalized memoir, "Two Years of My Life." The fact that
there are so many stylistic similarities between these
fictional works and the revised drafts of the diary suggests that Mary Chesnut chose to use techniques of fiction
in writing her diary, perhaps because she intended it to
be read by others and wanted to make her account as interesting and cohesive as possible.

To say that Mrs. Chesnut used fictional stylistic
devices in revising her journal is not to accuse her of
distorting the facts beyond recognition, though she did
sometimes change them. Nevertheless, even the revised
drafts of the diary can be a valuable tool for the historian who is aware of the nature of the work he is using
as evidence. It is therefore important to determine to
what degree her style--especially her organization and
presentation of material--affects her readers, and how it
affects the historical accuracy of her portrayal of people
and incidents.

Two of the most common and important stylistic devices
which Mrs. Chesnut employs in her journal are the dramati-
zation of incident, rather than straight narrative or
report of events, and the counterpointing personal reflection on the significance of the events. It is precisely
this combination of dramatic portrayal and reflection
which contributes to the diary's importance as an

historical document, for it not only reveals what the wife
of an important official of the Confederacy knew, and when
she knew it, but also how she felt about the events which
were occurring around her. And yet these same devices are
also what make the diary read at times like a novel of the
period.

In order to explore the effects of style on the
reader's understanding and appreciation of events, I have
chosen some of the journal's entries concerning one incident, the murder of Mary Chesnut's cousin Betsey Witherspoon, and I will attempt to explore the ways in which
Mrs. Chesnut treats the facts. My research has involved
a search of contemporary newspapers for stories relating
to the murder, as well as an examination of the diary
manuscripts for September through December, 1861. I have
paid particular attention to the differences between the
narratives of the original version of the diary, kept con-
temporaneously with the events, and the one revised version, prepared nearly twenty years later, the account
which is familiar to Mary Chesnut's readers in Ben Ames
Williams' edition of the diary.[2]

On the night of September 15-16, 1861, Mrs. Elizabeth
Witherspoon of Society Hill, South Carolina, was strangled
and smothered to death by her slaves. The crime is well
documented in surviving newspapers of the period, and has
also been of some interest to historians of slavery.
Eugene Genovese, for example, in *Roll, Jordan, Roll*, quotes
at length from Mrs. Chesnut's account of her cousin's death
as an example of the murder of a master or mistress by
slaves.[3]

The earliest located newspaper report records that
foul play was suspected in Mrs. Witherspoon's death when
"blood was found on a candlestick, and on a bed cover in
the room, and . . . marks of violence were found on her
person." The coroner's jury, however, had not been able
to determine who had committed the crime.[4] A more detailed
account which appeared in the *Charleston Daily Courier* the
next week reports that "On both arms at the elbows were
purple discolorations, such as might be made by hands
holding her down in bed by force." The *Courier* story,
furnished by a correspondent from Society Hill who signed
himself "T. S.," calls attention to Mrs. Witherspoon's
"never tiring attention to the wants and comforts of her
slaves in sickness and in health, . . . a beautiful

exemplification of the christian faith which ruled and regulated her conduct."[5]

On October 12, 1861, the *Courier* reported the outcome of this strange murder case. A Charleston police detective, Mr. Hicks, who had gone to Society Hill to investigate, found that Mrs. Witherspoon had been killed by a number of her servants: William, the carriage driver, Rhody, the maid, and Rhody's children Romeo and Sylvia. They had murdered their mistress "to escape a whipping for an offence of which they own themselves guilty." The incident had so outraged some of the townspeople that they wished to lynch the slaves involved, but they were to be tried and executed according to law.[6] I have been unable to locate newspaper accounts of the trial and execution, however.

These journalistic accounts of the Witherspoon case report the facts more or less objectively and completely. Mrs. Chesnut's diary does not at all conflict with these reports, but it does provide us with a far more detailed view of the events which not only communicates the facts in a more dramatic form, but also gives the reader a better indication of the emotional atmosphere which resulted from such an occurrence. The two surviving drafts of the journal do, however, differ in the amount of information they contain and in their manner of presentation.

The original version of the diary, which seems to have been written concurrently with the events it covers, reports Mary Chesnut's first information about the death of Mrs. Witherspoon rather matter-of-factly on September 19.

Heard yesterday of the death of Cousin Betsey Witherspoon--found dead in her bed--went to bed quite well--had been dead several hours-- her family troubles I fear killed her.

In the revised version, Mrs. Chesnut expands these few phrases, and also adds several important elements. She introduces the entry with the words "A painful piece of news came to us yesterday. . ."; yet "painful" was not the word she originally used to describe the news in this revised draft. Above this line is a cancelled false start which reads "A horrid piece of." This revision within the

revised draft seems intended to make the eventual discovery
of the homicide more shocking to the reader. "Horrid"
draws too much on Mrs. Chesnut's subsequent knowledge of
the events to be dramatically appropriate at this point;
at the same time, "painful" provides a personal reaction
to the discovery of her cousin's death which is not present in the original version.

The revised draft of the entry continues along the
same lines as the original, adding details about the
family troubles which plagued Mrs. Witherspoon, and, more
importantly, including a consideration of Mrs. Witherspoon's personal qualities.

> She was a proud and high strung woman.
> Nothing shabby in word, thought, or ~~dee~~
> deed ever came nigh her. Of a warm, and
> tender heart too. Truth and uprightness
> itself. Few persons have ever been more
> loved and looked up to.

This brief sketch of Betsey Witherspoon's character is
vital because it encourages in the reader feelings of
admiration and sympathy for the subject.

I do not think it is unreasonable, then, to conclude
that Mary Chesnut's revisions in this entry were made with
the intention of involving the reader imaginatively in the
incident she was recording. She goes beyond the mere
reporting of facts by preparing the reader for the horrible
tale which follows.

After this initial entry, Mrs. Chesnut tends to con-
solidate in the revised draft events and reflections which
she recorded over the period of more than a month in the
original version of the diary. Once again, her revision
seems aimed at intensifying the reader's reaction to the
story. By compressing the incidents in time and elaborating in detail, she dramatizes their importance and
increases the reader's interest. Had she chosen to delay
the reader's discovery of all of the facts of the murder
by retaining the original sequence of entries, the impact
of the tale would have been greatly diminished because in
the original draft of the journal the parts of the Witherspoon story are scattered among entries which have nothing
at all to do with Mrs. Witherspoon's death.

In the original draft of the entry for September 21,
Mary Chesnut writes that a letter from Mary Witherspoon
received the night before informed Mr. Chesnut that Betsey
Witherspoon had been murdered by her slaves--"she was
smothered--arms & legs bruised & face scratched." William
and several of the other servants were suspected, "people
she has pampered & spoiled &c."

The revised entry places the news in the context of a
dramatic situation.

> Last night when the mail came in, I was
> seated near the lamp, Mr Chesnut lying on a
> sofa at a little distance called out to me.
> "Look at my letters, and tell me. . . about
> them?"
>   I began to read one ~~of them~~ aloud; it
> was from Mary Witherspoon--and I broke down--
> Horror and amazement was too much for me--
> Poor Cousin Betsey Witherspoon was murdered!
> She did not die peacefully, as we supposed,
> in her bed--Murdered by her own people. Her
> negroes.

She then refers briefly to the murder of Dr. Keitt by
his slaves, an event which is not mentioned in the original
draft until October 19. She goes on to comment about the
murder of Mrs. Witherspoon--"Horrible beyond words"--and
comments on her cousin's treatment of her slaves. "She
knew, she said, that none of her children would have the
patience she had with these people who had been indulged
and spoiled by her." This comment nicely foreshadows the
fact which the reader learns somewhat later that Mrs.
Witherspoon's death has indirectly resulted from her son's
lack of patience with the slaves.

The entry for September 24 is much the same in both
the original and revised drafts. James Chesnut and David
Williams, husband of Mary's sister Kate, have returned
from Society Hill where they have learned that several of
the suspected slaves are in jail and that there is talk
of lynching them. The revised version adds: "But it is
all idle talk. They will be tried--as the law directs and
not otherwise. John Witherspoon will not allow any thing
wrong or violent to be done." She says finally, "He has
a detective there from Charleston." This detective, apparently the Mr. Hicks mentioned in the *Courier* story of

October 12, is never referred to in the original draft.

In the same entry, Mrs. Chesnut adds material which
occurs in the entries for September 27 and October 19 in
the original version of the diary. The first part, a personal reflection on how Mrs. Witherspoon's death has
affected her own attitude toward blacks is slightly
expanded in the revised draft, and is the first of
several considerations of the effect which the event has
on the lives of Mary and her family and friends. "Hitherto
I have never thought of being afraid of negroes. . . Two
thirds of my religion consists in trying to be good to
negroes. . . . Why should they treat me any better than
they have done Cousin Betsey Witherspoon?"

Secondly, she relates an experience of her sister
Kate. In the original draft, Kate had told Mary Chesnut
the story; in the more dramatic revised version, Mary
witnesses the incident.

> Kate's maid came in. . . dragging in a
> materass. "Missis I have brought my bed to
> sleep in your room. While Mars David is at
> Society Hill. You ought not to stay in a
> room by your self *these times*." . . .
> --"For the life of me" said Kate gravely
> "I can not make up my mind. Does she mean
> to take care of me--or to murder me."

Mrs. Chesnut then attributes to her sister a nightmare
which had troubled Mary herself in the original draft.
"Those black hands strangling and smothering Mrs Witherspoon's grey head under the counterpane haunted her."

The original draft of the October 10 entry provides
a very brief account headed "Circumstantial details of
Mrs Witherspoon's death." The version provided in the
revision is considerably longer, and also adds the story
of the detective's strategy in determining the guilt of
the suspected slaves.

The slaves had been threatened with a whipping by
Mrs. Witherspoon's son for taking his mother's silver,
china and table linens to their own party while she was
away from home. In order to distract the son from his
intention, they planned to murder their mistress, thinking
that, since her sister had died suddenly in her sleep, a

similar death would not attract suspicion. The plan failed
when the family noticed marks of violence on the body.

The story of the detective is particularly interesting
because it seems quite typical of the type of tale which
Edgar Allan Poe had introduced with his ratiocinative
stories of M. Dupin in the 1840s. The style of this passage is particularly noteworthy for its dramatic quality.

> The Detective dropped in from the skies
> quite unexpectedly--he saw that one of the young
> understrappers of the gang looked frightened and
> uncomfortable. This one he fastened upon and
> got up quite an intimacy with him. Finally he
> told this boy that he knew all about it. William
> had confessed privately to him to save himself
> and hang the others. But as the Detective had
> taken a fancy to this boy. If he would confess
> every thing he would take him as States evidence
> instead of William. The young man was utterly
> confounded at first--But fell in the trap laid
> for him and told every particular from beginning
> to end. . . .
> They smothered her with a counterpane . . .
> had no trouble the first time because they found
> her asleep and "done it all fore she waked."
> But . . . she came to!--Then she begged them
> hard for life. She asked them what she had ever
> done that they should want to kill her? She
> promised them before God--never to tell on them.
> Nobody should ever know. But Rhody stopped up
> her mouth by the counterpane. . . .
> That innocent old lady and her grey hairs
> moved them not a jot.

We know, of course, that there really was a detective
involved in the Witherspoon case, but we know nothing of
his methods except what Mrs. Chesnut tells us. Considering
her faithfulness to the facts in other details of the
story, we have no reason to doubt her accuracy here. That
her account of the detective's course of action sounds
fictional--though perhaps more like a present-day *Columbo*
script than like Poe or Conan Doyle--seems due to her
marvelous choice of words and her fine sense of proportion
in mixing comedy and tragedy in this passage, rather than
due to a departure from the facts.

There are too many other fascinating details connected
with the Witherspoon murder in Mrs. Chesnut's journal to
include a thorough analysis of them all in a paper of this
nature, so I will mention briefly only two more which have
particularly interested me in the course of my research.
The first is Mary Chesnut's descriptions of her mother-in-
law's reactions to the murder. A woman who has always been
afraid of slaves, but is called "their good angel" for her
many acts of charity toward them, old Mrs. Chesnut is
described as "treating every one as if they were a black
Prince Albert or Queen Victoria" after the tragedy. Still,
on one occasion, the old lady startles the family at
dinner by warning them not to eat the soup that she suspects is poisoned.

Secondly, there is the strange tale about Dr. Keitt
which is told in the context of the Witherspoon slaying.
Dr. Keitt, the brother of the secessionist South Carolina
Congressman, Lawrence M. Keitt, became aware of the fact
that he was gradually being poisoned by his slaves. One
day he confronted one of the servants with his discovery
and dashed a cup of poisoned tea in her face. "Next
morning he was found with his throat cut from ear to ear."
The maid who served the tea was hanged, but two other
servants who were suspected were sold to distant places.
Afterward, according to Mary Chesnut, Keitt's brother and
a friend, Mr. Taylor, separately claimed that each had
seen and spoken with Dr. Keitt, who informed them both
that "'you hanged the wrong person . . . you let the
rascals who cut my throat go--' and instantly--vanished."

It might be claimed that I have chosen for analysis
the most dramatic incident contained in the Chesnut journal. But certainly Betsey Witherspoon's death and connected events are no more sensational in their own way
than the bombardment of Fort Sumter, the romance of
General Hood and Buck Preston, the internal conflicts
among the Confederate leadership, the ravages of Sherman's
army, and the dissolution of the Confederacy, all of which
Mrs. Chesnut describes in great detail. Moreover, the
accounts of all of these events and phenomena are portrayed with the same combination of dramatic incident and
reflective aside.

There is a need for a full-length study of Mary
Boykin Chesnut's literary accomplishment in her journal,
a work which will require a good deal of patience and care,

but one which offers the prospect of making a major contribution to our understanding and appreciation of Mrs.
Chesnut's role as author. Until such a thorough analysis
is completed, we can only estimate her talent, and our
estimates are undoubtedly an inadequate measure of her
literary abilities.

Notes

[1]*Patriotic Gore* (New York: Oxford University Press, 1962), p. 279.

[2]*A Diary from Dixie*, ed. Isabella D. Martin and Myrta Lockett Avary (New York: D. Appleton and Co., 1905), contains a gap between entries for 19 September 1861 and 20 February 1862; thus, while the reader of this edition knows that Mrs. Witherspoon has died, there is no indication that she was murdered. The editors note that, "By reason of illness, preoccupation in other affairs, and various deterrent causes besides, Mrs. Chesnut allowed a considerable period to elapse before making another entry in her diary" (p. 130n). Ben Ames Williams, in his edition (Boston: Houghton Mifflin Co., 1949), observes that the omission was caused "presumably because the notebooks in which they were written were not found" (p. 139n). 19 September 1861 is the date of the last entry in the volume marked "no. 9" in Mrs. Chesnut's hand, and 20 February 1862 is the date of the first entry in volume "No. 13." Volumes 10 through 12 are not contained in the same box of manuscripts as volume 9 currently, though their arrangement before their deposit at the South Caroliniana Library is unknown. Thus, the true reason for the omission of this material from the 1905 edition cannot be ascertained; either the editors were unaware of its existence, or they knowingly suppressed it.

[3]New York: Pantheon Books, 1974; pp. 362-63.

[4]Columbia *Tri-Weekly Southern Guardian*, 24 September 1861, p. 4, col. 7. No file of the *Darlington Southerner*, from which this item was reprinted, survives for this period.

[5]*Charleston Daily Courier*, 26 September 1861, p. 1, col. 3; rptd. in the *Charleston Mercury*, 27 September 1861, p. 1, col. 7.

[6]*Charleston Daily Courier*, 12 October 1861, p. 1, col. 2.

Session V: Discussion

MR. POLK: Mr. Woodward, should all the stages of the diary eventually be published?

MR. WOODWARD: I frankly can't imagine that as a feasible effort, especially version two, which is for her own purposes and a rough draft in pencil, much of it scarcely legible, and notes and signals to herself, for her next version. And then the practicability is questionable, in the extensive duplication. Much of the later version is literally transcribed or very insignificantly changed from the early version. Versions four and five are polishings of version three and duplicate it often. When you are dealing with close to a million words, you know, you have to spare duplication.

MR. POLK: You're talking about things which, as a literary scholar, I'm deeply interested in, and I think you're answering from the point of view of the historian.

MR. WOODWARD: I guess so.

MR. POLK: Then there's nothing in the early versions that as a historian you would like to have in print?

MR. WOODWARD: No, no, I didn't mean to say that. I propose to draw extensively from the first version, and supplement the third version, as a basic text, with considerable parts of it. But often the third version is preferable in obvious ways. The haste and the circumstances of the hurried jottings of her original diary make it very difficult to edit in a publishable form, often, and she gives the editor more help in her third version. She gives him more trouble, too.

UNIDENTIFIED SPEAKER: Mr. Hayhoe, how would you characterize her tastes in reading? Was she influenced by particular writers? You mentioned Dumas.

MR. HAYHOE: I didn't mention Dumas. I believe Professor Woodward did. But it seems to me that she read a great deal of French and German fiction and poetry, and also a great deal of British poetry. I'm not sure that I see any absolute influences on her.

223

UNIDENTIFIED SPEAKER: Well, do you think she was more adventurous in her reading than most of her class at that time, men and women?

MR. HAYHOE: I doubt it.   I think she was probably reading more than other people were, but pretty much the same kinds of things.   I was surprised at the amount of seventeenth-century poetry that she talks about.   I didn't realize that period was as popular in her day as she seems to indicate that it is.   But aside from that, she seems to have pretty much the tastes of the readers of her period.

MR. POLK: It might simply have had something to do with what was available to her.   What about the book trade during the war?

MR. HAYHOE: She speaks at one point of not being able to get the English journals that she had subscribed to previous to the war, and notes that her mother-in-law doesn't seem to have that problem.   Old Mrs. Chesnut always seems to be able to come up with copies of things, without even buying them, by borrowing them from friends.

MR. WOODWARD: My command of French literature of the period is very limited, but she made a great deal of some authors no longer read, I'm pretty sure, especially French authors.

MR. INABINETT: Professor Woodward, were the other editors aware of her destruction of her original diaries?

MR. WOODWARD: Yes, in fact, some of my capable assistants will help me here, but I at least know of one or two quotations form the original journal, especially in the early parts of the Williams edition.   He had it avail-able, but he didn't regard his purpose as the consoli-dation or incorporation of it.

MR. INABINETT: I think you people have done a really masterful job of separating the five versions.   I didn't even really realize there were that many.   Professor Woodward, do you anticipate a change in the title for review, for publication?

MR. WOODWARD: Yes.   I don't like the title used by the
previous editors, and I don't think it's Mrs. Chesnut's
title.   I don't know what to call it, but not that,
anyway.

MR. INABINETT: And is it your hope that your work will
rule out the need in the future for any fourth?

MR. WOODWARD: One naturally has that hope.

MR. RICHARDS: Professor Woodward, when your new edition
appears, will there by any sort of material that will
help us separate the actual historical material from
the reworked literary treatment that we see sometimes?

MR. WOODWARD: Well, that's quite a question.   Of course,
I can't undertake to tuck in a history of the Civil War
in footnotes, and as she is rather casual about events
and checking the accuracy of them.   Where she makes a
blatant departure from fact, I think it's the duty of
the editor to point it out.   But, on the other hand,
when she, as she does in her original diary, reports an
extensive interview with Jefferson Davis, about fighting
around Atlanta, in which it was perfectly clear that
Jefferson Davis was wrong, she deletes that, I think,
because she knows he was wrong, after the event.   But to
me it's interesting that the President of the Confederacy could have had such a misconception.   It ought to
go in.   And you see, I, in other words, I'm interested
in inaccuracies, too.   But I can't straighten them all
out.   I just have to record her on impressions, often.

UNIDENTIFIED SPEAKER: If this manuscript version of the
first edition, as her first writing, is in existence
now, what was destroyed?

MR. WOODWARD: Well, I tried to suggest a range of possibilities in my paper, that she reports destruction but
she doesn't designate what she destroyed, often.   Of
course, it's perfectly obvious what's not there.   But,
on the other hand, in just recent weeks, a fraction of
the diary, covering a couple of weeks, which we have
reason to believe is original, was discovered tucked
away in version three, and it's possible that other
pieces might turn up.   Miss Martin, in a letter now in
the hands of Miss Kathy Hill, of Columbia, writes the
owner of the diary, returning the manuscript to him, in

April of 1905, when her edition came out, that unfortunately she's lost two or three volumes, and that it's
amazing that there haven't been more lost, considering
how they've been knocking around all this time, and she's
very casual about it. Well, one can dream of turning
those missing volumes up in somebody's attic sometime.
I've made a try at it, but not with any success.

MR. MERIWETHER: Professor Woodward, would there be justification for considering that there are two versions of
the journal, the original and incomplete one, and the
final, the third version, with its partial revisions?
Would it be possible to bring both versions out, as
separate or different versions, with whatever supple-
mentary material was appropriate to either? Could you
consider two works, then: a diary, or something very
close to a contemporary journal of events, and then a
very self-conscious literary work that records what she
thought of those years, later on?

MR. WOODWARD: You ask if I can conceive of it, yes, but I
don't think I'm about to undertake it. In fact, it seems
to me to do it separately would be to miss the utility
of bringing them together, and if you confined yourself
to version three, in a new edition, you would deprive
the reader of a lot that he ought to know about what
she's writing about, by enlarging, supplementing, con-
tradicting, elaborating, all those things. And, by dup-
licating so much in two volumes, or versions, are you
complicating the reader's task, or assisting him? It
depends on your conception of what your readership is.
If it's confined to professional scholars, I think
there's much to be said for your point of view. But I
think the professional scholars who are involved in
this---to this degree---are very limited, and that
raises a practical question.

MRS. ANDERSON: I was going to ask a quite similar question,
but I want to address it to both of you. Would it be
advisable, perhaps, in the light of what George is saying
about the literary possibilities of version three, to
have separate editions which serve two quite different
functions: one, your edition, which would print all the
historically relevant material from all the versions, to
be used by historians and any other reader who wants to
use it; and one which would exploit the literary form
that Mary was apparently working toward, although she

never finished it? Or do you think that your version,
Professor Woodward, would be usable for someone who
wants to study the literary form?

MR. WOODWARD: Well, I would hope so, but I have, of course,
in mind the example of my appallingly industrious col-
league at Yale, Fred Pottle. He's dealing with James
Boswell in somewhat that fashion, bringing out a trade
edition of the journal of Boswell, and then has in preparation a scholar's edition, done according to a
different and elaborate set of rules. For Boswell, I
don't know. I'm yet to be persuaded that Mary Chesnut
is quite in that league in this respect, you know. I
suspect there's enough of a Boswell clique to sustain
the great strain financially of this enterprise. It's
a very expensive business, what he's doing, and he
hasn't done it yet.

MR. MERIWETHER: Expensive of time as well as money, I'm
sure you mean.

MR. WOODWARD: Yes.

MISS KATONA: May I ask a question about the difference between version one and version three? I quite realize
that version three is a greater work of art, a more conscious work of art. But I'm interested in how great is
the difference, from the historical point of view. Does
she describe the same historical event in the same way
on a greater level of artistry, or is her point of view
changing?

MR. WOODWARD: This is your spot, Mr. Hayhoe.

MR. HAYHOE: If you boil the facts out of version three and
compare them with the facts in version one, they're
pretty much the same. Version three sometimes has more
facts, more detail. The facts are the same, but sometimes the way that she presents the facts is different.
A story that she has been told third hand in version one,
she might present as if she were present at the occurrence of the event. She might take her own thoughts
recorded in version one, and put them in someone else's
mouth in three. The facts are pretty much the same, but
it's the way which she presents them that is different,
and in that sense version three I guess is a less
historical account---

MR. WOODWARD: That's right.

MR. HAYHOE: ---and a more literary account.

MRS. MUHLENFELD: I wondered, Mr. Hayhoe, if in this very
self-contained section of the diary about Betsy
Witherspoon, if, looking at version three, you had to
make a judgment, would you say she was most concerned in
her rewriting with fidelity as an historian---or as a
journalist---or was her greatest concern as an artist,
a writer?

MR. HAYHOE: That's hard to respond to, because there's
some of both. She's concerned as an historian when she
introduces more detail. There's a lot more detail in
version three's narrative of the Witherspoon case than
version one's. On the other hand, she's concerned as a
literary artist with the way that she shapes her narrative. It's a much more conscious literary work than
version one.

MRS. MUHLENFELD: That's a good answer. She seems to have
the ability to combine these two fields. I really would
have to look a long time to find someone to compare her
with in that respect.

MR. WOODWARD: But she gives the historian the creeps and
shivers when she presents, for instance, a dialogue as
if she participated, when it's apparent that she did not
participate. In other words, she's forging evidence,
and I have to call her to terms on that, you see.

MR. POLK: It would seem that the addition of new details
would be more the literary artist at work, than the
historian.

MR. WOODWARD: Well, I'll have to wrestle with that one.

The Formality of Memory:
A Study of Literary Manuscripts of Mary Boykin Chesnut

by

Eileen Gregory

Mary Chesnut's diary is, as Prof. Woodward and Mr.
Hayhoe have indicated, a monumental work of its kind. I
would like to emphasize, however, that, like the work of
many of the women we have studied these two days, the
diaries are as well memorial: as Mrs. Chesnut said, they
are *"memoires pour servir."*[1] A monument testifies to a
particular achievement or event in time. But a memorial,
though signifying a specific moment of the past, points
forward; the time memorialized is continually reenacted in
the present. In establishing a moment of the past, a memorial artifact serves history; in making that moment accessible to the future it serves poetry. Memory herself is
impotent without the rich and contradictory recording of
ordinary life, yet she perpetually reshapes actual events
into an experience more abundant, original, and universal.
The memorial artifact--whether a tale, a shrine, a hastily
conceived record--captures that first shaping of events;
it is an elemental act of preservation. However, memory
bears fruit consummately in poetry. Hesiod tells us that
Memory (Mnemosyne) is the mother of the Muses, the god-
desses of poetic inspiration (*Theogony*, 915-18). Homer
says that the immortal Muses know what is really true in
the past, while we on earth know only Rumor; the poet asks
in an invocation of the *Iliad* that he be aided to remember
truly (*Iliad*, II, 485-93). That true remembrance, informed by memory, takes shape finally in the poetic artifact.

I think that we examine many of the writers at this

conference with such interest because they are to one degree or another necessary to the final preservation of history in literature. They are guardians and servants of
memory, but not of the muse. A good many of them, including Mary Chesnut, did not, I believe, aspire to be poets.
They wrote, they recorded--in diaries, scrapbooks, letterbooks, cookbooks, in literary journals of more or less
pretension--for private and for public reasons. But is
this not what women habitually do? They gather things--
memoribilia--fix them in time, accumulate and store fragments from the present moment. That effort might appear
futile and pointless, like that of the dying lady in John
Crowe Ransom's poem, "Here Lies a Lady":

> . . . her confident eyes would blaze,
> And her fingers fly in a manner to puzzle their
> heads--
> What was she making? Why nothing; she sat in a
> maze
> Of old scraps of laces, snipped into curious
> shreds--[2]

The lady of this poem gathers round her the "old scraps of
laces" in a delirium of fever; but the curious behavior
signifies an habitual action of her life which gains meaning in the face of death: gathering and attempting to
make something intelligible out of the "amazing," complex
patterns of the past. The accumulation of "curious shreds"
is not done from idleness but from a positive desire to
preserve something out of mutable reality--from an irrational tenacity to the concrete, we might say.

This feminine knowledge of the particular, preserved
and transformed in memory, is not in itself poetic, but is
essential to the final expression of the poet, just as the
tale-teller makes way for the epic bard. Not only Mary
Chesnut's diaries, in all their revisions, but other existing manuscript materials as well, show her to be a servant
of memory, recalling concrete instances of the past in
different forms and under different lights, attempting to
find an expression of their significance which would allow
them to come alive again from their fragments.

The quantity and diversity of Mrs. Chesnut's literary
manuscripts (even beyond the many existing versions of the
Diary) indicate an overwhelming activity during the last
years of her life. Though these papers cannot be dated

with certainty, the major portion appears to have been composed in the years between 1876 and her death in 1886,
during the same period in which she was rewriting her
Diary.[3] Her papers in the Williams-Chesnut-Manning Collection at the South Caroliniana Library[4] contain, besides
the scrapbooks, letterbooks, and occasional diary entries,
a biographical sketch of James Chesnut of 22 pp., originally commissioned by W. W. Butler for a proposed book entitled *Sketches of the Lives of the Leading and Prominent
Men of Our State 1861 to 1865.*[5] Several versions exist of
a memoir of approximately 30 pp. entitled "The Bright Side
of Richmond. Winter of 1864-Scraps from a Diary." As the
title indicates, this is a reworking of already existing
material. It may have been suggested to her in a letter
of 1884 from William Henry Trescott encouraging her to publish such a reminiscence as part of a collection of her
husband's papers.[6] This reminiscence may, too, have been
intended for separate publication. The Charleston *News and
Courier* was at that time paying for sketches about the war.
One such sketch by Mrs. Chesnut, entitled "The Arrest of a
Spy," was accepted for publication by the editor, F. W.
Dawson, on April 8, 1884, with payment of $10.[7] Another
more personal memoir of 42 pp. deals with Mrs. Chesnut's
family history and particularly with the figure of her
sister Kate.[8] Still another incomplete essay of 42 miscel-
laneous pages was written as an answer to and a correction
of a book by William Shannon on the history of Camden families which apparently gave undue praise of the Kershaw
family at the expense of others.

     There are also indications that Mrs. Chesnut during
this period was involved in preparing translations: an
eight-page MS. and perhaps another page numbered 70 are
fragments from a translation of a French work by Emile
Colombey entitled *Histoire Anecdotique du Duel*. Also, another letter from F. W. Dawson, dated July 2, 1880, expresses interest in a translation of "Pousckin's novelette"
which Mrs. Chesnut had evidently offered to submit for publication to the *News and Courier*.

     But by far the most significant of the manuscript
material other than the notebooks of the *Diary* is that com-
prising two lengthy fictional works: *The Captain and the
Colonel*, a romance whose action occurs largely during the
Civil War, and *Two Years of My Life*, a fictionalized memoir
centering around events of about 1836 through 1840.[9] The
manuscripts give evidence that Mrs. Chesnut devoted

considerable energy to these works. *The Captain and the Colonel* exists in an incomplete MS. of 346 pp.; there are as well 43 pp. of a later version of the beginning of the novel. *Two Years of My Life* exists in an incomplete MS. draft of 258 pp.; at least 115 pp. are missing from the first half of the work. This later manuscript is heavily marked in purple pencil, with rewritten passages on the versos of the pages. Besides this draft of *Two Years of My Life* are later versions of portions of the novel which might allow one to infer the existence of another complete MS. of the novel which has been lost.[10] But it is certain in any case that Mrs. Chesnut took great labor in writing and rewriting the work.

These various forms of records and writings suggest an enormous energy and literary curiosity, but more important-ly indicate Mrs. Chesnut's sophistication as a woman of letters: an educated and voracious reader of continental, British, and American literature, a writer possessing dis-cipline and seriousness and a refined awareness of the formal conventions which shape the tone, the texture, and content of any work. Of particular significance are the various forms of memoirs. The commissioned memoir of her husband, for example, seems in a classical Plutarchan tradi-tion--elevated, stylized, paradigmatic--while the memoir centering upon her sister Kate, and intended to be read by those who knew her, is an informal reminiscence, familiar and perhaps self-indulgent, yet still courteous, still a public document. The memoirs of life in Richmond are simi-lar in style to largely narrative passages of the diary from which they come. In general, however, the conventions of the diary would-- and did--allow a much more intimate and private communication with the reader, who is, theoret-ically, the author alone but who is actually anyone (pro-bably someone in the future) who would find access to the document.

Both fictional works, too, draw immediately upon Mrs. Chesnut's memories, some of them already written in the diary of the War and perhaps in a diary from her early years, mentioned in a fragment among the manuscript pages, but not surviving.[11] These writings show her to be respon-sive to the necessities of formal conventions. The form of *The Captain and the Colonel*, a war romance, limits, I would submit, her possible intention to make the story a serious study of various feminine figures in their response to the exigencies of war. The style as a whole seems artifically

elevated and rigid, the characters somewhat shadowy, since
there is not, as in her diary, that recording of a whole
concrete world through the presence as narrator of a wise
and discerning woman. However, *Two Years of My Life,* in
the form of a slightly fictionalized memoir and, in part,
a "western" adventure story, allows the intimate rendering
of character and detail and as well an imaginative play in
tale-telling. The existing portions of *Two Years of My
Life*, in that they are closer to a recollection of the
concrete experience of her past, seem a much more successful attempt to give the memories form than the chivalric
and somewhat insubstantial romance. Mrs. Chesnut's stature as a writer cannot be established on the basis of
these two explicit attempts at fiction: but they reveal,
in her partial success and failure, that the source of her
power is in recollection unmediated by imagined plot or
character.

The *Captain and the Colonel* is really an ambitious
attempt to write the story of the war, drawing upon experiences recorded in the diary and giving them focus in a
central plot. It comes from an explicit desire to remember
the complex experience of the war and draw from it some
final significance. In the novel, the commentary and in a
way the thematic intentions of the author are indicated in
epigraphs, usually poems or passages from literary works,
that precede most of the chapters. The first of these,
introducing chapter 1, indicates the presence, the viewpoint, of the author: "'The tide of time flows back with
me,/The forward flowing tide of time.'"[12] This and other
quotations, particularly in the beginning chapters, indicate the act of recollection, by one who sees the precious-
ness of a time now dead. One of the quotations preceding
chapter 2 reads:

> "You seize the flower, the bloom is shed,
> Or like the snow falls in the river,
> A moment white----then melts forever."[13]

The novel might possibly be the realization of a work
originally conceived of toward the conclusion of the War.
Mrs. Chesnut writes in a diary entry for January 1, 1864:

> The last night of the old year sent me a
> cup of strong, good coffee. I drank two cups
> and so did not sleep a wink. Like a fool I
> passed my whole life in review, and bitter

memories maddened me. Then came a happy thought.
I mapped out a story of the war. Johnny [Johnny
Chesnut, her nephew] is the hero, light dragoon
and heavy swell. I will call it FF's for it is
the First Families both of South Carolina and
of Virginia. It is to be a war story, and the
filling out of the skeleton was a pleasant way
to put myself to sleep.[14]

Perhaps the love romance *The Captain and the Colonel*
is the final fruit of that "happy thought" born at the New
Year of 1864 as a relief from "bitter memories" of a whole
life passed in review. However, by the time that Mrs.
Chesnut came to write the story similar to the one she out-
lined in 1864, the War itself and all those depicted in
the War diary are part of a more mature and comprehensive
pattern of memory. The romance does indeed contain in the
figure of Dr. Johannis, S.C.F.F., a character much resem-
bling Johnny Chesnut, who loves horses and ladies and who
is gallant and heroic. But other characters, as well, and
even whole incidents from the diary appear there: the romance between Buck Preston and Gen. Sam Hood and even a
bit of the exchange between the lovers, attributed in the
diary to Buck Preston, is echoed in the novel in the exchange between Frank Collingwood and Emily Effingham. Mr.
Team—possessing his own name—is also present, and the
novel includes as well anecdotes describing the care of the
sick and dying in the hospitals, the wagonloads of negro
babies that Scipio gathers to please his mistress, the
escape of slaves, a party at the home of Mrs. Davis, and
various hardships of the war.

But written as it probably was many years after the
war, the novel does not depict, as Mrs. Chesnut's original
"happy thought" might have, an idyllic, pastoral world of
the antebellum plantation. It rather portrays the fragil-
ity of that "garden" and rejects the possibility of re-
covering it. The work indicates that only those survive
the loss of a world and the investment of value within it
who are able to surrender their illusionary controls and
understand, as they are named in an epigraph in *The Captain
and the Colonel*, the "deities" of "Patience, Poverty, and
Despair," not less powerful than "Persuasion and Force."[15]

The central plot involves the life of Joanna Hardhead,
a willful determined woman from New York, accomplished and
efficient in all things, who contrives to marry a Southern

gentleman Frank Effingham, and comes south. She destroys
the life of her first daughter by consigning her to marriage with a "brute." Her husband submits to Joanna's will
after some resistance but despairs at the death of his most
beloved child. Joanna then takes over the management of
his plantation and the care of her three daughters. Later,
years after her husband's death, Joanna refuses to allow a
match between her daughter Emily and a Kentuckian Robert
Collingwood because she has determined to enforce her idea
of her daughter's future. The couple refuse her will
though they are thereby forced to endure separation during
the war and to undergo a test of their absolute fidelity
to each other; but finally after the war they are reunited
and marry.

Parallel to this action is Joanna's gradual submission
during the war to the uncontrollable elements of existence;
and in a way her recognition indicates the main theme of
the work: power which is forced to learn mercy. She possesses at first a somewhat scientific desire for order--
imposing her will upon her sister, her husband, and her
daughters and in effect molding their fate according to her
narrow materialistic conceptions of the good, symbolized
by her effort to "fix" proper marriages. But she is overwhelmed by fate, a power greater than hers, and by the
genuine, courageous devotion of the lovers. Her surrender
of power in both these instances causes her to learn sympathy and mercy. By the end of the novel she has gained
considerable stature in moving from a simplistic understanding of human behavior to one more complex and comprehensive.

Although finally unsuccessful, *The Captain and the
Colonel* is significant because Mary Chesnut wrote it:
after seeing in the pages of the diary her intense curiosity and scrutiny of everyone and everything around her, one
expects to find the same acute mind at work here. And
indeed it is at work, though it is not in its element. But,
although with only partial success, she does explore in
the novel some fascinating aspects of the feminine as embodied in Joanna, her sister, and her daughters. One might
also see in the relationship between Joanna and her weak
but noble husband Frank Effingham, and as well between
Joanna's daughter Margaret and Johnny Johannis, a representation in part of the complex union of Mary and James
Chesnut, Jr.: the woman, as she seems in the diary, intensely active and practical, tending to excess in talking
and doing, and, her husband, somewhat withdrawn and passive,

who, as she noted in her biographical sketch of him, "is, as he always was, inclined to stand back and let the world flow by him," who is "cool and dispassionate," tending to allow "his perception of the universal [to weaken] that of the particular."[16] She seems to be contemplating in this fictional relationship, as she constantly did in the society around her and in her own life, the mystery of that correspondence between the masculine and feminine in marriage.

Two Years of My Life, though fragmentary, is in many ways more interesting than The Captain and the Colonel. It is a fictionalized memoir: The narrator is Helen Newton, who is at the beginning of the work taken out of boarding school in Charleston and made to go with her family to her father's cotton plantation in Mississippi. We find out that her sudden removal is occasioned by her seeing too much of a young law student named Sydney Howard. The family in travelling westward encounters the rough hospitality of the frontier and experiences some authentic "western" adventures, one of which is an elaborate blood feud between a Col. Blueskin and a family called the Hamlins. Sydney, we find, has followed Helen into the wilderness. In the missing section of the work he has apparently been involved in an intrigue of some sort and is present when a man is killed. Mr. Newton then commands that Sydney cannot see his daughter for two years. Helen travels back to Charleston with her father, who leaves her then at Madame Talvande's school. We are given a marvelous description of a "boarding school of fifty years ago," as Mrs. Chesnut entitles this portion of the memoir. Some months later Helen's father dies suddenly on the plantation and Helen returns to Mississippi with her mother to help manage the estate. After a while Sydney Howard's penance is up, he returns, and the work ends with "a wedding of fifty years ago."

A great deal of this plot we know to correspond to events in the life of Mary Miller before her engagement to James Chesnut, Jr. The lengthy memoir of her family mentions her trip with the family to Mississippi in about 1836, her stay in Charleston at Madame Talvande's, her courtship by James Chesnut, and finally her removal to the west after the death of her father. The memoir as well tells about some of the experiences in Mississippi and Alabama which seem to be sources for events in the story. Besides the information provided in the memoirs is a poem,

apparently in James Chesnut's hand, in an early scrapbook;
the poem, entitled "To Mary upon Leaving for Mississippi,"
is dated October 1838. Mary Miller's father had died
several months earlier, in March of 1838. Evidently Mary
was embarking west with her mother at the time of the
poem's composition. In a letter from James Chesnut, Jr.,
to Mary Miller from Charleston dated May 9, 1839, he dole-
fully regrets that she is no longer present to charm the
boarding house on Legare Street. Mary Miller and James
Chesnut were finally married in 1840, several months after
his return from a trip to Europe.

Two Years of My Life, then, draws upon immediate
experience; for the most part the parallels between Helen
Newton and Mary Miller seem disguised in little except
name. An interesting exception to the believability of
this work as a memoir of Mary Chesnut are the wild and
somewhat grotesque adventures on the road to Mississippi
which have the bizarre flavor of Southwest humor. Whether
the incidents are fact or fiction, they are certainly as
delightful as much in Mrs. Chesnut's diary.

Perhaps a more significant portion of the memoir is
the account of life at Madame Talvande's boarding school on
Legare Street. It is remembered with concreteness and fond-
ness, and at times the author seems to break the loosely
assumed persona to express the power of the memories. She
says at one point, "with the garrulity of age I find it
hard to know where to stop. These people were so kind to
me."[17] Madame Talvande's school is seen in memory to be
structured upon discipline and control, and, consequently,
upon the adventure of disobedience. But the remembered
world is also composed of moments of abundant feasting, of
dancing and singing, accomplished within the comic action
of learning civility. Ruling over the kingdom is the Queen,
Madame Talvande, a refugee of the St. Domingo insurrection
who quickly established herself in Charleston. She is
described by Helen in regal terms:

At ten o'clock she appeared in the school
room, bowing, smiling, curtsying, flirting a
gossamer handkerchief, redolent of cologne. Her
widows cap strings floating airily - a boa grace-
fully wound around her throat, a fur lined cloak,
if it were cold. She was a true type of her
country women, most pleasing and attractive to the
eye. Her tiny shoes were lined with fur, and as

she crossed those small feet of hers on the bar
below her desk after seating herself on her
throne, she looked a queen - The tiny brown
hand, was then waved aloft - and business began;
in earnest.
        She had the fiercest eye I have ever seen
in mortal head. Once a dead hawk was brought
in and thrown on a table in the Hall - Later in
the evening the hawk came to life, and walked
in the parlour, to our amazement and unspeak-
able alarm. He was ruffled, and bloody, and
staggered, unsteadily on his feet. But with
what a powerful eye he regarded us; reproach -
rage, indignation, hatred, vengeance, it was
all there. I can never forget it. Madame's
eye was the counterpart of that hawks -- that
broken winged hawk. She had the faculty of in-
spiring terror to an untold degree. It was by
that power she ruled us so absolutely.[18]

Other aspects of that child's world are rendered elab-
orately: the subterfuge of reading basketfuls of forbid-
den novels smuggled to the girls on picnics, the experiences of learning under duress, the mercilessness of the
students in ridiculing their peers. But the dominant pre-
sences in the narrative are the several negro servants of
Madame. Among them is Maum Jute, the abettor of the girls'
wishes:

        "Juliet"--Madame called her when she was in
a good humour.
        "Cette Vilaine negrrresse" when she was
angry. We gave her the name, she chose for herself - Maum Jute. She was our friend. The servants were one with us against the tyrant. They
made common cause with us. Why Maum Jute dressed
as she did? Who knows! She was given the same
kind of clothes, they gave Maum Margaret - who
was as neat and trim a maid servant as heart
could wish. But the shoes of Maum Jute were
always down at heel - and you could hear them in
regular cadences as she flip flapped away. When
on any of her predatory expeditions she went
barefooted - she wore a linsey woolsey gown, very
short, always open in the back, revealing the
absence of every other garment - stockings were
never seen on those poor old husky legs in the

middle of her feet. Her much soiled handkerchief was always hanging over one ear, or
pushed back far from her forehead, or shoved
over her eyes. For whenever spoken to - she
began at once to scratch her head; and as she
did so the forlorn turban toppled over - and
yet it never fell.[19]

One wonders at Mrs. Chesnut's desire to capture the
memory of these particular two years in fictional form.
They would seem to be pivotal to her in a certain way, re-
presenting as they do the several events which mark the
child's entrance into adulthood--the experience of the
Mississippi frontier, the death of her father and the burd-
en of managing the plantation with her mother, her engagement to James Chesnut, and finally her marriage. The work
begins with the child's peevishness at leaving the comforts
of Charleston and the known world and ends in the frightened joy of a young woman confronting the moment of marriage.

But what is perhaps more significant than the story
of this transition is the meaning taking shape in the work
through the remembrance of the ever-present narrator--the
old woman, having endured the War and the Reconstruction,
writing of life "fifty years ago." She finds in these two
years not only her own intense experience but an "ancient"
way of life, not ideal by any means, but allowing nevertheless an abundant existence based upon codes of gentility.
The setting of the action moves from Charleston to the
frontier and back to Charleston, but wherever the characters settle, they establish and maintain an order of
hospitality and courtesy, the feminine virtues of a culture
inculcated in part through institutions like that of
Madame Talvande. At the end of the chapter describing the
life at that Charleston school, the narrator meditates
upon her love for Charleston; she asks, "Why did I then -
and why do I now prefer them [the men and women of
Charleston] to the whole world." She answers:

One always likes the best of its kind. I
will state the case prosaically and be careful
to let nothing "high-toned" creep in. A cart
horse is useful - but gives the palm to the
thoroughbred. If I were forced to be a cat or
a tiger - I should be a tiger if I died for it.
Lord Byron said everybody knew a gentleman when

he saw one, but he had never met anyone who
could define the creature. So I will not try.
But they are there still, and now, to be found
in the queerest places, and in the oddest em-
ployements. The fine flavor still lingers.
They are the best of their kind.[20]

This long meditation reveals that love of the valuable
quality of a past life that is in part the motivation for
Mary Chesnut's enormous endeavors in composing and rewriting her memoirs in various forms. Though both *The Captain
and the Colonel* and *Two Years of My Life* possess fictional
form, they are finally, I believe, like all of Mrs.
Chesnut's writings, accomplished in the service of Memory,
out of the need to give form to and preserve that past
which has rendered what is valuable in the present. Her
work shows her to be an imaginative craftsman, the kind of
writer whom Allen Tate in a recent essay describes as "the
archeologist of the memory, dedicated to the minute parti-
culars of the past, definite things--*prima sacrimenti
memoria*."[21] This is a fitting role for Mary Chesnut
and for other women writers of this conference. For, as
Tate reminds us later in the same essay, "St. Augustine
tells us that memory is like a woman. The Latin *memoria*
is properly a feminine noun, for women never forget."[22]

Notes

[1]Mary Boykin Chesnut, *A Diary from Dixie*, ed. Ben Ames
Williams (Boston: Houghton Mifflin, 1949), p. 196.

[2]*Selected Poems*, Third Edition (New York: Alfred A.
Knopf, 1969), p. 140. I quote here the original version
of "Here Lies a Lady," which Ransom reprints in this edition along with a revised version.

[3]A portion of *Two Years of My Life* is entitled "A
Boarding School of Fifty Years Ago" and another "A Wedding
of Fifty Years Ago." The "fifty years" is an approximate
number; a note on a separate fragment among the manuscript
pages indicates that *Two Years* relates incidents of "more
than forty years ago." The actions upon which the memoir
is based occurred during the time from about 1836 to 1840.
The fictionalized memoir was composed, then, sometime after
1876. Since I completed my work on the unpublished Chesnut
literary manuscripts, Elisabeth Muhlenfeld of the Southern
Studies Program has undertaken to prepare an annotated edition of these manuscripts as her doctoral dissertation.
Ms. Muhlenfeld suggests the following dates for these manuscripts: *Two Years* was probably written between 1878 and
1882. Mrs. Chesnut's novel *The Captain and the Colonel*
may have been begun as early as 1875. The brief memoir
focusing on Kate Williams (see note 8) was written in mid-
1876. "The Bright Side of Richmond" could not have been
written prior to 1883, and was more probably prepared in
1884. The dating of the manuscripts, however, is still
conjectural.

[4]The papers of this collection consist of those belonging to the Library and of those merely on deposit there.
Only the first portion possesses an itemized catalogue.
For any reference to a work within the collection I have
indicated where possible a page number within the manuscript, but I have not attempted to indicate the location
of the manuscript within the collection.

[5]I have been unable to determine the date of this ad-
vertisement or to locate any work published with this title
and author. However the biographical sketch was written
while Mr. Chesnut was still alive, perhaps sometime during
1879 or 1880. Within the collection is a book containing

diary entries by Mrs. Chesnut. A two-page note entitled
"Scraps for the Life of James Chesnut" exists among its
pages. The first date which occurs preceding this note is
April 17, 1879; the first date occurring after the note is
November 12, 1880.

[6]The letter from William Henry Trescot, dated December 6, 1884, was evidently written in response to a letter
of Mrs. Chesnut in which she had spoken of contemporary
histories and memoirs of the war. Trescot suggests that
she write her husband's history for him, and that "if you
would add your own recollection of the inside history at
Richmond, I think you would throw as much light upon our
troubles as the history of the battles--private or
public . . . ."

[7]Receipt of the sketch was acknowledged by the *News
and Courier* on January 21, 1884. It was evidently written
in response to a call for contributions. A series of reminiscences of the war appeared in the *Weekly News*, but I
have been unable to locate a sketch with this title in
issues of the *News and Courier*.

Editor's note: Mrs. Chesnut's sketch has recently
been located by Ms. Patricia Wall, a student in the Southern Studies Program currently preparing an edition of Mrs.
Chesnut's letters as her Master's thesis. The sketch was
published as No. 60 in a series entitled "Our Women in the
War" in *The Weekly News and Courier* of Charleston, and
collected the following year in *"Our Women in the War":
The Lives they Lived; the Deaths they Died,* presumably
edited by Francis W. Dawson (Charleston: News and Courier
Book Presses, 1885).

[8]This memoir seems to be addressed to the family of
Kate Williams, or to those who knew her well. Mrs. Chesnut
indicates at one point that "it is her [Kate's] life & not
mine that I am writing" (p. 10). But her own past is
interwoven with that of her sister. To my knowledge the
memoir provides more immediate biograpical information
about Mary Chesnut than any document besides the diary of
the war.

[9]The fictional memoir begins with the departure of
Helen Newton to Mississippi with her family and concludes
with her marriage. Mary Miller left Charleston for her
father's plantation sometime in 1836, one year after the

rest of the family had migrated with Stephen Miller (see the memoir of Kate Williams, p. 6); she married James Chesnut, Jr., in 1840.

[10]Besides the portions of the early MS. of *Two Years*, nos. 1, 4, 5, and 6, is a portion entitled "A Boarding School of Fifty Years Ago," numbered 267 through 309, a later version of parts 4 and 5; and a portion entitled "Two Years--or the Way We Lived Then No. 1," numbered 1 through 49, a later version of part 1 of the original. A separate fragment exists as well, entitled "No. 5 The Way We Lived Then." Other pages exist, numbered 411 through 419, which correspond to pp. 265-73 of the original MS. This evidence would indicate the existence of a complete or nearly complete revised version of greater length than the original MS.

[11]A note on the verso of the fragment, mentioned above, from a later version of *Two Years* states: "The greatest part of this is written from memory--though I used my diary, of more than forty years ago, freely. But no diary was possible in Legare St."

[12]*The Captain and the Colonel*, MS. p. 1.

[13]*The Captain and the Colonel*, MS. p. 25.

[14]*A Diary from Dixie*, p. 346.

[15]*The Captain and the Colonel*, MS. p. 25.

[16]Sketch of the life of James Chesnut, Jr., MS. pp. 20-21.

[17]*Two Years of My Life*, MS. p. 254.

[18]*Two Years of My Life*, MS. pp. 222-24.

[19]*Two Years of My Life*, MS. pp. 248-49.

[20]*Two Years of My Life*, MS. pp. 260-61.

[21]"A Lost Traveller's Dream," in *Memoirs and Opinions 1926-1974* (Chicago: Swallow Press, 1975), p. 12.

[22]"A Lost Traveller's Dream," p. 12.

Literary Elements in Mary Chesnut's Journal

by

Elisabeth Muhlenfeld

Until today, Mary Boykin Chesnut's Journal had been badly misunderstood; fortunately, Dr. Woodward has charted some very muddy waters, and Mr. Hayhoe and Dr. Gregory have further examined Mrs. Chesnut's use of her material. Nevertheless, it would be useful to reiterate here some of the basic points which have been made earlier today about the problems with the currently available edition of the Journal, and perhaps the simplest way to do that will be to comment on a brief four-line footnote in Ben Ames Williams' edition of *A Diary from Dixie*. In this footnote, Williams makes three bibliographical blunders, characterizes one passage inaccurately, and misquotes the original version of the Journal.[1] He says, in this remarkable footnote, that Mrs. Chesnut *copied* her original diary; she had instead re-written it. He says, "she destroyed most of the original;" in fact, we do not know what happened to some of the original, some of it was destroyed in 1863, some presumably after she had initiated her task of rewriting, but a good portion---between a third and a half of the original diary---still exists.[2] "But," says Mr. Williams casually, "one or two notebooks escaped." In fact, there are many groups of loose and stapled pages, and five bound books, two of these rather handsomely bound, on deposit at the South Caroliniana Library.[3] Such misinformation is lamentable, but not surprising: apparently Mr. Williams did not work from the diaries themselves, but from a typescript prepared for him by someone else.[4]

245

That Mary Chesnut was conscious of herself as author,
and that she fully intended for the product of her labors
to go to press, is evident from a letter she wrote to Mrs.
Varina Davis in 1883: "How I wish you could read over my
Journal. I have been two years over looking it--copying--
leaving my self out. You must see it before it goes to
print, but that may not be just now ... for I must over
haul it again and again."[5] And overhaul it she did. We
know that she reread the entire original in early 1865,
that she reread at least portions of it in 1866, that she
again worked on the material in 1875,[6] and that she devoted
large amounts of time in the early 1880's to the task of revision. Enough of an interim draft remains to suggest that
she revised large portions of the Journal very systematically at least twice in these last few years, and that in
all, she must have written well over a million words while
working on this book alone.

It is the reasons for and the product of these extensive revisions which I would like to examine today. Mr.
Williams makes a remark in his introduction which contains
an interesting idea. He speaks for a moment about himself
as an author: "The writer of fiction based on history is
free, as long as he seeks out and respects the truth, to
supplement that truth with details based on probabilities
and supplied by his imagination."[7] Obviously, Williams
applied some of his expertise as historical novelist to his
job as editor, for he saw fit to supply from his imagination
a small detail like the last sentences in the diary.[8] More
interesting, though, is that Mary Boykin Chesnut seems to
have operated on exactly the same principle---she too has
attempted to "seek out" the truth, but has felt free to
"supplement that truth with details ... supplied by [her]
imagination." The reader of her Journal is often faced *not*
with facts exactly as they happened---or even as she thought
they happened, but rather with an account of factual events
which has been carefully reworked, rewritten, rearranged
and in some cases interspersed with invention. The problem
of defining what the Journal actually is has been examined
earlier today by Dr. Woodward and Mr. Hayhoe. I would not
go so far as to say that what we have is fiction, or even
the "fiction based on history" of Mr. Williams' statement,
but on the other hand, neither is it quite what it seems to
be: the simple recording of events by a highly intelligent
woman. Whatever it is, however it is defined, in every
case where we have a portion of the original diary, as it
was recorded day by day, corresponding to the later version

as it was revised in the 1880's, the later version bears
no more than a close family resemblance to the former.

Mary Chesnut revised not only, as she stated to Mrs.
Davis, to minimize her own role in the Journal's pages,
but also to make the times of which she tells come alive.
By no means a slave to her own diary, she freely rearranged
incidents and thoughts within a given entry (or date) to
heighten their dramatic import. She transformed what had
originally been third person narrative statements into dialogue, often turning her own thoughts into the words of
others. When she wished to concentrate on a given per-
sonage, she sometimes assigned remarks to him which had
been made by someone else in the original, and she seems to
have had some definite themes in mind which she carefully
explicated by her arrangement of material.[9] In short,
throughout the revision of the whole, she was quite conscious of the journal *as a literary form*. In one of the
earliest volumes of the original, Mary gave her work a
formal title: "My Journal of the Secession of 1861."[10]
I am convinced that, from the beginning, she conceived of
her Journal as a literary work, and that the finished product was built not upon the lucky accident of a diarist who
happened to be fortunately placed in society and time, but
rather upon the careful craftsmanship of an author who intended all along to write a valuable book, to make a contribution to history, and to do so in the form of a journal
or diary.

To illustrate my basic contention, let me offer in
evidence the fact that there are extant no less than four
drafts or portions of drafts of what we now know as the
first entry in the Journal. Yet none of these represents
the actual first entry; that appears in a small book which
Mrs. Chesnut was keeping as a sort of commonplace book late
in 1860. On page 10 of this book, following several pages
of quotations and aphorisms, occurs an entry reminiscent of
those made in family Bibles:

> November 11th 1860
> James Chesnut Jr
> resigned his seat in
> the Senate of U.S.A--
> alas I was in Florida
> I might not have been
> able to influence
> him--but I should

have tried--.[11]

I suspect that at this point, Mrs. Chesnut had not decided
to embark upon her journal project, for the next pages of
the small blue book contain more notes and quotations un-
connected with national events written in December 1860.
Sometime in February, she apparently decided to begin a
formal journal, for she began to write in a handsome red
volume. The first entry is dated 25 February 1861, but on
the flyleaf, she wrote:

> November 10th 1860
> James Chesnut Jr
> resigned his seat in
> the U.S.A. Senate--
> "burnt the ships
> behind him"
> The first resignation--
> & I am not at all resigned--.[12]

I mention these two early entries in detail because they
seem to be the two earliest notations she made, and because
the first became the third paragraph of the published diary,
and the second, "I am not at all resigned," became transformed into "Said someone spitefully: 'Mrs. Chesnut does
not look at all resigned'" in paragraph eleven.[13]

Neither of these two early notes is one of the four
drafts or partial drafts of the first entry I mentioned a
moment ago---all four of those appear to have come later.
The earliest is a rather formal essay probably written in
February or March 1861 which contains most of the material
of pages 1-4 of the published book, but which conveys little
sense of "diary." The second, third and fourth appear to
have been written in the 1880's; they are all very different from each other and from the first draft. Only two of
them contain what we know today as the opening paragraph of
the Journal, a probably fictional "vignette" used by Mrs.
Chesnut to establish the tone of an eyewitness account: "on
the train just before we reached Fernandina a woman cried
out--'That settles the hash.' Tanny touched me on the
shoulder.--'Look out!' 'Lincoln's elected.' 'How do you
know?'-- 'The man over there has a telegram.'"[14]

These first pages over which Mrs. Chesnut worked with
such care are skillfully wrought: they contain within them
several of the themes which she treats throughout the

Journal, and they illustrate many of the techniques she uses to achieve both verisimilitude and dramatic interest. She deals with the character of the Southern soldier, with the inefficient leadership of the South, with her own character and her dislike of Mulberry. In one brief sentence (one which, incidentally, does not appear until the drafts of the 1880's) she illustrates the ambivalent and confused nature of grief which is to become such an important theme later in the diary, "so wild are we-- to day I saw at a grand parade of the home guard [a woman] . . . driving about to see the turn out of this new Company. though her father was buried yesterday."[15] Again, in another single sentence, she suggests the stoicism and strength of the Confederate woman and comments on the juxtaposition of momentous events on day-to-day matters: "Dec -- 27th -- Mrs Gidiere came in quietly from her marketting [sic] to day. And in her neat incisive manner exploded this bombshell -- 'Major Anderson has moved into -- Fort Sumter'."[16]

Most importantly, these opening pages establish Mrs. Chesnut's most identifiable technique which can perhaps best be described as a carefully constructed montage of scenes in which incidents of serious import are punctuated by anecdotes in an entirely different, often ironic vein. Thus, in the midst of discussions of her own politics, those of her husband, and the confusion rampant on all sides, is a flash, a picture of the ridiculous publicity posters of Judge Magrath, a local politician.[17] The entire entry, with its serious tone, is ended with a light anecdote about two people who accidentally get up and have breakfast before midnight, then set and wait for morning.[18] This last delightful little story should not be ignored, for Mrs. Chesnut often uses anecdotes metaphorically. Here, by portraying the incongruity of two people who prepare themselves for daybreak eight hours too soon, perhaps she also means for us to think of these two people in terms of the Confederacy. She has just described the disorganized activity of preparation for war, but it was to be a long wait before the South could really see daylight again.

Mrs. Chesnut strives throughout the Journal, both in the original document and more carefully in her later rewriting, to convey above all else the *feeling* of the times in which she lived. In the sense she gives us of the quality of life in the Confederacy, how people felt and behaved, what they worried about, how they dealt with the

constant bombardment of death and destruction which the war
brought, in this sense of what it was like to be alive in
the South in 1861 or 1865 lies the Journal's greatest value.
And the panorama of people and actions and motives is
achieved precisely by the use of the diary format. Mrs.
Chesnut was perfectly capable of writing very creditable
straightforward essays about the central figures in her
Journal. She did, in fact, write at least one such essay
on her husband in 1879 or 1880.[19] But the James Chesnut
of the essay seems hopelessly stilted in comparison with
the James Chesnut of the Journal. The formal James Chesnut
has birth and death dates, schooling, official position,
political leanings, appreciative friends, but the Journal
James Chesnut *lives*. He too has the dates and official
titles of formal history, but we see him as a multi-
dimensional man, one who fulfils his appointed duties im-
pressively, but who ultimately is only a small part of the
vast machinery of the Confederacy---one moment stepping
with irritation over his wife's endless stream of guests,
another moment gossiping companionably with her over a
plate of scrambled eggs in front of a late night fire. By
using the diary form, Mrs. Chesnut can place the major
figures of the day in an interesting perspective: brilliant
on the battlefield one day, ridiculous or bitter or egotis-
tical at the dinner table the next---or vice versa. The
elegant hostess becomes an angel of mercy at a Wayside hos-
pital, becomes a helpless and pathetic creature who goes
hungry because she cannot cook. An important topic of the
day is distorted by rumor and eclipsed by a funeral which
in turn is forgotten in favor of an evening of amateur
singing.

One feels when reading the Journal that its author has
recorded *everything*, and that the reader is to be congratu-
lated for bringing some kind of order out of the chaos she
offers. In fact, Mrs. Chesnut's major point, her central
theme in the diary, might be said to be the chaos itself,
the riot of emotions and events and people that *are* a dis-
rupted society. The montage technique to which I referred
earlier, clearly functioning as a device to produce in the
reader a sense of the hectic, the confused, the fluctuating
world of which she was a part, might almost be said to
approach something like an early conception of stream-of-
consciousness. A look at a holograph page of the Journal
reveals that Mrs. Chesnut uses a unique system of punctuation, the effect of which is to reproduce as accurately as
possible the mind casting back and forth over a day's

events, stopping now and then to ponder, veering occasionally from the moment at hand to the associations it evokes.
She punctuates almost exclusively with dashes of various
lengths and with spaces which, on the manuscript page, give
a very real feeling of spontaneous and unstructured
thought.[20]

To achieve this chaos, though, Mrs. Chesnut has
exercised a rigorous selectivity on her material. For
example, in one section of the diary for which we have the
original and the revision,[21] nearly half of the material in
the original version is *not* used---and we may assume some
selectivity at the time the original diary was written. At
the same time that she has cut out a great deal, she has
expanded what was retained so that in this segment of the
Journal, thirty-seven pages of original becomes fifty-two
pages of revision---in spite of the considerable amount of
material excised.[22]

A brief look at this section of the diary can illustrate well the kinds of literary techniques Mrs. Chesnut
applied to her original material throughout the revision
process. In the original, for example, no sooner does she
get settled in "Johnstones Hotel Lincolnton" than her maid
interrupts what Mary Chesnut describes as her own constant
state of weeping with a complaint: "Old Miss Jonson--'Say
in the kitchen--go away gal--dont stand there--My niggers
wont work for looking at you--Now Misses--aint I a *show*."[23]
In the revised Journal, the scene is very different, very
much longer, very much written with an eye to its humorous
potential. Furthermore, it provides insight not only into
the maid herself of whom we now get a vivid picture, but
also into the character of the hotel proprietor, one of
that ubiquitous class of people who profit by the misfortunes of others:

> after dinner Ellen presented herself--blue black
> with rage--She has lost the sight of one eye-- so
> that is permanently *blueish*-- opaque-- The other
> flamed-- fire and fury. --Heres my dinner. A
> piece of meat-- And a whole plate ful of raw ingans.
> I never did eat raw ingins and I won't begin now--
> dese here niggers say dis ole lady gives em to em
> breakfast and dinner-- Its a sin and a shame to do
> us so. She says I must come outen her kitchen-- de
> niggers won't work for looking at me--

I'se something to look at surely-- She threw
down her odorous plate-- held her fork and made a
courtesy
--"Ellen-- for pity sake?"--
Lord ha' mercy. She say you bring me and Laurence
here to keep us from running away to de Yankees--
and I say-- Name o'God Ole Missis-- If dats it--
what she bring Laurence and me for-- She's got
plenty more-- Laurence and Me's nothing-- to our
white people-- De ole soul fair play insulted me" --

Mrs. Chesnut has turned a remark of no interest into a
scene which lives in and for itself, but which also functions significantly in the whole Lincolnton section of the
Journal. In the original diary, Ellen is simply there---an
adjunct to Mrs. Chesnut's other possessions. In the revised Journal, however, Ellen provides comic relief and a
very human tone. In the midst of the grief which the upper
class Carolinians feel for the destruction which Sherman is
wreaking on their homes and property, Ellen is having the
time of her life. This is her first trip as lady's maid,
her introduction to the wide world, and she is delighted to
find that the prominence of her mistress gives Ellen herself
a superiority over the other servants in town.

The way Mrs. Chesnut uses her characterization of
Ellen is clearly seen in a passage describing the household's escape from the horrible Johnston Hotel. The original diary reads: "I moved here Yesterday-- friday morning--
I swallowed my superstitions-- so anxious was I to leave
the Hotel."[25] The revised diary, on the other hand, shifts
the superstitions to the comic Ellen:

"Lord, Missis we can't move to day-- it is friday--
bad luck-- all round' --
    but Ellen succumbed-- swallowed her super-
stitions-- she was too keen to get away from 'dirt
and raw ingins' -- and the raking fire of the Land-
lady's sharp tongue--.[26]

Ellen, in the revised diary, is given to singing "Massa's
in the Cold, Cold Ground," the very song which had been
sung as the Confederate flag was raised in Montgomery in
1861, and Mrs. Chesnut uses this touch symbolically and to
eerie effect by punctuating a "conversation" with Isabella
(a conversation which, incidentally, is the invention of
the 1880's, not an actual talk of 1865) thus:

M̲r̲s̲ Martin says-- "Only Genius can create
something out of Nothing-- Lee or Wellington could
not work without material-- Genius like love pays
its own expenses-- Stonewall was our genius-- He
was inspired-- Some say a little mad. We would a
Napolean to create an army and enthuse it-- We had
the best fighting material in the world-- but it
was not properly handled-- and our men could only
die in their tracks"
--"Don't you feel better now-- You have railed and
scolded so--" --No-- Not quite-- We have ceased to
look for gentlemen, when we elect rulers-- we fairly
rake them up from the Ashes, the Cinders, the
Gutters-- Stop Ellen-- "No more Massa in the
cold-- cold ground"-- Sing something else"--
--"Well so they are most of them" says Isabella.
                Times revenges--27

Touches like these represent artistic skill of a very
high order. But they are clearly fiction, and at this
point we must remember Dr. Woodward's concern with the degree to which the Journal can be relied upon as history.
Obviously, no one is likely to write a biographical sketch
of Mary Chesnut's black maid Ellen---if anyone did so using
this source, he would, unawares, be writing something much
closer to a literary character analysis. On the other hand,
though, historians might well wish to turn to the Journal
for source material on General Hood, whose portrait in the
revised diary suffers somewhat in comparison to his treatment in the original. Historians using the Journal should
be aware of the fact that Mrs. Chesnut's extensive rewriting has produced direct quotations somewhat after the fact,
has jumbled dates and characters a bit, and has eliminated
a good deal of material which might be of historical value.
Only in the original diary, for example, does a description
of General Wade Hampton appear, complete with a record of
his assessment of some of his fellow officers.28

Very much to be pitied is anyone who is so naive as to
write a sketch of Isabella Martin using the revised Journal
as a source, for most of what Isabella says and does in
A Diary from Dixie is fictional; Mrs. Chesnut uses Isabella
as a device to remove herself from its pages and to enhance
the underlying fiction of the book: that the Journal is a
spontaneous diary. In a passage which Dr. Woodward quoted
this morning, that of February 23, 1865, Mrs. Chesnut
testifies to the worth of her own work and to her fear that

it might have to be destroyed:

> for four days . . . I have been busily engaged--
> reading the *16* volumes of memoirs of the times I
> have written-- Nearly all my sage prophecies have
> been verified the wrong way-- & every insight into
> character or opinions I have given as to men turned
> out utter folly-- still I write on-- *for if I have
> to burn* [italics added]-- & here lie my treasures
> ready for the blazing hearth-- Still they have
> served already to while away for [sic] days of
> agony.[29]

The final revision seems to be pure invention designed to
provide a touch of drama and to preserve the fiction of
Mary Chesnut writing for her own amusement but unaware,
finally, of the value of her effort: "Isabella has been
reading my diaries. How we laugh [at] my sage ratiocina-
tions-- all come to naught. My famous insight into char-
acter-- utter folly. They were lying on the hearth ready
to be burned-- but she told me to hold on-- Think of it
awhile--." Then she quotes Isabella directly: "'*Don't be
rash.*'"[30] We can smile knowingly at *this* fiction. Mary
Chesnut was not about to commit her future masterpiece
dramatically to the flames.

When Mary Chesnut began her Journal in 1861, she approached the self-imposed task professionally. A comment
which appears only in one of the original segments indicates
that she saw herself as a journalist gathering source material, "I must regain the habit of regular writing in my
journal. Will be worthless--for I forget every thing if I
neglect it a day."[31] It is no accident, I think, that she
refers to the London Times correspondent Russell repeatedly,
has read his articles closely, formed definite opinions
about his reportorial ability, and is able to compare his
coverage of the Confederacy with his earlier assessment in
India. Her habit of clipping out items of interest to her
which she inserted in her revised Journal and her passion
for obtaining and reading magazines and newspapers all indicate strongly that as she recorded and preserved, she was
also deliberately studying her craft.

But Mary Boykin Chesnut is ultimately not a journalist
in the narrow sense. Rather, her achievement here can, perhaps, be compared to Thoreau's triumph in *Walden* or
Faulkner's brilliant fiction-essay "Mississippi."[32] In

Mary Chesnut's Journal, the techniques and inventions of
fiction superimposed on a historical record produce a
picture of reality which is both truer and infinitely more
alive than the simple historical record alone. So skillful
is the blend that I do not hesitate at all to return
finally to Ben Ames Williams who, for all his lamentable
faults as an editor, does not overpraise Mrs. Chesnut too
highly when he calls her Journal "a masterpiece of history
in the highest and fullest sense."[33] This is a big book,
a complex book, and I regret that today I have only been
able to scratch the surface of the artistry which informs
it. Many of the participants at this conference have discussed works which they readily admitted were not, after
all, unsung masterpieces. In my judgment, Mary Chesnut's
Journal, which is so hard to define because it takes a form
peculiar to itself, and which has therefore been so misunderstood, *is* one of the unsung works of art of the nineteenth century.

Notes

[1]Ben Ames Williams, ed., *A Diary from Dixie* (Houghton Mifflin, 1949), p. 14. Williams cites an original passage as reading "'counting months on their fingers.'" The passage, dated March 7, 1861 (rather than March 5 in the revised version) actually says "They were counting the time for her baby to be born with dreadful suspicions." This small error in quotation is, unfortunately, quite typical of Williams' approach to the Chesnut manuscripts.

[2]See C. Vann Woodward, "What is the Chesnut Diary?" in this volume, pp. 193-209, for a listing of extant portions of the original journal (Version I).

[3]Williams-Chesnut-Manning Collection, South Caroliniana Library, University of South Carolina. Hereafter, quotations from the Journal will refer to manuscript except where otherwise noted, and will be cited by version and date, in accordance with Dr. Woodward's system of description in "What is the Chesnut Diary?"

[4]Bell Irvin Wiley, "Mary Boykin Chesnut--Southern Intellectual" in *Confederate Women* (Greenwood Press, 1974), p. 6.

[5]Quoted in Wiley, p. 16, from a letter in the Confederate Museum, Richmond, Virginia.

[6]Mrs. Chesnut stated in an entry dated February 23, 1865 (Version I) that she had just finished rereading the entire Journal. A notation, "What a fool I was 1866" (Version I, 19 [February 1861]) indicates that she was rereading the material in 1866. A notation at the end of her entry for March 6, 1861 (Version I), is dated 1875, as are several other notations.

[7]Williams edition, p. ix.

[8]Wiley (p. 7) notes Williams' insertion of the final sentences of his edition of the Journal.

[9]The methods of revision Mrs. Chesnut used may be clearly seen by comparing a passage from the original Journal describing General Hood and its counterpart in the revision

made nearly twenty years later. The original version reads:

> "Sam" the *simplest* most transparent soul I have
> met yet in this great revolution came Yesterday--
> Isabella & I went to See him-- he can stand alone
> on his wooden leg & is So pleased. What a greeting
> he gave us-- how eloquently he talked of his plans
> & *that* aim [aims?] fall defeat-- he blamed nobody--
> We talked of the Bazaar & while Isabella was telling
> one of her merriest stories I looked at Sam-- & he
> perfectly abstracted was gazing in the fire-- his
> face livid-- spots of perspiration on his head--
> he was back evidently in some moment of his bitter
> time-- Willie Preston's death-- the fields of
> dead at Franklin-- the panic at Nashville who can
> tell-- but the agony of his face was fearful-- &
> when we were alone-- Jack told me Several times
> he had seen the intense gaze into the fire &
> accompanied by the Same agonized expression--

The revised version reads very differently and is, in this
case, perhaps not so compelling; Mrs. Chesnut has supplied
Hood with some dialogue, and transformed her own thoughts
into the words of Jack Preston, apparently to characterize
Preston as well as Hood:

> Hood came yesterday-- He is staying at the
> Preston's with Jack. They sent for us.
>   What a heartfull-- greeting he gave us-- He
> can stand well enough without his crutch-- but he
> does very slow walking. How plainly he spoke out
> these dreadful words. "My defeat and discomfiture"
> "My army is destroyed"-- "My losses" & & --
>   Isabella who adores Hood-- said--
> --May you attempted the impossible?--
> And then she began one of her funniest stories.
> "Sam"-- did not listen-- Jack Preston touched me--
> And we slipped away unobserved into the Piazza.
> --"He did not hear a word she was saying. He had
> forgotten us all. Did you notice how he stared in
> the fire. And the livid spots which came out on
> his face-- and the huge drops of perspiration that
> stood out on his forehead?"--
> --Yes-- He is going over-- some bitter hour. He
> sees Willie Preston-- with his heart shot away.
> He feels the panic at Nashville and its shame.
> --"And the dead on the battle field at Franklin

> they say-- was a dreadful fight." said tender
> hearted Jack with a shiver-- "And that agony in
> his face-- comes again-- and again. I can't keep
> him out of those absent fits. It is pretty try-
> ing to any one who has to look on"--   "When
> he looks in the fire-- and forgets me-- and seems
> going through in his own mind the torture of the
> damned-- I get up and come out as I did just now--"
>   (Version III, undated)

[10]Flyleaf, small bound book containing entries covering
4 August-9 September 1861.

[11]*Ibid*., p. 10.

[12]Bound book containing entries covering 25 February-
3 August 1861. The first entry in the book, that of 25
February 1861, has apparently been recopied from an earlier
entry made on loose pages.

[13]Williams edition, p. 3. In her revised manuscript
version, Mrs. Chesnut indents frequently, making no effort
to maintain standard paragraphing form. The manuscript
version of this passage reads slightly differently: "Said
one of them spitefully, 'M$\underline{^{rs}}$ C does not look at all resigned." (Version III, undated entry, loose pages,
Williams-Chesnut-Manning Collection.) This manuscript
version, the only revised manuscript version extant which
might be considered Volume I of the revised Journal, seems
to be an interim draft which Mrs. Chesnut intended to revise further. Moreover, there are indications that these
loose pages have been arranged and numbered by a hand other
than Mrs. Chesnut's. Possibly a Volume I in the same kind
of notebook as the other forty-seven volumes existed at one
time, but if so, it has been lost. We cannot, therefore,
place as much weight on the author's intentions for the
opening pages of her Journal as we can on other sections.

[14]The earliest draft is carefully copied in a group of
pages stapled together; the second is a series of loose
pages in pencil; what is apparently part of another draft
written about the same time as Version II is a single page
containing the "That settles the hash" passage; the last,
page one of Version III, corresponds roughly to the version
in Williams' edition. Page one of this latest version has
been lost, but was reproduced in facsimile in the first
edition of the Journal (Isabella D. Martin and Myrta

Lockett Avary, eds., *A Diary from Dixie, as written by Mary Boykin Chesnut, wife of James Chesnut, Jr., United States Senator from South Carolina, 1858-1861, and afterward an Aide to Jefferson Davis and a Brigadier-General in the Confederate Army* [D. Appleton, 1905], p. xxiii).

[15]Version III, undated entry, loose pages, Williams-Chesnut-Manning Collection.

[16]Version III, 27 December [1860], loose pages, Williams-Chesnut-Manning Collection. This sentence was revised by Mrs. Chesnut from the original journal (Version I, 18 February 1861): "one morning Mrs Gidiere coming home from market announced fort Sumter seized by the Yankee garrison."

[17]Version III, undated entry, loose pages, Williams-Chesnut-Manning Collection, and Version I, 18 February 1861.

[18]Interestingly, this anecdote is dated 30 January 1875, and appears on the last page of the booklet containing Mrs. Chesnut's first version of the opening entry. See footnote 14. The first entry occupies about half of the booklet; the remaining pages are blank with the exception of the last page. The final words of the anecdote, "stories of the times-- transition state," indicate that Mrs. Chesnut saw the incident metaphorically.

[19]Manuscript in Williams-Chesnut-Manning Collection, South Caroliniana Library, University of South Carolina. See Eileen Gregory, "The Formality of Memory: A Study of Literary Manuscripts of Mary Boykin Chesnut" in this volume, note 5, pp. 241-242.

[20]Although Mrs. Chesnut employed dashes more often than strictly grammatical procedure would warrant, her punctuation was not always so unconventional as that of the revised Journal. In her unpublished novel "The Captain and the Colonel" and in her memoir "Two Years of my Life" as well as in more formal letters and other writings, she punctuated far more nearly in accordance with standard practice.

[21][17 January]-23 February 1865. (The date 17 January is inferred: the first dated entry in the original version is 4 February, but it is preceded by a portion of an earlier entry. The corresponding entry in Version III is included under the January date.)

[22]This count is misleading because the manuscript pages
of the original are considerably smaller than those of the
revised version. It would be more accurate to state that
a typed transcription of the original version is nineteen
pages long, and a typed transcription of the revision is
forty pages long.

[23]Version I, 16 February 1865.

[24]Version III, 16 February 1865.

[25]Version I, 18 February 1865.

[26]Version III, 18 February 1865.

[27]Version III, 19 February 1865. Version I reads quite
differently, and a comparison of the original to the passage just quoted serves to further illustrate the way in
which Mary Chesnut reworked her material to imbue it with
life:

> I read Mad de Genlis-- contrast our country at the
> Revolution-- John Rutledge dictator *now* Magrath--
> we do not look among Gentlemen for our rulers--
> but in the dust & ashes we rake them from dung-
> hills-- enough for Sunday-- Oh bitter pill!
> "Massa in the cold- cold ground"-- The time they
> sung where they elevated our Flag at Montgomery--
> They are *most* of them there-- young & old--.

[28]Version I, 8 February 1865:

> Gen Hampton was here last night-- said Longstreet
> had behaved magnanimously he commended him for
> Leut *Gnl* for [winning?] the battle of Chickamauga--
> Said he liked Hood-- that he was a good soldier
> &c but decried his *ability*-- When JC said either
> Hood or Johnston would do-- he said the people
> here educated by the press would not hear it-- he
> said H had given him a most interesting account of
> his western Campagn-- just then I was called out--
> When I came back he was telling that Hood left
> 18,000 muskets in the Western Army-- & had not
> lost more than 8000 all told-- dead wounded &
> prisoners! Gen Hampton is a Johnston Wigfall Man
> out & out-- Says *Joe* is equal to even Gen Lee--
> if not superior.

[29]Version I, 23 February 1865.

[30]Version III, 23 February 1865.

[31]Version I, 4 February 1865.

[32]In William Faulkner, *Essays, Speeches & Public Letters*, James B. Meriwether, ed. (Random House, 1965), pp. 11-43.

[33]Williams edition, p. ix.

Session VI: Discussion

MR. RICHARDS: I highly endorse the rhetorical approach, the analysis of artistic invention, that Mrs. Muhlenfeld gave us. It's abstract to say that this journal is fiction, and I certainly think that the historians have taken a very concrete approach to the work, but I think it's now our obligation to take the same type of concrete approach that Mrs. Muhlenfeld has taken towards it, and the approach that Mr. Arnold used yesterday towards one of his works. I would like to ask Miss Gregory, in light of this, if we could not go one step further and make a comparative study between those works which she discussed and the diary with respect to the rhetorical techniques, the rhetorical art, of Mrs. Chesnut?

MISS GREGORY: I think that it would be very interesting, because it seems to me they are quite different. I think even "The Captain and the Colonel" is very much more formal than "Two Years of My Life," and "Two Years of My Life" is slightly more modulated and less terse than the diary. I think it would be very fruitful to have that kind of analysis.

MRS. MUHLENFELD: I'd like to ask Miss Gregory a question, if I can. You postulated that most of these pieces of work that you were discussing were done during the 1880's. And you cited some evidence for that. Do you think it's possible that either this version of "The Captain and the Colonel" or an earlier one could have been done sometime between 1865 and 1880? I ask that because of my feeling that she was writing this journal as a sourcebook, and I wonder if maybe she might have first tried her hand at the novel and realized that that was not her *forte*.

MISS GREGORY: It's possible, but there's no way at all of dating it. I was really going on intuition---the handwriting, the paper that was used and that sort of thing---but I think it's very possible that it could have been written earlier.

MR. MERIWETHER: Professor Woodward, has your search among other family papers turned up any evidence about the dating of the novel, and of the fictionalized account of the early years?

MR. WOODWARD: No. I don't pretend that that search has
been exhaustive, but I can't add anything to what Miss
Gregory---

MISS GREGORY: She does, you know, say it is a boarding
school of fifty years ago, and if it were 1835 when she
went to that school, that would make it about 1885.
But that's a loose date, because in another place she
says, "This is composed largely from memory, although I
did use my diary of more than forty years ago," and so
it could be, I think, anywhere from 1875 to 1885.

MR. MERIWETHER: That would make it roughly around the
same time as your version two?

MR. WOODWARD: Version two, the part that is available and
capable of being dated, all came out in 1881, but
there's another batch of 800 pages or so that's impossible to date, because it doesn't come under the
same binding. But considering the sheer number of
words that she wrote, I think she's bound to have had
projects that she turned back and forth from, at one
and the same time, and that there was a concentrated
literary enterprise along about the early '80's, when
she was doing a lot of things.

MR. RICHARDS: Was the style of those things done at that
time roughly the same? Does her style change from one
year to the next? In other words, does it mature, does
it progress, or do we see her when she is working on a
number of things at one time, exhibit different styles
peculiar to the different things she is working on?

MRS. MUHLENFELD: I think we do.

MR. WOODWARD: I guess so. We'd have to assume that. We
don't know when she was doing these fictional accounts,
but---

MISS GREGORY: I was thinking of some mythical title for
my paper, and I thought of---you know, it sounded a
little too cute, so I just forgot about it, but I was
going to call it "The Formality of Memory," because all
of the memoirs that I named, the memoir of James Chesnut,
and her family memoir, and then these two large works

that do draw from memory, each of them seems to have a
particular form, and a particular style; and it's
partly, I think, because of the pressure of working
within a certain convention for each of them.

MRS. CHILDS: I thought when I was reading the account of
her being at Madame Talvande's school, that the real
intimacy, the real friendship, that she and some of the
other students had with many of the mulatto servants,
was an influential factor in some of her attitudes.
They really knew them as people, and they talked to
them and knew about their lives, and I think that
probably broadened Mrs. Chesnut's sympathy and influenced her later thinking about the whole question of
race, in which she was so different from most people.
Because the French had and have a very different attitude, I think, and as Madame Talvande mentioned, she
really knew those mulatto servants extremely well. Not
just as nurse and maid and all that sort of thing. And
then the other thing I was wondering about, is the "Two
Years." Her accounts of going down the Mississippi,
and the Choctaw country, all seem so fresh---I mean it
doesn't seem like something she's just remembered from
fifty years ago. I wonder if she might have had some
source that she had kept at the time.

MISS GREGORY: I think she might have had a diary for that,
because she mentions in---there's just a loose sheet,
and I don't know exactly where it belongs, but it's in
one of the revisions of a part of Part Five of "Two
Years of My Life," and she says, "This is written mainly from memory, although I did have my diary, more than
forty years ago, but, of course, I couldn't keep a diary
at LeGrande Street." She didn't have a diary at the
boarding school; but indicates, then, that there was
another diary she used later.

MR. WOODWARD: You've got to admit, though, you don't know
when she's kidding. When she pretends to have a diary
sometimes, you know pretty well she's not.

MR. INABINETT: Eileen, where does she get LeGrande Street
from?

MRS. MUHLENFELD: Must be Legare.

MR. INABINETT: Talvande is a real name, and was her
teacher. But the Talvande school was not on any
LeGrande Street. There was no LeGrande Street in
Charleston that I know of. Did she change that deliberately?

MR. HAYHOE: I haven't looked at the manuscript, Eileen,
but it seems to me that there's a note in your transcription, a prefatory note to the memoir, which mentions Legare Street, and it seems that since the rest of
the memoir is so much fictionalized, she may have
changed that.

MR. WOODWARD: But the building still is on Legare Street.
You can still see it there.

MR. MERIWETHER: I'd like to follow up a remark I made to
Professor Woodward yesterday, concerning T. E.
Lawrence's *Seven Pillars of Wisdom*, which seems to me in
some ways very much like Mrs. Chesnut's book---a very
carefully wrought literary masterpiece by a very talented and ambitious literary craftsman who felt at the
time of writing it that he would live only through this
work, which he made from the direct materials of his
experience, during a major conflict. He made many notes
and jottings at the time. He had diaries and letters
and a few published accounts to work with. He made
three or more versions of his book, constantly revising
towards a more finished and polished literary accomplishment. He lost the first version, after destroying the
notes it was based on; and its disappearance necessi-
tated the writing again, from memory, of almost the
entire work, without the benefit of those notes---which
he said he had burned. It seems to me that you can
almost see Lawrence setting himself free to create
finally the work that he really wanted to write, by the
process of burning those earlier notes---and perhaps by
the loss of that first draft based on the notes. What
he ended up with was not a history of the campaign in
Arabia but something much more personal, with himself at
the center. He called it a "personal narrative pieced
out of memory," which I suppose provides the excuse to
overlook his occasional historical slips, as well as
calling attention to the fact that he is himself at the
center of the work. I don't want to labor the analogies
between Lawrence and Mrs. Chesnut---he was a very active
participant in the events his book records, and she was

for the most part a spectator. But I find the similarities between the two authors and two works interesting
in quite a number of ways.

MISS GREGORY: Can I make one more comment? There are
about forty-nine pages of "The Captain and the Colonel"
that are, I think, an earlier draft of it, that are
burned at the edges, some of them.

MR. WOODWARD: You know, I think we shouldn't blur something here. I suppose ideally the object of the conference is to reach a consensus. I don't think we're
doing that. I think the tension here---my concern is
that between the two, that there's a danger to the
integrity of the project. I'm in the curious role, as
editor---my first duty will be partially to destroy
Mary Chesnut's reputation as a diarist. That's lamentable. My second duty, it seems to me, as historian,
is to preserve such integrity as her diary has, not to
forfeit it or to destroy it. But when I inform my fellow
craftsmen that what they've been reading really is a
bunch of fiction, well---

MRS. MUHLENFELD: Well, remember when you said this
morning that you had a great deal of respect for her as
an editor of her own work, that she did---

MR. WOODWARD: Well, that's a somewhat different thing.

MRS. MUHLENFELD: Right, but you went on to say that she
did not distort facts, where it seemed to be important,
that she had a good sense for what to leave out. It
seems to me that in every instance that I ran across---
and Mr. Hayhoe's paper about Betsy Witherspoon backs
this up---whenever she's talking about an event of some
historical significance, over and above its picture of
the life and times, she takes real care, although occasionally she'll get sloppy, as when she rearranges a
date. But she takes care to keep things, at least facts
and people, straight. It seems to me that she felt free,
when she was talking about an incident which, rather
than being of any newsworthiness, was instead a picture
of the times, a picture of a person's grief or a person's
folly, sketches of the types that she ran into, there I
think she felt perfectly free to conflate people, to
blow up incidents so that they had some dramatic
interest---

MR. WOODWARD: And invent them.

MRS. MUHLENFELD: And invent them.

MR. WOODWARD: But you see, Betsy, we're dealing with two
    sets of values here. Part of them are those of the
    courtroom.   Your diarist is a witness on the stand,
    and being cross-examined. "You mean to tell me that
    this is a first-hand account of what you saw?" "Oh no,
    I made this up twenty years later. I really wasn't
    there at all." You see how easy it is to destroy a
    witness's credibility there. And granted, often her
    inventions are not of moment so far as the authenticity
    of her account is concerned. There are questions where
    she does raise that point.

MRS. MUHLENFELD: Yes, I've seen a couple of them.

MR. WOODWARD: She has taken the license of fiction in a
    work of reputedly historical nature. It's a very shaky
    situation, and I don't want to pretend that I have found
    the answer. I haven't.

MISS GREGORY: You mentioned this morning that one of the
    ways out of that dilemma is simply to place her within
    a tradition of diarists. There are certain conventions
    and certain ambiguities, as you were pointing out, that
    belong to all diarists. Or is this a more extreme case?

MR. WOODWARD: I think it's pretty extreme; at least, I
    wish I knew an analogy that could be made.

MR. MOLTKE-HANSEN:)
MISS GREGORY:) Thucydides.

MR. HAYHOE: Boswell's biography of Johnson is much the
    same. He placed himself in situations where he actually
    was not present.

MR. WOODWARD: I have talked to Fred Pottle about this, and
    there is some comparability. Boswell will, in his
    journey through the Hebrides, make a record from day to
    day, although sometimes he'll do what Mary did and sit
    down and catch it all up. And that represents two
    versions, often, of the same conversation. Here is a
    work supposedly of interpreted or evolving sort, and I
    don't---there must be other diarists who have done this,

but I think---

MR. MERIWETHER: Could I suggest a different context for
this for a moment? I plead guilty for having brought
the twentieth century into the discussion a little while
ago, and though I think that there's some comparison to
be made between her Civil War journals and *Seven Pillars,*
it would be perhaps a greater favor to Mrs. Chesnut to
compare her work with that of the many nineteenth
century books which are actually fiction but which go
through an elaborate business of pretending to be
fact---novel after novel masquerading as the memoirs of
so-and-so, left in manuscript, turned up accidentally
somewhere---perhaps in a desk in a custom house. Here
is someone who has a great deal of skill, not only literary skill but fictional skill, the basic fictional
skill of characterization. She characterizes all these
other people, an enormous variety of people, through
dialogue, characterizes herself through dialogue, yet
she is writing what purports to be fact and is actually
to some extent fiction. Her talents and ambitions place
her close, I think, to a great many of the novelists of
her time, except that she has a much better mind than
most of them.

MR. INABINETT: Dr. Woodward, it seems to me you've partially solved your problem there, anyway, when you said
you were anticipating a change in title. But what if
you just stayed clear of the word "diary"?

MR. WOODWARD: Oh, well, I wouldn't want to use that.

MR. INABINETT: To call it something else with sufficient
explanation of what you found---

MR. WOODWARD: On the other hand, there *is* a diary, and it
exists in---

MR. INABINETT: But if you're going to use the third
version---

MR. WOODWARD: Yes, but I'm going to use the first one,
too.

MR. POLK: It seems to me that a useful analogy is Henry
James. If somebody wanted to tackle the problem of editing James---to do an edition of *The American*, you don't

combine the first edition and the last, the New York
edition text---

MR. MERIWETHER: I have one more literary reference to make.
I think of Defoe, who had a lesser mind than Mrs.
Chesnut, and perhaps also a lesser talent. He wrote a
Journal of the Plague Year that isn't very much of a
journal, and he wrote *Memoirs of a Cavalier* that are
most certainly not the authentic memoirs of a cavalier.

MR. WOODWARD: These things you are calling up don't have
an original there, you know. They are made out of the
whole cloth. She didn't make up much, many of these
things. She reconstructed them, but out of materials
that are valid.

MISS GREGORY: It seems to me that you cannot ever employ
the memory without reconstructing, and without reimagin-
ing a fact.

MR. WOODWARD: You're getting into the epistomological.

MISS GREGORY: No, I don't want to get into it. But the
point I was trying to make is that I think that you have
to draw the line between what is intended to be poetry
and what is not. And it seems to me that one of the
things that you work with as a primary assumption in a
literary work, a poetic work, is unity, or some sort of
economy, that is, in which nothing within it is wasted,
everything within it contributes to a meaning. The
meaning is intended. It has a plot, however it may be
unfolded. You have to fall back on traditions of some
sort, or else you'll be calling everything---you could
call a phone book fiction, you know. It's as little
fact as anything else.

MR. WOODWARD: Some of my best friends are fiction writers.

MISS GREGORY: If you define fiction as untruth, that seems
to me a very narrow definition of fiction.

MRS. MUHLENFELD: I would like to just throw in the fact
that she says in the diary that she has been rereading,
at one point, I believe it's 1863 or '4, she's been
rereading Ramsay, McCrady, Tarleton, and Lee's memoirs.
This would have been a nice thing to think of when I
was writing my paragraph about preparation for her craft.

I think she saw herself, at least at that point, interested in the very question.

MR. INABINETT: There's no similarity, though, between those authors and Mary Boykin Chesnut.

MRS. MUHLENFELD: Not at all. She was looking at various kinds of eyewitness accounts. They're not too similar to each other either.

MR. HAYHOE: I wonder if it might not be profitable to consider the similarities and differences between what we know as *A Diary from Dixie* and "Two Years of My Life." The fictionalized memoir of her school days is supposedly based on an earlier diary. Yet it has been fictionalized to an extreme degree, I think, in comparison with the Civil War diary.

MISS GREGORY: She was intending, I think, to talk about, not just any two years, but the two years that were two of the most important in her life, especially from the point of view of an old woman. At one point I quoted that moment in which the old woman, you know, kind of intrudes into the narrator's voice and breaks through. But the book as a whole is written from a certain point of view and with a certain end in mind---that is, re-constructing something imaginatively that doesn't have to have any basis in a particular fact.

MR. HAYHOE: But isn't there more of that imaginative re-construction, at least as far as we can determine it, in that memoir, as compared to the Civil War diary?

MISS GREGORY: Yes, but she had the freedom to do it in "Two Years." You know, I think the difference is a matter of scope, to a large extent. These questions could go on and on.

MR. MERIWETHER: I'd like to suggest a possible narrowing of the gap that Professor Woodward has called attention to. Surely we've all agreed that the journals of Mary Chesnut represent a conscious work of art, and any work of art of that magnitude surely compels its own defini-tion. If there is no immediately available term to describe it, I think that's very pleasing---this is a measure of our insufficiency, and of Mrs. Chesnut's sufficiency. Here is a work which is quite different

from what it has been thought to be before. Professor
Woodward has made it clear that whatever it is, the
final version is not, is no longer, a diary. So far,
the literary critics and literary historians here have
not come up with a satisfactory term for it either.
Despite its fictional elements and fictional techniques,
I certainly don't want to call it a novel.

I'd like to suggest that Mrs. Chesnut's Civil War
journals, in their final form, are a dramatic and truth-
ful account of the war years as she saw them, based on
her earlier diaries and her memories, of course, and
perhaps on a certain amount of later research or reading. The final form is still that of a journal, but
the vision is that which she had achieved two decades
later, and so has become a commentary upon history
rather than a contribution to it. She made her comments
by editing, revising, rearranging, and dramatizing her
material, rather than by discussing it in the light or
from that viewpoint of her later understanding of those
earlier people and events. So her commentary is implicit, rather than explicit. But something of the
sort---on a much lesser scale---may have been involved
in those original, on-the-spot and at-the-time diary
notes too. We can prove she revised and changed her
earlier diary, in writing up the later versions, because
we have the earlier version for comparison. But that
doesn't mean the earlier version was always strictly
factual---she may have been a very biased and unreliable
witness, to follow Professor Woodward's legal metaphor,
when she first set down what she saw and heard and
thought.

It seems to me that by the time she wrote the final
version she was attempting to write a social history of
a significant part of the Civil War, telling it in the
first person and using the diary form. This is the war
behind the lines, or on the home front; this is in contrast to the many military histories and accounts that
were already appearing. She was untrained in the sense
that a modern historian is trained, and apparently did
very little research, so perhaps I should use the term
memoir rather than the term social history. In either
case, though, I think we should permit her the same
license that the memoirists or historians of her own
age were permitted.

Session VII: Round-table Discussion

Needs and Opportunities for Research

MR. MERIWETHER: This session has a lot of ground to cover,
although many of the papers at the conference have already suggested possibilities for further research.
The discussions following these papers have also suggested further contributions to the field that would be
useful, and there is no need to cover again here any of
this ground.

I'm going to ask Les Inabinett, if he will, to begin by
suggesting some of the materials in the South
Caroliniana Library which have been neglected and which
have to do with this subject of our women writers.

MR. INABINETT: Jim referred to those which have been neglected, and perhaps some of them have been justifiably
neglected, but I don't know that it's my place to determine that. I was surprised, for instance, at the excellent paper Mrs. Scafidel presented on Mrs. Carson.
I had never thought of Mrs. Carson as a writer. One of
the problems facing me is that Jim Meriwether, in
putting this conference together, has so broadened my
conception of the term "women writers," that I'm really
at a loss as to where to begin.

The opportunities for research in this field in the
Caroliniana Library are great. Perhaps the needs are
even greater. All one has to do, for instance, is to
take a very outdated book, one that is far from adequate
for our present purposes, Wauchope's *Writers of South
Carolina*, quickly thumb through the index and come up
with the names of at least twenty-five women writers,
most of whom have never really been studied. Writings
of these women are represented in the South Caroliniana
Library in published form, and in some instances by
small collections of manuscript material. Then add to
that the fact that Wauchope's book came out in 1910, and
a great deal of work by women has been accomplished
since then. One can see immediately the need---and
opportunities---for more South Carolina Women Writers
Conferences. In the area of unpublished letters of
literary significance by our women writers I could come

273

up with a list that would seem endless. Our collection
of unpublished diaries by women is not extensive, but
there are certainly several that merit attention and
further study. Half a dozen come to mind immediately;
I must confess that many of them are known to me only
as names. I have learned so much more here about Susan
Petigru King than I had ever known before, for example.
Even as familiar as Julia Peterkin is to me, I can't
confess to having read all of her books and the same is
true of so many other writers---Penina Moise, Catherine
Poyas, Beatrice Ravenel, Sophia Hume---I could go on
and on with names of writers whose works and lives have
never been adequately studied.

MR. MERIWETHER: Do we have papers for those you have just
mentioned?

MR. INABINETT: No, I'm afraid not in all cases---I was
just mentioning some of the better known who are represented in our collection by published works. We have
supporting manuscript material for Frances Guignard
Gibbes (Mrs. Oscar L. Keith), who was a prolific drama-
tist, who has never really been studied. Perhaps her
works have deservedly been relegated to obscurity. I've
tried to persuade some eager graduate student to edit
the letters of Anna Marie Calhoun, the daughter of John
C. Calhoun who married Thomas Green Clemson. I think
she's a great letter writer.

MR. MERIWETHER: Did she do a volume of poems, Les?

MR. INABINETT: That was her daughter, who did the volume
of poems. Coming into the twentieth century, Grace
Lumpkin, a native Columbian who has incidentally just
come back to Columbia, has an established reputation; I
understand that one of her early novels is now being reprinted, to appear next year.[1] Our library in the last
few years has acquired a small collection of Grace
Lumpkin manuscripts, and they should be looked into.
But I can't claim that the Library has any collections
of the papers of women of the stature of Mrs. Peterkin
and Mrs. Chesnut.

MR. MERIWETHER: You're being too modest about your resources, Les, since you like to be able to talk about an
entire archive in connection with an individual writer.
But I think of the many letters that are scattered

through other collections, the great number of letters
from our women writers, important or unimportant, which
you have. Some of them are already in process of being
edited. Mrs. Hampton is hard at work on her edition of
the letters of Sally Baxter Hampton.[2] Mr. Arnold is
already under pressure to bring out that epistolary
novel of the Revolution, the Eliza Wilkinson letters,
with a critical introduction demonstrating the novelis-
tic structure of the work. In the Peterkin field, Noel,
we have the short stories collected in Frank Durham's
edition. Is there further work that should be collected
and published?

MR. POLK: There are probably a half a dozen sketches that
were not published in Durham's book. I suspect that
there are some book reviews in the Charleston papers,
and perhaps even in the Columbia papers, that haven't
been tracked down. And there are some poems that merit
collecting. What we most need is an edition of her
letters.

MR. MERIWETHER: An edition of her letters, and an edition
of Josephine Pinckney's letters---these seem such obvious needs. Herbert, is there Pinckney material that
you think should be brought together and published,
besides her letters?

MR. SHIPPEY: It's possible that a volume of her essays
could be assembled. The most urgent need would be for
the letters, those that relate to her writing, I would
say.

MR. MERIWETHER: If we turn to Susan Petigru King, Jim, for
how many of her novels would you like to write critical
introductions, in process of reissuing them by photo-
offset from the original editions?

MR. SCAFIDEL: You get the publisher, I'm ready.

MR. MERIWETHER: When we deal with works of a very limited
marketability, like these, we should be looking at the
possibility of the simplest kind of photo-offset reissue,
if the work has existed in an acceptable text. Nothing
could be more simple and practicable than to type neatly
a new critical introduction, and have it microfilmed
with the original book text. One could keep a negative
microfilm and advertise the availability of the work at

a reasonable price. The reissued work would be manufactured and sold one copy at a time, as it is with
University Microfilms---a positive microfilm of Mrs.
King's novels, with your introductions, would seem to
be an obvious possibility, Jim. I'm suggesting a step
up from University Microfilms, which only gives you the
original work; here we could offer additional material.
There are many works by our women writers which are neglected and are unavailable, which have some significance
but only limited sales potential. We should do a little
bit more than just call attention to them. We should
make them available at the same time if we possibly can.

MRS. CHILDS: Well, you know the bibliography by Lyle
Wright of American fiction from 1776 to 1900---aren't
all those on microfilm?[3]

MR. MERIWETHER: That series, like others of the same kind,
doesn't always do a good job of picking the right text
to make available. A good deal of bibliographical research needs to be done before bringing out a reissue of
many of these novels.

MR. POLK: Also Wright lists only fiction, and that would
leave out many works that we are considering here.

MR. MERIWETHER: I think that Mary Moragné Davis is in very
good hands now. It's perfectly clear that her novel,
that the unpublished portions of her diary, and that her
uncollected but published fiction should be brought out.

MRS. CRAVEN: Also, I would like to urge the University of
South Carolina Press to reprint *The Neglected Thread*.
I've had a number of requests for it.

MR. POLK: It may be worth noting that a manuscript and
typescript draft of *Scarlet Sister Mary* have been in the
library at Wofford College for about a year now.

MR. MERIWETHER: What about Mrs. Peterkin's other manuscripts?

MR. POLK: So far as I know, there are none.

MR. INABINETT: She claimed that she systematically
destroyed them.

MR. MERIWETHER: I don't want to skip past something else
that requires attention, but Mrs. Chesnut is waiting
for us. The rather free-wheeling literary discussion
awhile ago concerning the definition of this historical
and/or literary masterpiece has already focused attention on our need for one or more new editions of that
material. And it is certainly pleasant for everyone
else here in this room to recommend to Mr. Woodward what
he ought to do in order to satisfy our own needs. I
might begin by saying that in an ideal world, Professor
Woodward would be editing---or perhaps would already
have edited---that collected edition of all of her
works, in which every manuscript word had been recovered,
presented in its pristine textual purity, properly annotated and introduced, and---how long is your index going
to be, Professor Woodward?

MR. WOODWARD: This is your story.

MR. MERIWETHER: Even with ample funding from some foundation or the government, it may be awhile before we
arrive at that millennium, and in the meantime, as much
of her work as is practicable should be brought out
soon---practicable in terms of time, of scholars' time,
practicable in terms of publishing and printing costs.
What can be done now with the Civil War journals is what
Professor Woodward was describing to us this morning. I
don't want to add to your editorial burdens even by implication the earlier material, the material that was
being described for us by Miss Gregory, Vann. Clearly,
this is of lesser importance. In your opinion, should
the editing of these materials await the completion of
the major task? Do you have any interest in the other
manuscripts?

MR. WOODWARD: I am interested in anything she wrote, but
that's not my job. That's somebody else's, Miss
Gregory's, perhaps, not mine.[4] No, I don't know them
well enough, just haven't faced that one. I've got
enough to face as it is.

MR. MERIWETHER: Are there enough of her letters extant to
make it worth considering an edition of them?

MR. WOODWARD: Well, I haven't made a systematic search.
But I would say that there's not enough in the collection. She kept letters in copybooks, and so you don't

have the original often.   You have only a copy of it.[5]

MR. MERIWETHER: Obviously the editorial problems of the
other materials are considerably less.   Let me ask those
who have read them more carefully than I, beginning
with Miss Gregory: do you feel that there's a need for
these works to be published?   How do they compare with
similar materials by other hands that have been published?

MISS GREGORY: Well, I've thought about this a little bit.
As I think I mentioned in my talk, "The Captain and the
Colonel" is of interest largely because we're interested
in that mind that's at work there, and because we know
it through the diary.   I don't know whether it can stand
on its own.

MR. INABINETT: Could passages from it which are autobi-
ographical be extracted for inclusion in the new edition of the *Diary from Dixie*.

MR. WOODWARD: If I prepared a biographical treatment, and
I think I ought to do so, I'd make use of it, and clearly indicate, of course, that it's fictionalized.   I
think her description of the frontier life in the '30's
in Mississippi is rich and useful for biographical purposes.

MR. INABINETT: I think you made it quite clear that she
was really consulting early diaries that no longer
existed when she wrote that---

MISS GREGORY: Well, that's what she said, but it's just a
note, you know, a hastily written note, that seems to be
addressed to someone, perhaps, that she was lending a
portion of the thing to, saying this was written mainly
from memory.   But there are no actual pages of the early
diaries themselves---

MR. WOODWARD: I have recovered some copybooks from that
period, from the Camden members of the family.   They're
more or less commonplace books, but they were made in
the '30's.

MISS GREGORY: I was going to say, though, that of all that
fictional material, I think that the description of the
boarding school is really the best.   One of the sections

that exists in a later version is a substantial part of
the boarding school episode and it is much better than
the version in the complete early version.

MR. HAYHOE: I think the "Two Years of My Life" is infinitely superior to "The Captain and the Colonel."

MISS GREGORY: Yes. She worked a lot harder on it, really
worked hard in revising it.

MR. HAYHOE: "The Captain and the Colonel" is largely a
first draft, in appearance. It's not very well written.

MISS GREGORY: It doesn't make sense in places.

MR. HAYHOE: It is not cohesive. It does not read well,
and is of interest only because she wrote it, and because it may shed some light on her life. Whereas I
think the "Two Years of My Life" is an extremely interesting memoir. And it is a shame that the entire
memoir is not available, and perhaps the two missing
sections will be located among other papers which are
not in the Caroliniana Library.

MISS GREGORY: I think they could probably be found in
some attic---

MR. INABINETT: How many pages are missing from "Two Years
of My Life"?

MISS GREGORY: One hundred and fifteen. That's about a
third. There are six sections, and there are two sections missing, so that's about a third.

MR. INABINETT: This is a problem that I'm sure all users
of our Williams-Chesnut-Manning Collection have faced.
The collection is complicated by the fact it falls into
two types of acquisitions: one, an outright gift; the
other, a deposit. And the two sections are kept apart.

MISS GREGORY: Dr. Woodward, did you find any sign of any
other literary papers among the diary, among the papers
of the diary?

MR. WOODWARD: Twenty minutes or so before this session,
Betsy Muhlenfeld showed me a version of the opening
paragraphs of the diary that I had not seen. That's

version what---number four or five? And I had seen a
Xerox of the other side of those pages, but this was
the verso of the same pages which somebody forgot to
turn over, so I hadn't seen them. Here again is an
illustration of her indecisiveness. I haven't gone into this thoroughly, but here are four versions of an
opening. I don't think she ever made up her mind which
she was going to use, and my suspicion is that she decided not to start there after all, but later. I think
she never completed anything, and I think that exoner-
ates me from this charge of infidelity to the author's
intent. She didn't know what she intended.

MR. MERIWETHER: None of them ever do.

MRS. MUHLENFELD: Isn't that just like a woman?

MR. MERIWETHER: I have a biographical question to ask.
In what sort of health was she in her last months? If
she left incomplete the task of preparing the final
version of her masterpiece, was it still something that
she was continuing to work on right up till the end?
Or was it something she had abandoned?

MR. WOODWARD: She couldn't have written the amount she did
without filling those years pretty actively with literary
work. You asked how was her health. Her health was always failing, all through her life. It was psychological for the large part, I think. But she was healthy
enough to square off and do a good day's work pretty
late in her life. I know that she did a great deal in
the last five years of her life.

MISS GREGORY: Her husband died less than a year before she
did, and in the same month that her mother died. And
it was quite a blow; there are a couple of entries that
talk about being despondent, so I wondered whether she
died of a broken heart?

MR. WOODWARD: I don't know. She was a pretty tough
customer.

MISS GREGORY: What was their income after '65?

MR. WOODWARD: I ought to know better than I do about that,
more exactly than I do, and I've got James Chesnut's
copy of his accounting of his father's estate. He was

made literary executor, along with two others. But he was the one who actually had responsibility, and he wasn't much of a business man, and he---oh well, there are a lot of charges about how he handled that estate. But I have no evidence that they were in desperate circumstances. They sold three Gilbert Stuarts---

MISS GREGORY: She had some problem about getting something from the estate after her husband's death, I remember, because there is a letter from Varina Davis that talks about that, and that was when Mrs. Davis suggested that she publish her diary, and make some money on it.

MR. WOODWARD: Well, she was---

MISS GREGORY: I think that might be the reason for those translations, if they do in fact exist---

MR. WOODWARD: She was also peddling butter and eggs pretty vigorously, until there were complaints about the quality of the butter from Charleston.

MISS GREGORY: Her heart wasn't in it.

MR. WOODWARD: There wasn't enough salt in the butter, they say.

MR. INABINETT: Speaking about opportunities, as long as the Chesnut diary is around to be studied, whatever approach Dr. Woodward takes in the final editorial structure of the diary, there will be plenty of opportunities for individual studies of certain passages or sections that could turn out to be any number of papers of the sort that have been read here today, or of those for graduate credit.

MR. POLK: I would try to answer the question that you directed at Eileen awhile ago, by saying unequivocally that everything Mrs. Chesnut wrote ought to be published, somehow.

MR. WOODWARD: Come on, Noel.

MR. POLK: Sure. She's an important writer and the amount of material that we have by her is finite.

MR. WOODWARD: It may be finite, but with a hundred and
fifty pages missing out of a three hundred and some-
thing---

MR. POLK: Well, we've established, I think everybody
agrees, that she's a writer of major importance, and
therefore I, as a literary scholar, am very interested
in everything that she wrote.

MR. INABINETT: Dr. Woodward, couldn't the materials extraneous to the diary be a companion volume, a third or
fourth volume?

MR. WOODWARD: I've got enough troubles as it is. But,
honestly, I can't believe you mean that literally,
Noel, because---

MR. POLK: Yes sir, I do.

MR. WOODWARD: Okay. Frankly, if you literary types want
to recognize a major literary figure in Mary, okay, but
I can't really buy that. I have to think of major
literary figures in quite other terms---

MR. POLK: Well, again, why do we have to think of her as
either one or the other, historical or literary? Why
can't she be both? It seems to me that I've finally
worked my way back around to my Henry James analogy.
It seems we are dealing not with two different people,
but with two different books. You don't edit Henry
James' *The American*, as I was saying, by combining the
two versions of it, which were written and published
twenty-five years apart. They are clearly two different
books, written by two basically different people.

MR. WOODWARD: False analogy. I don't know the real
history of that novel, but I do know that the author
authorized the publication of two different versions.
But Mary Chesnut never authorized the publication of
anything, as a complete version. Instead, she had fragments from a workshop, which are scattered over twenty-
odd years, and nothing is really authorized as completed.
And we're putting together, taking much liberty and
license about what we decide to do with it. We're performing a function which is normally sacred to the
artist herself, if she can be so described.

MR. POLK: Well, the textual principle that I would follow
then, if I were in the unfortunate position of editing
the diary, as you are---the principle I would follow
would be, since you can't really determine what her intentions were, what you have to deal with is what she
actually did.

MR. WOODWARD: She did many contradictory things.

MR. INABINETT: Why couldn't you come out, though, with a
series of volumes, or set of volumes, called *The
Writings of Mary Boykin Chesnut*, or *The Works of Mary
Boykin Chesnut*? I think it's pretty well established
that even her diary is not a single work, but at least
two works, possibly three to four.

MR. WOODWARD: Well, art is long, you know, and life is
short, and I have a limited objective.

MISS GREGORY: I was thinking of some sort of softbound
edition that could be typed, and proofread, and annotated, if possible, and given some sort of limited dis-
tribution.

MR. MERIWETHER: Is this a suggestion along the lines that
we were discussing for a collected edition of the works
of Susan Petigru King? Something adapted to the needs
of the modest number of literary scholars of the quality
of Mr. Polk? There are so few of you, Noel, that you
can't be counted on to make possible an edition of the
works. What about a transcription, a carefully typed
transcription, of the collected works, that could be
introduced, annotated, and even indexed? Then copies
of the typescript deposited at a few major centers, and
Xeroxes or microfilms made available at cost, or something not too extravagantly beyond cost, to the research
libraries and scholars which want something more than a
practicable publishable edition?

MR. WOODWARD: Why not a microfilm of the whole thing?
Honestly, I question the practicability of publication.
I know the difficulty I've had correlating the work of
several people trying to transcribe the manuscript, and
their inability to agree among themselves on, for
instance, capitalization. There won't be any authentic
transcription; there'll be somebody saying this is the
best we could do.

MR. MERIWETHER: But that's no different from a printed and published version, is it? Ultimately somebody has got to decide what it is. Can't that be done just as well with a complete typescript, as with the partial typescript that goes to the printer to make the new edition that you are editing?

MR. WOODWARD: I defer to your wisdom on that.

MRS. MUHLENFELD: I have read large parts of "Two Years of My Life," and agree with you that, in spite of the fact that there's a hole in the middle, it's nevertheless a good piece of writing. And I think somebody ought to edit it for publication.

MR. INABINETT: If her description of Maum Jute that you read this morning is typical of the quality of that entire manuscript, I think it ought to be published *in toto*.

MR. WOODWARD: It's that good.

MR. MERIWETHER: I have read the whole thing, thanks to Eileen's industry in transcribing it. It is a work of fine quality. Yes, it's got a hole in the middle. So what?

It's five o'clock. I feel sure that the audience will join me in thanking all the people who did the work of the conference, by giving the papers and by joining in the discussions, and also in thanking again Mrs. Reynolds, who made these labors possible.

Notes

[1]Grace Lumpkin, *The Wedding*. Carbondale: Southern Illinois University Press, 1976. Lost American Fiction series, ed. by Matthew J. Bruccoli. (Reprint of 1939 ed.)

[2]Publication of this volume is planned for spring, 1978.

[3]This microfilm series is published by Research Publications, New Haven, Connecticut.

[4]All of Mary Boykin Chesnut's unpublished literary manuscripts are being edited by Elisabeth Muhlenfeld and will be submitted as her doctoral dissertation at the University of South Carolina early in 1978.

[5]Her letters were edited by Allie Patricia Wall for her 1977 M.A. thesis at the University of South Carolina.

CONTRIBUTORS TO THIS VOLUME

At the time of the conference, James B. Meriwether
was McClintock Professor of Southern Letters and Director
of the Southern Studies Program, University of South
Carolina. . .Delle Craven was a resident of Knoxville,
Tennessee. . .Ann Hampton was a resident of Columbia,
South Carolina. . .Thomas Landess was Professor of English,
University of Dallas. . .Noel Polk was Visiting Bibliogra-
pher, Southern Studies Program, University of South
Carolina. . .C. Vann Woodward was Sterling Professor of
History, Yale University. . .Eileen Gregory was Assistant
Professor of English, University of Dallas. . .Dianne
Anderson, Karen Endres, Beverly Scafidel, David Moltke-
Hansen, Herbert Shippey, J. R. Scafidel, G. Michael
Richards, Edwin Arnold, George Hayhoe, and Elisabeth
Muhlenfeld were graduate students in the Southern Studies
Program, University of South Carolina.